American Social Science Series

GENERAL EDITOR

HOWARD W. ODUM

*Kenan Professor of Sociology and Director of the School of
Public Welfare in the University of North Carolina*

A
SOCIAL INTERPRETATION
OF EDUCATION

BY

JOSEPH KINMONT HART

Professor of Education
The University of Wisconsin

NEW YORK
HENRY HOLT AND COMPANY

PRINTED IN THE
UNITED STATES OF AMERICA

To the Memory of

LUCY KINMONT

IN WHOM TRADITIONS OF SCOTCH UNIVERSITIES
AND EXPERIENCES OF THE AMERICAN FRONTIER
MINGLED TO MAKE HER A TEACHER UNEXCELLED.

PREFACE

This book was begun when the author was assistant professor of education in the University of Washington, nearly twenty years ago. Through ten years of university teaching; a year of teaching in a back-woods country school; seven years of editorial and research work in New York City; and now more years on the campus—the study has been carried on. It is not complete. The task undertaken in this book is, by its very nature, not capable of being completed. It seeks an understanding and explication of educational processes in a world that changes the incidence of its educational influences with every new invention, scientific discovery, international re-alignment and social or economic dislocation.

But the thesis, presented first in any considerable fashion in *Educational Resources of Village and Rural Communities* (1913), is slowly making headway toward recognition even in the schools. To all who are interested in the progress of *education,* this book will probably seem a welcome addition to this growing discussion. To those who care not so much for education, but who seek the prestige of the schools, the book may well seem almost an impertinence. But so be it: if only thereby the intelligent discussion of education is furthered. This book is not addressed to schoolmen only, but to all who are concerned with either the successes or the failures of schooling and education, to-day.

Grateful acknowledgments must be made to Professor Boyd P. Bode for his careful, critical reading of the manuscript, even though not all his suggestions were accepted; and to Professor Howard W. Odum, editor of the series, whose critical editorial suggestions saved the author from many mistakes, both of substance and of style.

J. K. H.

Madison, Wisconsin,
March 8, 1929.

CONTENTS

PART THREE

How We Are Educated

PART FOUR

A Community Interpretation of Education

INTRODUCTION

THE ARGUMENT OF THIS BOOK

Our philosopher . . . is like a plant which, having proper nurture, must necessarily grow and mature into all virtue; but if sown and planted in an alien soil, becomes the most noxious of all weeds . . . Do you really think, as people often say, that our youth are corrupted by Sophists, or that private teachers of the art corrupt them in any degree worth speaking of? Are not the public who say these things the greatest of all Sophists? And do they not educate to perfection young and old, men and women alike, and fashion them after their own hearts?

When they meet together, and the world sits down at an assembly, or in a law court, or a theatre, or a camp, or in any other popular resort, and there is a great uproar, and they praise some things which are said or done, and blame other things, equally exaggerating both, shouting and clapping their hands, and the echo of the place in which they are assembled redoubles the sound of the praise and blame—at such time will not a young man's heart, as they say, leap within him? Will any private training enable him to stand firm against the overwhelming flood of popular opinion? Will he not have notions of good and evil which the public in general have—will he do as they do, and as they are, such will he be?—PLATO, in *The Republic*.

Education began, and begins, before school. The human race existed for untold generations before anything like our academic school came into being. All early civilizations, all early eras in the life of nations, e.g., pioneering America, were educated without the help of schools. Children now live two, four, six years before they start to school; and they usually live many years after school is done with. Education is more than schooling; it does not inhere in schools alone.

The Old School.—As will later appear, the human race has subjected itself to some two or three thousand years of academic schooling—out of the two or three hundred thousand years at least that it has probably existed upon the earth. The academic school first appeared in Greece, but it has reached its culmination in modern America with our universal compulsory attendance laws, our intellectualistically trained teachers, our curricula made up of the finished materials of old cultures, and our academic tests, which are not the tests of life and the world, but purely institutional and academic tests, useful only in determining further school promotions. In general, the products of this academic schooling adequately reflect the character of their training. Here and there are some who rise above that training into generous emotional and intelligent living.

Presuppositions of This Old School.—Two presuppositions underlie and defend this schoolish training. The first is that the child is a natural barbarian, or even a bit of an animal, and he must be humanized and civilized. The school is society's instrument for this essential purpose; and no matter what happens, civilization is so much more important than any individual impulse that the child must be made to accept the "long results of time" whether he wants to or not. The second assumption is that "education" is something already in existence: it is made up of patterns of behavior, and a certain content of culture; it is sacredly treasured in schools; and the individual, if he is to get it at all, must go to a school to get it. This assumption that education is a pre-existent culture which the child, as pupil, must take on justifies and rationalizes all the intellectualistic processes characteristic of the academic school.

The New School.—This program of the Old School, with its institutional tyrannies, has ceased to be universally convincing. Children rebel against it; adults make light of it—after they are safely beyond its reach; and most communities find themselves in the curiously ambiguous position of paying large sums for the support of schools for the products of which they have very little use. Hence, in recent years, something called the "new school" has appeared. This new school holds that education is not a pre-existent culture: it is something unique in the case of each individual; it must be newly achieved by each new child coming into the world. Although the doctrine of these schools is at least as old as the times of Socrates, the development of new schools has not yet become widespread. The programs they propose have an allurement for large numbers of people; but these programs have been practically worked out in a very few cases, only.

Presuppositions of the New Schools.—Two fundamental presuppositions underlie the proposals of the new school movement. The first of these is that children are young human beings and, if given adequate chance, will naturally develop into adult human beings, in good time. The second assumption is that education is an affair of the specific individual: as a process it lies entirely within his experience, even within the mind of the specific child; it must never be imposed upon him from without. Education is entirely sub-integumental: it goes on within, under the skin, or not at all. Hence, the new school becomes a place where the individual child is stimulated to develop his own "personality," and his "own intellectual outlooks," in his own uncontaminated way, carefully defended from antique institutions, until such time as, having developed and organized himself, he is able to defend himself. This the theory.

How We Are Actually Educated.—Not many children, however, have the chance to enjoy the sort of education theoretically provided in these new schools. Some who have had that chance have not quite fulfilled the hopes of the supporters of those schools. On the other hand, large numbers of children who have gone to the older schools leave school before they are fifteen years old, with most of their years and their real education still ahead of them. Those who remain in school several years longer spend more time out of school than in, and most of their interests lie outside the schoolhouse. Few people have ever been educated in schools. School plays some part in the education of each of us to-day, but so does every other social institution, and the whole life of the community. In the case of a few, school plays an enormous part: they became "schooled," "schoolish," "schoolmen"; in rare cases they become *educated*. In the case of most children school plays a negligible part; in the case of many its impacts are harmful, and even disastrous.

The fact, simply stated, is that we are educated by our experiences, of every sort, whether those experiences accrue to us in school or out of school. School has its place in education, of course, but *no one knows* to-day just what that place is. It does the school little good, and education no good at all, to give the school more credit than it deserves for whatever its share in education may be. We shall do much better to attempt to discover just

how education does actually go on, and what influences
are responsible for its actual effects. Such knowledge
will better serve the real interests of the school, the individual and the community.

The Modern Disorganized Community.—Industrial
development in the past century, with the growth of huge
factories and the piling up of congested populations, has
destroyed the old-time community, which was ever the
chief support of the individual child in its efforts to become a mature and well-organized human being. That
is the most important fact for all educational discussion
to-day; and it is the fact most completely ignored by
schoolmen. The modern "community"—rural, village,
town, small city, large city—is *disorganized*. It has no
integration. It knows little of neighborliness, or common
interest, or community spirit or aspiration. Its inhabitants are little aware that such a spirit ever existed. Likewise, our institutions are fragmentary and, therefore,
predatory and war-like. They compete for the allegiance
of the young people, often with almost obscene indecency,
with the inevitable and obvious result that they succeed
in helping to turn out individuals almost as completely
disorganized as the community itself is. They blame
these results on the school, usually.

It must be seen to be supreme folly to expect a school,
whether an old school or a new school, to provide an education that will turn out integrated and intelligent adults
in the midst of these inescapable disorganizations of the
modern community. The community of to-day knows
no community of mind or of spirit, no integration of its
anarchic impulses. How then should any specific institution within its area be expected to assure community
of mind and spirit and integration of personality to any
of its inhabitants? The expectation exists, but it is ab-

surd. That fact appears in the results that we can see all
about us. We are educated by the community disorganization within which we live and grow up to-day; and only
an occasional individual is able to escape that disorganization, into an integration that he may spend all his life
to achieve. What wonder if, when he has achieved it,
he finds it antiquated, lop-sided, unbalanced, erratic?

How We Shall Be Educated.—There are those who
hold that our academic school system could yet provide
effective education for our children, even in the midst of
all this social disorganization, if only the technics of
pedagogy were more definitely worked out and more
efficiently applied. These assume that a more "scientifically" organized school will be able to secure the results we desire, even without the support of a human
community. This assumption accounts for the feverish
activity of "schools of education" and the development
of innumerable types of tests and measurements and systems of classification. If the kingdom of education can
be taken by adding an inch to the length of a "test," the
thing will be done!

But it seems likely the assumption is unfounded. The
most efficient school can't keep the world entirely out of
the experience of the child who, after all, must come and
go through the city streets. Regret it as we may, the
world will intrude. Education is a function of the whole
life of the individual, not merely of the hours spent in
the schoolhouse. *We may as well face the fact*. We
shall never again know a satisfactory general education
until we shall have again created a more completely organized community life—a community that will provide
infinitely varied social patterns of individual growth and
development; that will offer wide ranges of intellectual
stimulation and broad vistas of physical and moral de-

velopment; but that, at the same time, will be a real community, within which the plastic spirit of the child and growing youth may find a habitation and a home.

Education is not primarily a function either of institutions in general, or of a specific institution, the school, in particular. These all have their parts to play, but they play only parts, and to-day those parts are usually fractional and fragmenting. No institution can play the whole orchestra of personal development. Education is the resultant of the whole community's endless impacts upon the growing individual; if his community is integrated, his education is likely to achieve some final integration. If that community is over-organized, his education is likely to become complete habituation. If the community is stagnant, that education is likely to be stranded in some dank past. If the community is disorganized, his education is likely to end in a disorganized personality that will endlessly seek through the world for a wholeness it will never attain. No mere school is ever likely to be able to cure with a few words, during a comparatively few moments of the individual's whole career, the ills inflicted upon that individual by the deficiencies of the community through the total moments of his life!

Now, it may be that if and when our educational statesmen have become able to see the problems of education from this community point of view, they will be able to envisage and, with adequate inquiry, to create an educational instrument, something like a school, which will assure the development and integration of personality even in spite of the disorganization of the modern world. But such an instrument will not be "academic": it will be real. It will be less like a school, and more like an Athenian playground, with adequate provision of materials, creative opportunities and resources, and with plenty of good pedagogues (in the Athenian sense: vid., Chapter IV) who will know, not too many books, but the rich and varied and disorganized life of the community; and they will know that life in such a way as to give it, still, some spiritual organization, which can be communicated to the growing spirit of the child. But this will come after we have escaped from *schooling* and have begun to think about *education*.

After School.—All this means that both the "old" and the "new" schools are factors, both of help and of obstruction, in our efforts to understand and to deal with our current social disorganization in educational terms. We shall have to get beyond both of them—in good time. The problem of education is not being solved, to-day, by the schools. The curriculum of the schools is, even now, in multitudes of cases, something to be escaped from by most alert children and youths, in order that their *real education* may get ahead—by means of *extra-curricular activities*. Harvard has long been said to harbor the doctrine that "a gentlemen's grade is C." Men of the world, and that means seventy-five to ninety percent of the population, cannot afford the time or the energy to get "A" grades. Broad experiences of life and the world are far more important than scholastic standings, to most of us.

There is nothing shocking in this fact. Youth must be served, and every sort of youth, at that. The shocking thing is that there are many schoolmen who are making strenuous efforts to capture all these "extra-curricular" activities and make them over into cut-and-dried modes of the school, for which "credits" may be given. They would even give "credits" for all out of school experiences, if those experiences could all be cut and dried in the same way. They argue, with admirable academic fallaciousness, that "if those activities produce such effective educational results in their present unorganized and unmeasured condition, how much more effective they may be made by being organized and standardized by men who really know what education is!"

The education which childhood and youth is working out for itself—in despair of institutions—under the leaderships of its own chosen and free pedagogues of all ages —most of whom also are youths, even if their heads are gray—is, of course, looked upon with suspicion by all institutionalists who would, if they could, bring all such enterprises under the control of the academic régime, even though that should mean the dry-rot of all those enterprises.

Education and Social Progress.—It is the custom of cynics and pessimists, and institutionalists, these days, to speak a bit patronizingly about "those naïve persons who still believe in progress." The universe, itself, must be a bit naïve, for it still is able to change, now and then— if there be any truth in the doctrine of evolution. But schooling stands for an education which, already in existence, is used for the purpose of making the new generations copy the patterns of the past, the errors with the truth, the evils with the goods. So history is made to repeat itself. The new schools, shocked by these follies in the older schooling, seem intent on cutting the new age adrift from all the past, destroying the truth with the errors, the goods with the evils, throwing out the baby with the bath. To a somewhat disinterested bystander, it would seem the part of wisdom to undertake to discover all the factors that enter into the processes of education, whether those factors lie within schoolhouses or outside; or if not *all* the factors, then at least as many as may be found. For education is the present stage of social progress. Education is to-morrow in the making. The future of society does not lie in the keeping of the schools, but in the keeping of education. We have made the task too simple. It is taking *all* of the past and the present to make the future, not merely that part of the past and the present that is found in schoolhouses. Education is compact of *all of to-day,* not merely that part of to-day that is in the keeping of the schools.

It is to be the task of this book to examine, as far as may be within limits, all factors and situations within the contemporary school and community, in order to discover, if possible, the conditions within which a genuine education may be envisaged and, it may be, eventually developed.

PART ONE

THE INSTITUTIONAL INTERPRETATION OF EDUCATION

CHAPTER I

SCHOOL

> The common school is the greatest discovery ever made
> by man. It is supereminent in its universality and in the
> timeliness of the aid it proffers. Other social organiza-
> tions are curative and remedial; this is preventative and
> an antidote. They come to heal diseases and wounds;
> this, to make the moral and physical frame invulnerable
> to them . . . The common school can train up children
> in the elements of all good knowledge and virtue.—
> HORACE MANN, in *Common School Journal*, 1841.

The universal public school, which provides a common
opportunity to all the children of all the people, is an
American invention of the nineteenth century. It is
probably the most generous gesture ever made by any
people in behalf of a common aim. The public school
did not spring into existence fully organized and complete; it is the product of a century of effort, experimentation and—fear. For a century, too, though not
quite the same century, this universal public school has
been widely praised. Statesmen and generals have
joined with educators and clergymen in teaching the
public to think highly of this "greatest discovery ever
made by man."

The School in the Nineteenth Century.—In the
course of the nineteenth century, some seven specific
arguments were developed and used to defend free, tax-
supported schools against the attacks of the few who
opposed them. Those arguments as given by Professor
Carleton, were as follows: 1. Education is necessary to

3

the preservation of free institutions; 2. It prevents class differentiation; 3. It tends to diminish crime; 4. It reduces the amount of poverty and distress; 5. It increases production; 6. It is the natural right of all individuals; 7. It will rectify false ideas as to the unjust distribution of wealth.

Helped by such arguments, public school systems spread over the whole nation, except certain limited areas of the old South, during the nineteenth century, and they became the "hope of the country." Then, during the later decades of the nineteenth century and the early twentieth, school attendance was made universal and compulsory—under varying conditions and with various age limits. The human race, long starved under the dominance of feudal institutions, was avid for "education." Schooling was believed to be the solution of this long problem; and the whole nation "went in for schools."

Yesterday, most Americans took the public school as a matter of course—as if it were as native to the soil as trees and flowers in June. They praised it to all "aliens"; they defended it against all critics—and their own doubts. They were bewildered by any serious suggestion that all was not as it should be in education. Impressive school buildings were being constructed everywhere, and a building is proof of the reality of the idea it is to house. Said the defenders of schools: "People don't build such fine buildings for things that are not real. There may be something wrong with education; but, if so, the fault is in those being educated, not in the system. How can anything be wrong with our schools? They're The Schools, aren't they?"

The School in the Twentieth Century.—But a considerable change has come over the world in recent years.

Opinions have been much modified. After all, the "common school" of the nineteenth century was a rural and village school. But in ever-increasing numbers we live in cities now. Life in cities differs from life in the country and the village, at least for children. We admit as much when we think of modes of earning livelihood, of transportation, of sanitation and water supplies. But we like to argue that "home is still home, whether in the city or the country," though a country home is not exactly the same thing as a city apartment. So, too, we should like to believe that school is still school, whether it is in one room, or in a hundred. But the belief is fallacious, even though the number of rooms in a schoolhouse does not make it so.

The justification of the country and village school was the country and village life. The city school has no such justification. The city school is still, for the most part, just the old country school brought to the city, and it cannot do the work it was able to do in the older country conditions, because it is working within an entirely different sort of environment. The present city school is not less efficient than was the older country school. But the conditions of its work have changed, and the city needs a different type of school just as it has needed, and secured, new types of houses, new means of transportation, different forms of water supply. We must become as realistic about education as we have become about sanitation and housing. When industry changes, education is compelled to change, willy-nilly.

The Doctrine of School.—Owing to an historical accident, as we shall see, the academic school developed as an instrument for the teaching of "knowledge," and the inculcation of "learning." Hence, in the course of history the school has gradually come to be regarded as the intellectual institution of the community; and the children who attend its offerings have come to be regarded as "pupils." Now, a pupil is that part of a child that is amenable to the intellectual disciplines of the school. That is, it is the "intellect," if any, of the child. In the older rural and village days, children sometimes became satiated with work on the farm and play and isolation; and they gladly went to the school house where they had opportunity to learn, to read, and to enter into mental feats with other children and the teacher. Hence, it was not difficult for educational theorists to believe that the school had a natural place in the education of children, at least of most children, or that "schooling" could be practically identified with "education." "Education" trains the "mind"; it develops good mental habits; it provides useful information; it teaches "how to think"! That is what education *is*—and the *school* is its instrument!

This doctrine was adequate, even inevitable, as long as the village and rural community provided all the other fundamentals of education—work, play, social life, emotional enrichment, the sense of community, and the framework of a personal career. But this doctrine ceased to be adequate and became obstructive as soon as the city began to take the place of the village and the country-side as the community. The city tends, more and more, to take away from children the old community materials of education: work, play, social life, emotional enrichment, the sense of community and the framework of a personal career. As we shall see, the city tends, more and more, to substitute *talk about things* for the old actual experiences with things. City children see many things; they handle very few. They look on at much; they participate in little. They read about work; they get their hands into little of it.

It must be obvious that a school, or a doctrine of school, that was adequate under old-time conditions will prove far from satisfactory under these new conditions. We need a new *doctrine* of school, in order that we may escape from the old doctrine, now outgrown, and thus take a real step toward escaping from the older institutionalized school, now also long outgrown as almost everybody feels assured, to-day.

In this First Part of this book we shall develop the social history of the academic school, in order that we may disentangle it from its present social acceptance and bring it out into the open world where criticism may be made to play freely upon it. Not everything we shall find in schools will be futile or undesirable: some things will seem necessary, some things unnecessary; some things will be desirable, some things merely ridiculous. Theory and philosophy have not forced this critical issue; it is the changed life of our times—our removal from the country to the city that has forced the issue. We have faced this issue in the matter of tallow candles and kerosene lamps, and most of us are willing to accept the electric light. We must face the issue as fearlessly in the matter of education—even though in this field the issue is so much more complex, the outcome so much less ascertainable. The school has boasted of its contributions to the cause of "mind," and "understanding." Here is its chance to prove its boasts, by helping to clarify the conditions of its own existence, and to establish the range of its own constructive criticism; that is, to let *mind* play upon the school itself.

We turn, first, to the beginnings of education in the human story, in order that we may discover the beginnings of the school as a social institution.

CHAPTER II

THE PRIMITIVE GROUP AS EDUCATOR

The boy imitates the work of his father, and the girl learns household duties by imitating her mother. The end to be attained in both cases is the same, the exact reproduction of the knowledge or skill of the parents. Variation has no place in this scheme of education, for the children are not supposed to make any advance beyond the attainments of their parents. . . . The theoretical or inventive field remains an unknown land. The learner has placed before him a model which he endeavors to reproduce exactly. No time or material is wasted in attempting to improve upon the model, rude though it be. The one desideratum is the acquirement of a certain amount of skill in doing just the things his ancestors have done century after century before him. Indeed, in all their occupations requiring skill, such as building, weaving, basket and pottery making, the forms have become so conventionalized by their beliefs that a religious sanction is placed upon them, which it would be a serious desecration to disregard. . . . The priests have been for centuries the real rulers of the Pueblos. They have successfully stemmed the tide of progress and held their people to a given level of achievement.—SPENCER, in *The Education of the Pueblo Child* (1899), v.p.

A friend of mine, Fontana, of Buenos Ayres, who has a life-long acquaintance with the Argentine Indians, expressed the opinion that at the age of twelve years the savage of the Pampas has completed his education, and is thereafter able to take care of himself; but that the savage of the Gran Chaco—the sub-tropical Argentine territory

8

bordering on Paraguay and Bolivia—if left to shift for himself at that age would speedily perish, since he is then only in the middle of his long, difficult and painful apprenticeship.—W. H. HUDSON, in *Idle Days in Patagonia*.

Human education is at least as old as human living. But *the school* is the latest of our major social institutions. Education is, therefore, far older than schooling. If, then, we are to understand education—and the school, too, for that matter—we must go far back of schools, to the origins of education; or as near to those origins as present knowledge will permit. Hence, we shall begin with life and education in the primitive human group *before school was invented*.

At the Crossing of the Trails.—Human history began with the emergence of small groups, bound together by blood ties and living within small and usually precariously held habitats. The first groups of which we have valid knowledge were a bit advanced beyond this stage. These groups were more complex, but they were still of blood kin and living within limited environments. They lived by hunting, fishing and collecting wild plants; some practiced simple tillage of the soil; they probably built crude shelters of sorts; and they may even have known some very simple metal work.

Such groups had no organized government, but they had much *control*, which was exercised, for the most part, by the older men and women in strict accord with ancient precedents—the "folkways." Often, however, there was in the group some one man or woman of unusual attainments in the way of skill or genial traits of character who had much personal influence, but no authority. Age, skill in hunting or warfare, liberality of personality, all tend to increase influence, or to confer prestige: youth always respects such qualities—in the primitive world.

These primitive groups were closely knit together by ancient standards of behavior and belief, any violation of which provoked a social disapproval that was more than a primitive person could endure. "My punishment is greater than I can bear," said Cain, when he was banished from his group. These group standards were expressed in custom and ritual, wrought into the fiber of individual activity by persistent habit, and justified by elaborate myths dating from time immemorial.

Usually the primitive group was small, consisting of from 20 or 30 persons to a hundred or two hundred, and its existence was always precarious. When it became a part of some larger federation of groups, its existence was a bit more secure, but such arrangements were not characteristic of the primitive age. When the conditions of survival were not too insecure, the lodges of the group may have stood near the crossing of the trails that led to favorite fishing or hunting grounds, or to traditional battlefields on the barrier hills. Usually, at the best, life was insecure. Enemies, seen and unseen, lurked everywhere. Epidemics, floods, earthquakes: these could not be foreseen. Food supplies might fail. Hostile neighbors might descend upon them in the night. Against such ever-present dangers, the group had no defense save its courage, its solidarity, and the help of its mystic allies, its invisible members, including its gods!

The milieu of this primitive group was *fear*, and out of fear were born the gods and such solidarity and courage as the group possessed, as their gods could induce. Out of this fear came, therefore, such educational efforts as the group had developed, as we shall see presently; the very existence of the group depended upon the maintenance of an eternal vigilance against all its foes—both within and without the group.

For we must see that this little group was a fairly complete society within itself. It must supply all its own needs, physical and cultural, without help, save such as might come from its own folkway past in the way of experience. Within the group there was little division of functions. There were no institutions, as we understand that word. All members were, by and large, participants in all the forms of living. The group was one large family. It was a single industrial unit: each member had a share in the work by which life was sustained, and in the results of that work. The group was a religious organization: it had a rich and storied past, with sacred traditions and rituals, and with ceremonials surrounding every activity and event, and every individual must observe these ceremonials and rituals sacredly and literally. The group had survived in the past by reason of its reliance upon these sacred ways; and its future survival would, of course, depend upon the same literal observance of them through all time. These ways were the pledge of the gods to the group: in them were bound up the revered past, the precarious present, and the glorious future; they were held in trust for the generations yet to come. Life itself might be uncertain at the crossing of the primitive trails, but "the group," with its past and its future, was something permanent.

The Children of the Group.—The importance of children in such a social order is readily apparent. Death being certain, birth must be equally certain, if the group is to endure. This means that the child exists, not for itself, but for the sake of the group. It perpetuates the group; it must perpetuate the group; it may not have any private life of its own; it must consent to serve the needs and purposes of the group. Any deviation from this rule endangers the safety of the group; the child's own existence is dependent upon its subordination to the group. If the group perishes, the individual will certainly also perish. Subordination to the group will secure not alone the group's survival, but the survival of the individual, as well. The individual gets his reality from the reality of the group. Education is rooted in these obvious facts.

Hence, education was the most important interest of the group. It may even be said that the primitive group was primarily an educational instrument. Children must be absorbed into the sacred ways of the group, and completely indoctrinated with the spirit and purpose of the group. Education, however, was of two types. The one type was casual, informal: the child grew up within the folkways and activities of the group and absorbed those folkways and activities by the very processes of living; the other type was a bit more formal and conscious: the child must be taught the attitudes of subordination, and shaped to complete emotional acceptance of the ways of the group.

No School in the Primitive World.—There was no school in this primitive group life. Yet education was inescapable and adequate; adequate, that is, to the survival of the group. The years of childhood and youth were spent in active participation in the ways of the adult generation: in work, and play that imitated work; in conversation and listening; in sharing and being instructed; in growing up into the interests, activities and skills of the adult world. All children thus absorbed the infinite details of nature, and the primitive skills by which the group kept itself going. They learned to do— by doing; and they learned to know—by watching, listening and participating. They absorbed the legends and traditions, the myths and folk-lore, the tales of gods and

heroes, immediately, uncritically. They were present on
all occasions that were permitted them, when the group
gathered for celebrations, feasts, camp fires, story-telling
or other public events. They lived with the group, subject to the limitations of their ages. They got the group's
sense of order, its relationships to nature and the social
environment, its whole round of life. They came to be
made of the stuff of group living. And when they were
grown they were prepared to do the things that elders of
the group were expected to do. They had no need of a
school: the community was the educator of its own young
in far more effective fashion than any school could provide. Life and living was education!

One Organized Factor.—There was, however, one
formal factor in this primitive education. This formal
factor had developed out of primitive group fears, and
had survived because of its social utility. The security
of a group depends not alone upon what the children
learn, but the spirit in which they live what they learn.
After all, skills and knowledges are not enough; youth
may know and be able to do, and may still play havoc
with the ancient folkways. The most important aspect
of education is emotional: what will youth do with its
knowledge and its skills? Unless youth accepts the folkways irrevocably and unquestioningly, knowledge and
skill may be turned against the safety of the group.
Youth may become resentful of control—unless the emotions are fixed in the "right" direction. Children, especially boys, are ever a possible menace to stability, unless
they are caught young, and their emotions brought under
the domination of group custom. The adult generation
must make sure that these emotions are so set—beyond
recall—else the group may be destroyed from within.

How can this complete fixation of the emotions of

youth within the customs of the group be brought about? The answer is found in the primitive initiation ceremonial. This ceremonial was practiced in some form practically everywhere in the primitive world. Groups that never learned to deal with youth in this way perished, and are forgotten. At least the exceptions are few and unimportant.

The initiation ceremonial was always performed during the period of adolescence, when youth is most susceptible to emotional impressions. In the experiences that were gathered into this ceremonial the adolescent found himself submerged irresistibly in the intimate life of the group. He became identified with the group. After feeling these experiences, he could never be a hanger-on, a critic, or a mere spectator of group life and interests. The group's goods became his own goods; its evils became his evils; its life his life; its death his death; its friends became his friends; its tasks his tasks; its problems his problems; its enemies his enemies; its gods his gods! He passed over from childhood into manhood, and from passive acceptance of the security provided by the group into an active defender of that security as an adult member of the group. These results were the climax of a series of experiences, which covered—depending upon the ways of various groups—anywhere from two or three weeks to four or five months.

The Initiation Ceremonial.—The ceremonials of initiation absorbed the attention of the whole group. The ceremonial would include days of public feasting and rejoicing; a period of the severest physical tests of courage and endurance, even to the extent of torture for the initiates; and a period of fasting in some lonesome lodge far in the woods, perhaps. Each candidate might be left alone in this secluded lodge, to fast and pray, and wait for events. With extreme hunger come dreams; in dreams come the revelations of guardian spirits, the totem animal; and the Great Spirit himself may speak. All this was very real and inescapably impressive to the youth. His emotions, stirred to the deeps by solitude, hunger, silence and vivid dreams, were ready for permanent attachment to objects that promised safety, to activities that promised security and to purposes calling for life-long devotion and control. Thus he was ready for the final revelations of the intimate secrets of the group and for induction into the counsels of the impressive folkway past.

These revelations were made by the elders of the group who sedately opened to him all the precious lore of the past. This wisdom came to him, under the circumstances, as from the very mouth of the divinity. These secrets were of many sorts: of family relationships and inter-relationships; of industry and the magic modes by which agriculture could be best promoted, or the means by which the fleet deer could be brought to earth; of war, and the means by which the enemy could be conquered; of religion, and those magic processes which even the gods cannot disobey; of social control, and the means by which rebellious individuals can be brought to submission—all these and more. And these revelations might be further "clinched" and made far more emotionally impressive by some form of physical torture applied at just the right psychological moment in the midst of the revelations. Also, as this experience marked the actual passing of the youth over into the ranks of the adult part of the community, there was always some changing of his clothing: he put away childish things and put on the marks of the man! In Greece and Rome, this ancient practice lingered until late historical times as all school boys know. Some fragments of it linger with us still.

After these experiences were consummated, the youth "belonged." He had become a member of the inner circle. He had passed emotionally from boyhood into manhood and citizenship, and a great gulf lowered between him and his youth. He gives up playing with the children and lives henceforth with men. He begins to assume, as he can, the responsibilities of the adult member of the group. He begins to think about marrying. He will be present in the future on all occasions when the group engages in deliberation. Eventually his voice will be heard and respected in the group deliberations, if he becomes worthy of his new destiny. So, in this ceremonial, the group has extended its life, enlarged its power, provided against the contingencies of the future; and this youth has lost his *individuality*, but found his *citizenship*, in the community. In the primitive sense, he is educated. He has taken the group for his world, and he will live, or die, as the case may be, with his group. Primitive education ends in the complete identification of the group and the new individual.

Characteristics of This Education.—This primitive education, it will be noted, was absolutely *thorough*. The youth was educated when he had become an absorbed, capable, dependable member of his adult world. That education was *practical*. It was wrought of the materials and activities and skills used and needed in everyday living in the group. It was an education that was useful because it had developed under the conditions of use. It came out of no irrelevant text book, taught by remote and indifferent teachers. It was life and living—no less!

Moreover, this primitive education was completely *moral*, in the group sense. It did not have to be moralized after it was taught. Its processes made the youth a

member of the group. If morality be defined as personal
capacity and the will to carry effectively one's full share
of responsibility for the common welfare, this primitive
education was indubitably moral.

We must note, too, that this primitive initiation ceremonial had specific social meanings. It was a civic ceremonial. It marked the "coming of age" of the young
people of the community; and it was a civic experience
through which they became recognized members of the
group.

That ceremonial had economic meaning also. The
initiate became a worker having a share in the group's
industrial organization. From that time forward he
shared with the elders responsibility for the support of
the whole group.

It was a religious ceremonial. In its process the youth
definitely foreswore his own private will, his "selfish" desires, his "sins," and gave himself, or was given, in complete devotion to the ideal will—the will and spirit of the
group. This made him acceptable to the gods of the
group.

Argument can be made, arguments have been made,
arguments will be made that education must be something
other than this supreme devotion to, and absorption into,
the traditional folkway group. The argument is that
such an education makes the individual nothing: he is
but a repetition of a pattern—nothing in himself. All
that may well be true, and still be beside the point. The
fact is that human education began in primitive groups,
more or less as here described; that early education was
developed in the structure and activities of the group;
and its results were, by and large, much as those here
set down. Whether that education was "good" or "bad"
is now beside the point. It was "good" in its time, as is

shown by the fact that groups practicing it survived. Whether "good" or "bad," it *was* the sort of education the human race first knew, and it demonstrated its uses. It was wrought into the nervous systems of the young in narrow patterns of behavior, adapted to narrow and fearful areas of behavior, the primitive groups. Being of the nature of habit, it operated automatically within its group areas, and operated not at all outside those areas; or, it attempted to compel outside areas to conform to the patterns that were familiar.

Moreover, this education has not ended. Throughout the course of our study we shall come upon evidences of the persistence of this same primitive education, up to the time schools came into existence; since that time, outside the school, and not infrequently within the school, as well. We live in larger worlds, and larger groups, requiring more inclusive behavior patterns and, not infrequently, developing situations with respect to which *no behavior patterns do now exist*. None the less, the narrow, provincial, prejudicial behavior patterns persisting from primitive times, offer themselves as adequate for these new and more complex situations, and even at times, propose to call in the authorities to secure their unquestioning acceptance. We shall see much of this as we go on.

What Is Education?—From this vantage we may consider briefly what education is. Is it an accumulation of a certain number of experiences? Is it a round of sensations? A mass of facts? A measure of ideas? Accumulated knowledge? Each of these probably, in part, but none of them exclusively, nor all of them put together. In the primitive group education meant the development of each child to a share in the life, the activities, and eventually the control of the group. Education is a *whole:* an outlook, a point of view, a sense of mastery, skill in the circumstances of life and action. It is organized experience which can take care of every particular experience which may happen along.

These are large words. In a simple society the results they connote were outwardly narrow and entirely to be contained within the range of custom and habit. None the less, education then meant grasp and mastery of the circumstances of group existence, action and control: nothing less. Not all achieved such mastery. But more achieved it under those conditions than do now achieve it under our more complex modes of living, even with the help of our more complex instruments of "instruction."

This is partly because the problem is so much larger to-day. It is also partly because that old past persists and interferes with our free analysis of this larger present problem. The task of education is larger to-day; but the definition of education should remain much the same. It is a gradual achievement, by the race and the individual, of an understanding and mastery of the conditions of existence, so that action can be relevant to conditions, and so that the future can be foreseen, at least in its larger aspects. But, because the *definition* of education is much the same, we are inclined to assume that the *processes* of education must be identical; at any rate, that our old primitive group patterns of behavior should be used just as much as possible: new patterns must be ever on the defensive. That is "natural." It is too natural. It is obstructive.

But we must return to further study of the primitive methods of education, and seek the fate of the primitive initiatory activities.

Remnants of the Initiatory Ceremonials.—If, as is here assumed, those initiatory ceremonials were so im-

portant, why have they so completely disappeared? Two
answers appear. First, they have not wholly disappeared.
They have, like the old group life, been broken into fragments, and the fragments are all about us. Second, the
school has come, and education has become academic.
Those old activities were largely emotional, and we suspect emotions to-day. Education is of the intellect, not
the emotions, to-day!

None the less, fragments of those ceremonials are still
with us. The nearest approach to the ceremonial itself
may be seen in initiations into lodges and secret societies
to-day. All such initiations are lineal descendants of
primitive ceremonials. Most people long, primitively, to
be initiated into something. They want to "belong."
But just as any secret society, to-day, is but a fragment
of the community, so its initiation ceremonial is but a
shadow of those primitive ones. We do not initiate our
youth into the whole community, to-day; hence, we have
no use for community ceremonials. We content ourselves with fragments of old ways. We initiate adults
into fragments of the community.

And we have many fragments to-day. The primitive
initiation was a civic affair: the youth "came of age" and
was publicly taken into the adult world. Young people
"come of age" to-day, too; but society makes little of
such events. A political machine may make much of it,
but "the community" seems but little interested.

The primitive ceremony was an industrial affair; the
youth became a factor in the industrial organization of
the group. Young people "get jobs" to-day, too. That's
an important fact. But the community is but slightly
concerned.

That primitive ceremony was a social event: the can-
didates, after that experience, belonged to the adult social

world. In some social areas we have "coming-out" parties for young people, young women particularly. But most children enter "society" without any public recognition of the event.

That primitive ceremony was a religious event. In it the candidate gave up his individual will, his selfish desires, and expressed his devotion to the ideal will, the will and spirit of the group. Young people "join the church" to-day, too; they are "converted" and "confirmed." This is usually a very private experience to-day. It ought probably to be the most significant experience of life, both for the youth and for his community. But because it has lost its significance—it seems to have lost its significance!

The Attitude of the Community.—But the attitude of the community is severely changed from that of the old group. The adult community to-day pays little attention to any of these needs or experiences of its youth. A girl in "society" may "make her début" into her special group, but not into the community. A young man may "get a job" or "go to work," but there is no civic celebration of this important event. The political party which a young man joins may put his name on the books as an additional voter for their candidate at the next election. That is as far as his coming of age is likely to be noticed in the civic life. At present, religious conversion and confirmation do not seem to have much effect on the actual social outlooks of men and women. The youth gets small social meaning out of a religious experience; and the age would scarcely know what to do with a *real convert*.

There is, however, one modern occasion which is more nearly reminiscent of the educational and civic significance of the primitive ceremonial than any of these. That is school "commencement." This fact is significant. There was no school in the primitive community. Hence, there could be no school "commencement." None the less the initiation marked the "commencement" of adult living. To-day education is about the only thing the community as a whole finds interesting. Even the modern community tries to get a thrill out of the aspirations and achievements of its children. As of old the community needs to feel its own future dramatized in the prospects of its youthful generations. Graduation from a school comes nearest to providing for the whole community the thrills of that original initiation ceremony—and an eighth grade or a high school graduate, looking down from the platform on the thousand faces of friends and neighbors, goes through some of the same experiences which the primitive youngster went through in the original initiation ceremony. At least for a few moments he feels the same old primitive thrills.

A great tragedy has happened here, however. That old ceremonial has been broken into fragments as we have seen, and this new ceremonial, graduation from school, has almost no community meaning. It is a "graduation," an end, not a commencement! It is a "social" event, little more. The diploma given on that occasion has no real community significance. It has nothing to do with the possessor's civic position. It doesn't assure him a job. It is not a certificate of good behavior, or character, or dependability, or of social acceptance. It is a formal thing. It opens up nothing to its possessor except one gateway; namely, the gateway to another school and to more schooling. So far has schooling lost the ancient realities of education.

The most important period in the life of any child is adolescence, when he passes over from childhood into

adulthood. The primitive community felt that importance and utilized the period; in very primitive ways, it
is true, but in the interest of the future of the group.
Those hopes were very narrow, even repressive, and from
the standpoint of progress, undeniably obstructive. But
we have swung to the opposite extreme; we seem to assume that adolescent experience has no significance at all.
We seem to have no concern whether boys and girls come
through to manhood and womanhood devoted to the common good, or to the meanest, most sordid, the most individualistic ideals. We have built our schools; we have
filled the schools with stores of accumulated knowledge.
We have turned education over to these schools. We
seem to believe that schooling can take the place of education; that schooling can prepare for living; that in the
schooling of our youth the foundations of the future
are established. And so we have washed our community
hands of the whole task, theoretically. We believe a
theory. We refuse to face the facts!

Do the Schools Educate?—Yet boys and girls play,
as of old, wherever they can find or make a corner of
freedom. They follow up such industries as the community has not completely hidden from them. They look
in at the open doors (there are not many!) of shops and
stores and factories and offices. They listen in on conversations. They take courses of instruction with hired
men and chauffeurs, street-car conductors and policemen,
alley cats and society poodles. They do not wait until
the school bell rings to begin their inquiries into the nature of life and they do not stop getting an education at
four P.M. They are fed by the streets and the movies,
by the filth and the folly as well as by the beauty of city
and country. They are parts of all that they have met—
and to them:

"All experience is an arch wherethrough
Gleams that untraveled world whose margin fades
Forever and forever . . ."
                                        as they move.

The education that they assimilate, the experiences
that actually become determinative in their destinies are
but partially the products of their school years, and even
less the product of the schools. The life of the community, the folkways of the family, the neighborhood, the
playground, the school-yard, the whole city, are the atmosphere, the background, the fundamentals of all their
actual characters and destinies. There is no reason why
the school should be praised or assailed, abstractly. The
school is an objective institution. What it is doing can
be seen and appraised. What it is failing to do can be
determined. We have given credit where no credit is due.
We have withheld credit where we should have paid.
The facts are needed and the facts can be secured.

Meanwhile if we are to be able to consider education
impartially, we must ask history to tell us how the race
came to lose that complete, though narrow, primitive education of the group, and to set up this academic substitute of the modern school. The story is long, but not
without a definite interest and a tremendous social significance. We turn to the story of the breakup of the
primitive community.

CHAPTER III

DISORGANIZATION OF THE PRIMITIVE GROUP

"Yes, sir," said the talkative man on the street car. "I guess I know this town as well as anybody could. There isn't a street or an alley I'm not familiar with. I've been living here for twenty-five years, and I know the old town like a book."

One can learn a good deal in twenty-five years. A city soon grows familiar. It is not hard to imagine that your home town never can surprise you again. Yet the talkative car rider was wrong. He doesn't know the town. Nobody does. Not one of us even knows his own street. Any collection of human homes, from a cross-roads settlement to a great metropolis, is a mystery, and we are mistaken if we brag of easy familiarity.

Consider the street you live on. You walk down it every morning and evening of your life; its physical aspects are seen so often that you could get to your house with your eyes shut. But the street for all that is a mystery. Each house in it is a dwelling place for two or more people like yourself, with secret hopes, hidden struggles and unknown dreams like your own. You do not know the street at all. It is not simply a commonplace highway lined with ordinary frame and brick buildings. It is the temporary resting place of some scores of aloof human beings, each of whom has his own victories, his own defeats, his own aspirations and his own heartaches.
—Editorial in the Rockford (Ill.) *Morning Star*, March, 1928.

The primitive community which we have been studying had a geographical and psychological unity. Its territory

25

was limited. Its numbers were few. Every one knew every one else. There were no extraneous elements. Everybody and everything belonged. Prof. Charles H. Cooley calls such communities "primary." Everything is directly present to everybody. Nothing has to be taken at second hand. All the territorial and personal factors in the community are perceptible to all. For our purposes we may call such communities *perceptual* communities to distinguish them from others which we shall presently come upon, and which we shall call *conceptual*. In such a perceptual community, practically all education of children takes place as part of the natural processes of development, as we have seen. The children are educated not by teachers, but by life—in and of the whole community.

The Fracturing of a Primary Community.—But, in the course of world history, populations have increased— at least in some areas. As new methods of food supply emerge, population grows. The little group at the crossing of the trails finds itself crowded, both within and from without. New lodges have to be built, new trails laid out, many trails laid out; until in good time, the earlier primary community grows into a city, which lies at the crossing of many trails. Instead of fifty or a hundred members, the community now has ten thousand, twenty thousand. And in such a community, few if any can know any considerable part of what exists or occurs—at first hand. The perceptual community is gone. It has been broken up, fractured by its own growth and prosperity. The characteristic of this larger community is that it cannot be known at first hand. This fact produces most of the educational and social problems of the modern world. Though we live in *conceptual* communities, we are educated to the levels of *perceptual* living, only.

No one can know at sight ten thousand people, or know what they are doing, feeling, believing, thinking, saying. No one can know where they live, how they live, what they live for. No one can know their family ties, their social and traditional backgrounds, their folkways and their moralities. No one can know how ten thousand people make their living, or fail to make it. No one can know the relationships and attitudes of ten thousand people to civic order and control. No one can know what ten thousand people think is beautiful, or moral, or honest, or sacred. In short, when a community has grown to a population of ten thousand, it has become what Professor Cooley calls a "secondary" community, and it can be known, or comprehended, or apprehended only in parts, in fragments, in generalizations, in statistics—*in concepts!*

In such a community, any one can know a fraction of it, but knowledge of a fraction of anything is *never* valid of the whole. He can know a few people, more or less intimately, in the old ways. He can know something about the geography of the place. He can know a bit about the industry—about some of the industries; a bit about the doings of the politicians and the courts; a bit about some of the religious ceremonials. For him, it is plain, the old community has been fractured, and all that he can know is something about some fractional parts of it. He can, probably, get statistics of the population, the industries, miles of streets, number of churches and church members, policemen, criminals, millionaires and paupers. But these are *facts*—not experiences. And if he should try to get a view of this large, fractured community as a whole, that view would have to be built up out of many details fitted together into a background that was only partially perceptual. Such a picture would be of the na-

ture of a *conception,* not a perception; and we may call
this "secondary" type of community a *conceptual* community. It will be known, if it is ever really known by
any one, in conceptual fashion, not in immediate perceptions.

The Fragmentation of the Individual.—A small community can be a unified world. A member of a small
community is likely a unified human being, however small
the unit. But with the growth of the community in numbers and size that original unity inevitably breaks up;
and always thereafter continuous fracturing takes place.
The community breaks up into neighborhoods and "quarters." It increases by "additions." In time "select residence districts" develop, and "industrial quarters" grow
up. "The Harbor" comes to have a character of its own.
"Villages" of various sorts will remain, or appear. The
larger "community" will not be a community at all, but
a congeries of lesser groupings all bound together by ex-
trinsic bonds of territory or political authority. A "civic
center" with courts and jails may seek to dramatize this
arbitrary unity. But the echoes of the footsteps of soli-
tary sightseers about the "civic centers" will reveal how
little place such arbitrary "centers" have in the actual
lives of men.

But not alone is the old community broken into fragments by this growth of the city; the individuals who
make it up are also fractured similarly. The "residence
district" that dislikes contact with the "industrial quarter" may develop an individual who dislikes the implications of industry. The "village" (in the city) emphasizes
its own distinctive, and hence fragmentary, character and
selects, or produces, individuals who are fragmentary in
the same directions. Left to itself this heaped-up city
would produce specialized, fragmented, eccentric, lop-

sided personalities. But when we consider the part which institutions play in any such situation the result becomes still more complicated. This is true even though institutions were developed largely for the purpose of providing against any such undesirable outcome.

Maybe the unity of the original, primary community has been over-stressed. After all, no person, no group, no community has ever been completely unified. Any individual or group has needs. These needs seek satisfactions. Not all persons have the same sense of need in every direction. The efforts to satisfy needs will probably always lead various members of a group in various directions, as they feel their needs. Probably each person will be torn a bit between this need and that. Such competitions of needs were latent and implicit even in the primitive group life. They became increasingly explicit in the expanding life of the city, when the old unity could no longer be maintained.

In the course of history, "human nature" has become sufficiently differentiated and dramatized to reveal at least five great fundamental needs. As children we need care and nurture; as active, physical beings, we need the chance to be active, to work, to create, to produce; as members of social groups, we need social experiences, and at the same time, protection from the misdirection of social ambition; as possessed of more or less curiosity and as facing problems and tasks in the world, we need to know; as something more than mere organisms, we need assurance as to the meaning and destiny of life. In the primitive community, all these needs are satisfied without questioning, in the common life of the group. The group itself is family, industrial organization, civic experience, educational opportunity, and religious realization.

But the larger community cannot and does not immediately provide these resources. In the breaking up of the primitive group, these primitive needs will be overlooked, or ignored, if they are not imperious. Hence, these needs, themselves, take charge of events. They make their own organizations and instruments. They set up their own outlets. They erect institutions: The Family; Industry; Government; The Church. They even seize upon fragments of the old community, and attempt to mold those fragments into psuedo-communities, which will retain something of primitive unity and resistance to change. Certainly, they tend to "select" individuals from the community for their own uses and memberships, the net result being that, at least in the larger community, we find "business" men, "church" men, "industrialists," "politicians," and even "family" men, but not very many men or women who are *citizens of the whole community*.

That is to say, the fracturing of the primitive group has its correlate in the fragmentation of the individual. This is not entirely loss: the "fragment" of the individual that passes for a man in the new city is larger and more important than that corresponding fraction of the primitive group member would have been. But in getting these more important *fractions* of men, we have lost the "whole man." In getting specialized *members of institutions,* we have let *humanity* slip through the fractures and escape. We have lost "humanity," but we have gained institutions —if that is adequate compensation. We have lost the primitive *community,* but we have gained incipient "individuals," if that is adequate compensation.

The Social Significance of Institutions.—We live, we say, in an institutionalized social order. It is difficult to see how life could get on without these institutional developments. The larger community cannot attend to

everything for everybody. We must have specialists and
specialized functions; division of labor and services, and
exchange of labor and services. All this is true. But, is
it so certain that our institutions have to be just what
they are? Do they have to maintain just the attitudes
they do maintain? Our institutions, to-day, have acquired certain *vested rights*. Historically and genetically,
they are not entitled to any such rights; they have those
rights merely because they have taken them; and because
our *theory* of institutions enables them to bully the community into permission to retain those rights.

Let us see where our institutions came from. All our
institutions have grown out of needs. *The needs of the
child* produced the family. Man's fears and man's needs
produced the gods and religion. Our need of creative
activity and economic security produced all forms of industry. Our need of social order either produced or
lulled us into accepting the various forms of social order,
association and control.

If, therefore, our major institutions have grown out of
human uses and needs, *they have no rights,* except the
right to serve the needs for which they were developed.
They have no absolute rights. They were not created in
some supernal way and handed down to men, ready made.
They all represent emergence, growth, development, use;
and they ought to have the fluidity of human use and
need. Why do they not?

Because of the general human tendency to habit and
custom, and to the reign of precedent. Our institutions
ought to be as fluid as time; but they build themselves
into molds, into structures, into vested positions with
their own rights and wrongs; and they resist change, just
as every habit resists change, until they identify changelessness with the sacred, and change with anarchy and

destruction. Every one of our institutions was once as vividly alive as is a tender, newly sprouted blade of corn. It probably was necessary, but not irrevocable that they should become old, ripe, fixed, growthless.

How Institutions Defeat the Community.—The normal man cannot live without some sort of community, some *fatherland* of his being, some *patria*, some group of congenial and protective friendliness. But when the large city grows out of and beyond the small primitive group, fracturing that group, the "member" of the group loses most of his former sense of membership. He retreats into some fraction of the whole, or he becomes a derelict in the city wastes. Some continue to cling to some idealized past, as we shall see later; but most find the task too difficult, too uncongenial. They find their "community" thenceforth in some fragment of the larger whole, some fraction of the city. A small neighborhood within the city may serve for a social world. Or some social group having common interests may save the sense of community. *The home* is "all the world" to some city individuals. The church becomes the community for some. Industrial and business fellowships provide community for others. Political cliques offer refuge for many. Clubs, lodges, brotherhoods, social and professional groups of many sorts afford other avenues of escape from the wilderness of the city into something that feels like the close-knit relationships of the primitive group. Our modern communities are filled, even cluttered up, with these efforts to escape from the complexity of the city into the simplicity of the primitive. One does not have to go to the woods to "return to nature." Though we want to live in *cities,* we want to *live by* the habit and feeling patterns of old groups.

It should not be difficult now to see the *great gulfs* that exist in the city which is made up of these overgrown fragments of the former community. New York City is not a "community." It is a wilderness of antagonistic villages in which both the "city" and the "individual" are lost. Nor should it be difficult to see the defects in the education that is likely to result from such developments of the world. *We are made by the lives we live.* He whose community is merely *the home* will carry everywhere his infantile traits. The business man and the worker may come to be nothing but smooth shuttles sliding back and forth in their grooves. The church makes churchmen. Politics makes politicians, not statesmen. All these lose that old-time sense of community. They spend their lives not in a community, but in fragments or in institutions. The comedian asked: "Who wants to live in an institution?" The answer, which he did not anticipate, was: "Nearly everybody!"

But growing up among institutions, or in institutions, makes fragmentary persons. Institutions are necessary in the modern great society; but *no institution* hesitates to manhandle persons in the service of its own prestige. Even the school, invented as we shall see presently for an entirely different purpose, tends to turn out "graduates," and to make "school men" out of its workers.

More than all this, *Loyalty to these fragments of the human* has almost universally taken the place of the former feeling for the community as a whole. This is pretty generally admired. A "good churchman" is usually regarded as a far better man than is a citizen of the whole community who is not a churchman. We produce few "citizens," men and women who belong to the whole city, to-day, and we don't mind. Business men feel that business men should run the city, and the world. Politicians assume that the city naturally belongs to them. Churchmen feel that if all the world would join the church, the world would be "saved." The "common weal," we rather hold, is unorganized, inchoate, and therefore probably an evil, a bog. Man's safety lies in his membership in, and loyalty to, institutions. That is to say, the *servant* of humanity's earlier existence has become the *master* of man's later years.

By reason of this subordination of the community to its own institutions, the community is further broken up into fragments; and the individual is thereby kept from anything approaching full development. No institution, nor any sum of institutions, can produce the full stature of a man. Nothing but the whole life of the community, playing in organic completeness over and through all his being, can produce any such result. An institution can produce nothing but fragments of personalities.

Moreover, these same results tend to take on geographical bounds, too. Our cities break up into "quarters," as we have seen. Industry is segregated in an "industrial section"—though some people have to live there, too. The civic life gathers into the court house, the police station and the jail. Religion remains quietly in churches. Once children grew up in the company of their elders, in the midst of work, surrounded by social controls, with a share in religious ceremonials, and looking eagerly ahead to the day when they should be initiated into full membership in the common life. Now, a child growing up in a "residential quarter" is not permitted to see any real work going on. His contact with government is an occasional sight of a "cop." He may get an unintelligent experience with "religion" once a week. He has been abstracted from the old time realities of group life, and he gets his "humanity" by being passed around among institutions, much as if he were an article being manufactured in a modern mass-production plant. "Education" in the form of schooling, is just another bit of this same processing by means of which institutions finally mold and shape social products.

The Escape of Institutions from the Community.— Institutions once were, as we have seen, necessary and inevitable developments, meeting great social needs. They developed as the primitive group grew too great to provide complete life in the old communal way. But the insidious factors of established prerogative and vested right are nowhere more obvious than in the after-history of all our institutions. Institutions were developed for service: that was their origin; that ought to be their history and their present status.

But service to individuals and the community is vague, irksome, unremunerative. It calls for faith in human nature and for a devotion which, though beautiful, palls upon us after the first glow of enthusiasm is past. It is so much easier to assume that, by their very existence, our institutions are serving men. It is even easy to assert the doctrine. It is not difficult to take the position that to call an institution to account is of the nature of disloyalty. "All good people should believe in marriage, the home, the state, the church, the school, business." And most good people would not think of doubting them, or examining them.

Hence, *all our institutions* have erected themselves into *ends* in themselves: they have accumulated their own customs and folkways, organized their own programs, developed their own vested interests, set up their own tests of personal loyalty, and embarked upon their own furtherance of their own position in the world, with little thought as to the actual bearing of their procedures on the individual or the community. They are dedicated to service: therefore, they serve! They do not have to show results: they have to show credentials only.

They compete ruthlessly for the allegiance of individuals. They publish statistics of the growth of their own private clientele. They have escaped from the community and forgotten it; or if they do remember it, it is to ask for support: they identify their own growth with the good of the community. This is just the reversal of the old legend of Chronos, who devoured his own children. Here is actual fact: the children have torn their mother to pieces and made themselves gorgeous in the remnants of her garments. Each of them has taken some part of her being and magnified itself by magnifying that fragment. There are those who hold, to-day, that the sum of our institutions makes up the whole of the community. But these are unaware of the fundamental biological doctrine that The Whole is always more than the sum of its parts.

All our institutions have gone their own ways, including the newest of them all, the school. For each of them, one can find some historical or psychological excuse for these results, except for the school. In this respect, by following in the ruck of the other institutions, the school has utterly failed of its true nature, has denied its origins, and has abdicated its proper functions. The fact of the failure of the school, in these respects, is one of the most important and serious of historical facts. This will become apparent as we consider the breakdown of the old group life and the emergence of the larger community with its complications. But, there is an interesting intermediate stage, which we shall first have to traverse. We take up this intermediate stage in the next chapter. It has to do with a personality and a function not properly recognized in the History of Education.

CHAPTER IV

THE FUNCTIONS OF THE PEDAGOGUE

You may like to know something of the person and character of my father . . . his great excellence lay in a sound understanding and solid judgment in prudential matters, both in private and public affairs . . . I remember well his being frequently consulted for his opinions in affairs of the town . . . He was also much consulted by private persons about their affairs when any difficulty occurred, and frequently chosen an arbiter between contending parties. At his table he liked to have, as often as he could, some sensible friend or neighbor to converse with, and always took care to start some ingenious or useful topic for discourse, which might tend to improve the minds of his children. . . . I continued employed in my father's business till I was twelve years old . . . But my dislike to the trade (of tallow chandler) continuing, my father was under apprehensions that if he did not find one more agreeable for me, I should break away and go to sea, as his son Josiah had done to his great vexation. He therefore sometimes took me to walk with him, and to see joiners, bricklayers, turners, braziers, etc., at their work, that he might observe my inclination, and endeavor to fix it on some trade or other on land. It has ever since been a pleasure to me to see good workmen handle their tools, and it has been useful to me, having learned so much by it as to be able to do little jobs myself in my house when a workman could not be readily got, and to construct little machines for my experiments, while the intention of making the experiment was fresh and warm in my mind. . . . From a child I was fond of reading

... I had a thirst for knowledge ... This bookish inclination at length determined my father to make me a printer.—FRANKLIN, in *Autobiography*.

Humanity is real. Men are neither accidents nor aliens in the universe. Human life is rooted in the reality of the world. Our personalities are woven of the stuff of our experiences. Hence, if we are to be completely human we must grow up in a completely human world. That is to say, a developing personality must have a complete community to furnish the stuff of its growing life. Anything less than this complete community will tend to produce something less than complete humanity. We have seen that the primitive community provided in general ways for all the essential human needs: the nurture of childhood; the social security of the group; some part for each individual in the industrial life; whatever the group had achieved in the way of knowledge and understanding; and some more or less convincing interpretation of the ultimate significance and destiny of human life. Humanity cannot be completely human without having some share in each of these great interests.

The Fragmentation of Personality.—But when the primitive community was broken up under the pressure either of growing population or the crowding in of competing tribes; when the little primary community at the crossing of the trails became the greater city at the crossing of many trails, those primitively unified human beings were inevitably broken to pieces, in the same way. Most of them naturally identified themselves with some fragment of the former community and so found a wistful completeness in this fragment of the world.

Children growing up in such fragments of the former world had little chance to attain unity, integrity, completeness of personality. The growing city gave them myriad opportunities to have experiences. By way of contrast we may say that in the primitive community a child enjoyed a certain number of experiences; in the more complex larger world, of which this child could touch only a fragment, we may admit that he got quite as many experiences, if not more than in the earlier small community. But life is more than a collection of sensations. Education is more than experiences. Education is understanding; and understanding is apprehension of unities, wholes. These wholes are not made up of parts put together. The whole must antedate its parts. No one ever understood an automobile by beginning his experience with the separate parts. Understanding begins with the whole—and it is the whole that gives meaning to the parts.

In the primitive group the child found that completeness of experience which alone we can call an education. That is to say, he found his life in the whole world about him, not in some isolated fragment of the world. That world may have been small—but it was a whole world and he knew his way about in it.

But in the more complex later community, with all his taking on of experiences, he did not always develop that *complete organization of experience which assures understanding and which alone can be properly called an education.* He did not come to be at home in the whole city. He did not understand the world outside his immediate experiences. He could not find his way about. It is evident, therefore, that it is not the number of experiences that determines an education, but the final outcome of experience in the way of an understanding of the world.

Education is not a matter of learning two or three new facts each day. Indeed it may be said of most people that the more facts they know the less educated they are. Education is understanding. This can be achieved, at least by most people, only when there is something of the nature of a complete community which provides the individual an integrating background for his experiences. What shall it profit a child if he gain the whole world of sensations and find no way to organize those sensations into understanding and control? The growth of the Great Community was not, therefore, all gain; at least not for the children of the lesser community.

Modern Parallels.—This problem is not academic and ancient. We live in the midst of like conditions. Our children grow up under similar influences. Our cities show little that is unified to any of us. Few of our communities present anything that serves as the organizing background of a completely human experience. Practically all our communities offer us nothing but fragments of living. A few among us who have imagination may be able to rise above the fragmentariness of our environments and achieve a certain degree of wholeness of outlook. If so, it is because we really live in an imaginary social community that is complete. But for most of us, especially for us who live in cities, living is either filled with whirlpools of bewildering sensations which tear us to pieces if we get caught in them; or it is made of narrow grooves of isolated custom and habit in which we slide back and forth all our days, unknowing and unknown. "A great city is a great wilderness," to none more so than to the growing child.

Two contradictory comments upon our modern city civilization will help to make this educational difficulty more concrete. One type of commentator never tires of telling us that western civilization is exceedingly complex, a technological civilization, he calls it, which none but a technologist can adequately understand. On the other hand, another type of writer continuously reiterates that the city easily becomes the refuge of the incompetent. One of these writers says: "It was never so easy before in the history of the world for the simpleton to live." The "simpleton" can find a little groove in some corner of the city's life and industry in which he can slide back and forth safely, asking nothing more. Such simpletons are highly prized by our machine civilization. They know enough to turn on the switch when they want a light. It is assumed that that is enough for them to know about lights. If the light fails to appear when the switch is turned on, the technologist must be called in, the man who understands the structure of this technological world we have built up. Between these two—the simpleton and the technologist—there is a great gulf fixed. It is not merely the gulf of knowledge. It is coming to be a gulf of social esteem, if not of actual social classification. Each lives in a fragment of the community. Each is on his way to becoming a fragment of a human being. A fragment of a community will produce and will select for survival fragments of human beings. We shall come upon this "great dichotomy" again.

The Primitive Fact.—Not in a single generation anywhere, save perhaps in Athens, but in the real experience of the race this breakdown of the primitive folkways took place, and groups of people faced a more or less disorganized world. The task of those disorganized ones to find a way of living in the larger community of the city is still our task to-day.

When our actual community fades, we feel naked and lost and we must seek for it somewhere else: if not in some other community, then in some substitute, in some institution, some underworld, or overworld, in some annex to the world, or some after-world—wherever we can find a fatherland for our living and our hopes. This reality of community and our need of it is not a cogitated fact of our experience; it is a deep and primitive feeling of need. Most animals are uneasy when left alone; some part of their environment has been shorn away, and that means some part of their real selves.

When the family is the community the absence of a single member leaves a painful gap. Not only is one member gone but the "community" is broken; the sense of wholeness is lacking; the "all" is not there. As any community grows larger, such disintegrations become more numerous and inevitable. If they are to be obviated they must be offset by processes of integration. But in no growing community do the integrating processes keep pace with the additive processes. That is to say, in all our cities populations have grown to metropolitan size, while our minds have remained of village dimension. We have achieved bulk, but not understanding, or integration.

In the primitive life this sense of community was very important. A story from the Old Testament Book of Samuel illustrates it: David was afraid of Saul. He decided to run away to his old home at Bethlehem for a few days. Jonathan, his friend, objected, saying, "The King, my father, will find all this out, and he'll blame me. What shall I say to him?" David replied: "Tell him it's our annual feast day and family reunion at Bethlehem, and it is absolutely necessary that all members of the family should be there. The King will understand."

Any one but the madman King Saul seems to have been would have understood. When every member is present "the family" is present. When any one member is away, not only is *he* absent, but the "all" is absent. This sense of the "allness" of the group was, and is, very real to all primitive peoples. The "all" gives strength and courage, beyond the strength and courage of the mere members taken severally. Hence, in some perspectives, this "allness" was the reality of the Deity. The true group includes not alone the obvious members, but that Allness which is the invisible part of the group. This Allness includes past, present and future. It involves the loyalty of every member, and the help of the group deities. It is thus a moral and spiritual "atmosphere" which the children and youth of primitive groups take in with every breath they breathe.

Children can never get this sense of community "allness" by doing intellectual tasks at school. Background of life is a social experience, and comes of a social background. There is, as we shall see later, a very close correlation between the reality of community and the development of real individuality. With rare exceptions, members of communities are small replicas of their communities, shadowy copies of the world about them. With rare exceptions, the nature of a community can be read in the lives of those who grew up in that community. A community may have a fairly definite "center," and still fray out around the edges into bedraggled fringes. The individual who grows up in that community may have some central integration, but he also is likely to fray out into bedraggled fringes corresponding to the fragments of world in which he lives.

The Solution in Athens.—A valiant effort to solve this problem of integrating education in a disintegrating community was made in Athens, in the age of Socrates and Plato. Athens emerges out of the prehistoric as a village. It grows into a city under our eyes. Its early education was essentially of the primitive sort we have been following. In the great days of the empire, under the stress of changing conditions and the growth of population, that older education had all but disappeared. What did Athens do in the midst of these disintegrating conditions? What invention, if any, met the educational needs of Athens at that time. The answer is the *pedagogue.*

Who was the pedagogue? The very word now bears a burden of obloquy. But not in its own right. The pedagogue was not a school teacher. Never, in Athens, did he perform that function. The earlier Athens had no schools in our sense of the word. The pedagogue did not belong inside any institution. His function was far simpler and more real. He performed a social and educational service in the life of the Athenian child, and therefore in the whole life of Athens, which we must first envisage; and this service had an intellectual significance which we must grasp if we are to understand education to-day.

As the city grew and became differentiated into areas, districts, neighborhoods; as interests deviated and institutions developed; as temples were gathered on the Acropolis and the shipping was isolated at the Piræus: in short, as the city broke up into fragments, there were still a few men who maintained something of a complete acquaintance with all that had been and with all that was coming to be. Their minds still grasped the growing city as a whole. For them it was still Athens, the single community. Such men were excellent pedagogues. The test of the pedagogue was: Does he know the city, old and new, and can he make the child see and understand the city: not in some fragment of the city nor many fragments, but the human community, broken yet still real, the background of his life and character and destiny?

The Work of the Pedagogue.—The task of the peda-

gogue is natural enough. Ben Franklin tells in his autobiography how his father was his pedagogue in Boston
village when Ben was a boy. The pedagogue led the
Athenian child through the streets of the growing city,
and helped him get something of the city as a whole.
With the help of the pedagogue, the child saw homes, industries, religious edifices and ceremonials, government at
work. He came to see *the city*. He rose above the
houses and the streets, the temples and the courts; these
did not stand in his way. In spite of them all, by means
of them all, with the help of the pedagogue, he found the
city—the community as a whole. And in such seeing and
finding he escaped the fragmentariness that would otherwise have been his fate. He achieved, with the help of
the pedagogue, completeness, integration, background, experience, unity in the midst of the multiplicity of details.
For a little while, in Athens, the pedagogue saved *education*. He assured understanding and intelligence to the
child who was born into that Athenian world after the
city had lost its primitive unity of organization and experience. Intelligent integration, that is, real education,
was still secured in the midst of disintegration.

How Did the Pedagogue Help?—Athenian government was ignorant of the fact that that primitive unity of
experience was disappearing. Government was rapidly
becoming the perquisite of the politician who had no
thought for posterity. Industry was willing to see the
whole structure of the past disappear—for the indus-
trialist has no understanding of the *moral* and *intellectual*
meanings of work. For him work is an economic matter:
he fails to recognize the educational responsibilities of industry. Religion suffered most from these fractionings of
the community, because religion is primitively just the
emotional fulfillment of the complete community life.

But religion easily takes refuge from world problems in temples where it can indulge in other-worldly hopes and deny its real nature.

So through the crevices made by these institutional fracturings, any individual child, or adult, might easily fall to his doom. The child, avoiding the crevices, and keeping to his own fragment of the community, must grow up a fragment of a person, nourished on the experiences of a fragment of the world.

One thing alone saved civilization in so far as it was saved, namely, the education fostered by pedagogues. Some of these pedagogues were semi-official: they actually led the children through the streets to the playgrounds and the music schools. But many of them were unofficial: the elders of the community who were intelligent enough and interested enough to devote time and energy to helping youth find itself and its world in the mazes of a disintegrating social order.

There is here no argument that the pedagogue fully understood what he was doing, or that others appreciated the nature of his task or his service to the community. In fact, it was Socrates who first made the work of the pedagogue intelligible. Socrates revealed the meaning of that service to Athens, and when they understood the Athenians would have none of it. That meaning was lost in the succeeding centuries. It was covered deep under the institutions of the Middle Ages. But within the last fifty years it has been rediscovered. The western world begins to believe that though the word "pedagogue" has become obnoxious, the solution of our educational problems may still lie in the direction of the methods once followed by those old Athenian pedagogues.

The Meaning of the Pedagogue's Work.—What was this work of the pedagogue? The pedagogue attempted to maintain the integrity of the child's world as the means of assuring the integration of the child's growing experience. This effort was made when the Athenian community was going to pieces; when the city itself was breaking up into institutional groups and other fragments. He tried to help the child grasp the feeling of a unified community so that that child might achieve a unified personality. He helped the child overcome the fragmentation of the community by leading him up to a high vantage from which he might still see the community as a whole. The process was groping, impulsive, tentative. But it was very real, and it did actually happen.

The old pedagogue is not to be confused with either the modern "pedagogue," or the school teacher. That ancient functionary assigned no lessons, worked in no building, heard no recitations. He wandered the city with his protégés, talked with them, answered their questions, called their attentions to points of interest and problems, and so called out their active mental powers. He did not give them books or lessons. He gave them the city, the whole community—long after "the community" had ceased to be.

The Intellectual Meanings of This Development.— We have already seen that in the primitive group the mental life of individuals was simple, concerned mostly with experiences on the perceptual level, and with taking on the skills and habits necessary to the perpetuation of the group.

But the growing city soon got beyond those old perceptual bounds. The city community called for more than immediate perceptions. It introduced materials and conditions and problems new to human experience. It called for the exercise of mental powers theretofore dormant or but little used. Generally the city community is, for the individual, a maze of concepts, jumbled, tangled, only partially accurate or dependable. One cannot *perceive* the city; one can only *conceive* it. Education for life in the city community must largely be by means of concepts. Now concepts are abstractions, and abstractions are always precarious: they are so easily fallacious or false. But if they were wrought out in the actual presence of perceptual materials upon which they are based, and under the questioning of a real pedagogue, they might still be very real, even to children. They might answer the child's own problems and bind together and explain for him the world that seemed breaking to pieces before his startled eyes.

Sheer unreality appears when the pedagogue does not understand what he is doing, or when he becomes pedantic; that is when he becomes a school teacher. He answers the child's questions with meaningless phrases. He attempts to cover up his own ignorance by the use of words. His real success in helping children overcome the distractions and disintegrations of the growing community will always depend upon his knowledge, his honesty and his ability to understand what is going on inside the child's mind. He must have enough sympathetic imagination to understand the questions children try to ask, for children do not always know how to formulate the questions they really want to ask. The task of the pedagogue, rightly understood, is the most important and interesting educational task in the world.

The pedagogue herein described was a real teacher, though not a school teacher. Children had problems. The pedagogue had understanding. He put his understanding under conscription to their needs, and helped them build for themselves a unitary experience out of the fragments of worlds about them. This sort of pedagogue was fundamentally responsible for the glory of the

great days of Athens. He was the real educator all
through the fifth century. All through that century he
helped Athenian children find their ways out of class and
group and neighborhood fragmentations of living which
otherwise would have destroyed them in the changing
Athens of that century. He helped them find that spiritual Athens which alone could make them human beings
—that Athens which glows in the orations of Pericles and
which shines like a steady flame through the centuries.
He helped them find it, and in that *finding* they in sober
fact *created* it.

This Athenian pedagogue occupies a unique position in
the history of education. In primitive times he was not
needed; or rather he was just any elder of the group, and
the group life of habit and perceptual experience was con-
cretely real enough to nourish the growing experience of
the children without much help.

But when the city became too large for any child's
immediate grasp and understanding, human nature, working inventively, defensively provided this wise man of the
community, whether slave or freeman, to help the children through the mazes of the unintelligible world.

He did not survive in Athens or in history for reasons
that we shall presently see in more detail. Enough to say
here that as the city became broken into factions and
fragments, "prudent" men took refuge from this chaos
in the fastnesses of institutions. Even the pedagogue was
quickly institutionalized. His social function was forgotten, his integrating service not being understood was
ignored. The institutionalized pedagogue became the
school teacher, the remote academician, with his irrelevant materials, his endless lessons, his intellectualisms,
and his bedraggled history. How this wise pedagogue
became the bookish school teacher we shall discover as
we proceed.

CHAPTER V

THE PEDAGOGUE OF THE COMMUNITY

I went to one who had the reputation of wisdom and observed him—he was a politician—and the result was as follows: When I began to talk with him, I could not help thinking that he was not really wise, although he was thought wise by many, and still wiser by himself; and thereupon I tried to explain to him that he thought himself wise, but was not truly wise; and the result was that he hated me . . . I left him, saying to myself: Well, though I do not suppose that either of us knows anything really beautiful and good, I am better off than he is—for he knows nothing, and thinks that he knows; I neither know nor think that I know . . . I went to another who had still higher pretensions of wisdom and my conclusion was exactly the same . . . After the politicians I went to the poets: tragic, dithyrambic and all sorts . . . I took them some of the most elaborate passages of their own writings . . . there is hardly a person present who would not have talked better about their poetry than they did themselves . . . At last I went to the artisans . . . They did know many things of which I was ignorant . . . but even the good artisans fell into the same error as the poets—because they were good workmen they thought they knew all sorts of high matters, and this defect in them overshadowed their wisdom . . .

I shall never cease exhorting anyone whom I meet, saying to him: You, my friend, a citizen of the great city of Athens, are you not ashamed of heaping up the greatest amounts of money and honor and reputation, and caring so little about wisdom and truth and the greatest improvement of the soul? . . . This is my teaching, and if this doctrine corrupts the youth, I am a mischievous person.—PLATO, in *Apology of Socrates.*

The work of the pedagogue, suggested in the preceding chapter, was a natural attempt on the part of a disintegrating community to protect its children from its own disintegrations while they were still too immature to understand and to withstand those influences. Perhaps it is scarcely correct to say that this was an effort of the community. Most of the Athenian pedagogues were not public officials. They were servants of particular families or family groups, and they undertook the task of giving the children of the more thoughtful citizens such education as the city still afforded.

Adult Isolation in the City.—The activities of these pedagogues in education shows that the community was growing so rapidly in numbers that its intelligence was not able to keep up with that growth. As has been pointed out, each section, or group, or class, or institution of the city might easily become an exclusive community for its own members. In fact each social class did essentially become such an isolated group. The result was that individuals, especially children, became more and more cut off from those community-wide contacts which formerly gave the growing individual his feeling of membership in the whole life, and which alone could give him any sense of complete freedom in the midst of confusions. This suggests that not only did children need the help of pedagogues in escaping these fragmentations, but that the Athenian community itself needed a pedagogue—some one who could envisage all fragmentary elements and all disintegrating factors and bring them together in a creative unity, and so save civilization itself from complete social and moral disintegration.

For a century the Athenian world kept on living on its capital of old habits and customs, long after that capital had been discredited, merely because group isolations kept the various factors of discredit from becoming aware of each other. This appears most clearly in the lack of contacts between those who assumed to do the thinking and those who did the work.

The common, uninteresting work of the community was done by slaves. Somewhat above the level of the slaves were the artisans who carried the crafts of the community. Both slaves and artisans were close to actual conditions of living. They dealt with the materials and forces of nature. They were still largely subjugated to old religious doctrines, but disillusioning processes went on at a very rapid rate.

At some considerable social elevation above these working groups we find those leisure class groups whose interests were intellectual: artists, statesmen, and perhaps a few struggling philosophers. As Prof. John Dewey has pointed out, this isolation of these superior groups from contact with the workers meant that they were also denied significant contacts with the forces of nature and physical things. Hence their points of view and their knowledge were for generations denied the criticism of actual fact.

But when political crises broke in upon the old city as in the Persian wars and in the building of the Athenian Empire, the gulf between the aristocratic and the servile social groups could not be maintained. Consequently, the gulf between intellect and experience or between theoretical and practical knowledge became narrower and narrower. The artisan and the artist—the worker and the thinker—could no longer escape each other. Criticism became inevitable.

The Work of the Sophists.—Presently we find in Athens a considerable group who insisted upon closing that gulf entirely. They brought the old legends of the aristocratic groups into life and death grips with the realistic knowledge possessed by craftsmen, even by slaves. This death struggle had for long been inevitable. None the less, the Sophist who precipitated it was regarded as a particularly detestable person. It must be admitted that he was ruthless once he got started. He insisted, for example, that under the new conditions of the far-flung Athenian Empire, real citizenship could not be achieved by merely growing up within some fragmentary local group. The empire had developed a great system of competing parts, and if one was to become a true citizen of such a world, he must *study the elements of that citizenship.* He could not achieve citizenship, as under the old local folkways, by merely growing up.

But this doctrine was particularly obnoxious to the superior groups in Athens. It assumed that the old method of education by experience had ceased to serve. It indicated that the old experiences themselves were no longer trustworthy; that the old traditions and customs and habits were to be discredited; and that something new was called for if society were to survive.

We must remember that the Sophists were working toward the future; but we must also realize that they were pioneers in social criticism and that they did not really understand what they were doing. Hence they committed many excesses, not primarily because they were corrupt or immoral, but because they felt a sense of intellectual freedom, which was new in the history of the human mind, and which had as yet no adequate safeguards. The Sophists said: "Old customs and habits are no longer convincing. The past must no longer be allowed to rule the minds of individual men. The individual man must be the judge of his own conduct. The individual must measure all his own experiences. The individual's own opinion is the only good for him. But he must not ever be permitted to dominate any other man. Argumentation is permissible. It is perfectly proper for one man to persuade another man. It is not only permissible; he should do it if he can. There is no such thing as absolute right or absolute wrong. Success is the only test of a fact or a doctrine. The individual is justified in taking that side of any question or that attitude toward any situation which seems to him most likely to get him ahead." This was scandalous doctrine, of course, but somebody had to say it!

The Attitudes of the Athenians Toward These Doctrines.—The work of the Sophists threatened to undermine all old folkway attitudes, traditions and customs of the Athenian world. The Athenians held a number of diverse opinions in respect to these doctrines. Some insisted that the Sophist was a detestable agitator who should be banished so that the community might once again reorganize its old folkway mind and social life, and go on being happy as before. A leading spokesman of this opinion was Aristophanes, the author of many comedies in which he ridicules the pretensions of the Sophists to wisdom, and shows the ends to which such wisdom leads.

At the other extreme from this reactionary type of citizen we find many irresponsibles of whom Alcibiades perhaps was an example. The disintegrating effects of sophistic irresponsibility are dramatically portrayed in the career of this brilliant youth who played fast and loose with the feelings of the people of Athens, both in peace and in war. Thucydides tells much of the story illuminatingly.

Both these groups failed to grasp the problems emerging in Athens, and envisaged for the first time in the history of the race. The reactionary assumed that the people could be brought back to the "good old ways" if only the agitating Sophists could be banished from the land. The Sophists, on the other hand, held that complete individual freedom could be achieved if men were allowed complete freedom of discussion. They held that the old customs and folkway controls could be destroyed in the fires of dialectic, and that with such destruction of the bonds of servility, the "freed" man would automatically emerge.

Both groups failed to understand the situation. The conservative failed to see that the released individual can no more be forced back into the old forms of behavior than a scrambled egg can be put back into its former shell. The Sophist failed to understand that the "freed" man is not a *free* man; that freedom is not something that can be given to men; that it is something it will take the race centuries to discover and more centuries to achieve; and that the way to such real freedom will be long and bloody with many battles. The free man is not merely the folkway man released from external controls. Released from external bonds, he is still tied hand and foot in the toils of his own limitations: he must escape from those limitations; he must overcome his fears of freedom; he must overcome and emerge from nature, and still be natural; he must overcome and emerge from old social orders, and still be social; he must rise to levels of understanding without cutting himself off from levels of "mere" experience, if he is to be free. In this struggle to be free, men will find much help in "nature," for in nature are materials and processes, crude hard facts, that can neither be forever denied by old folkway "minds," nor easily dissolved in a Sophist dialectic. But such understanding of nature is still two thousand years in the future, at the very least!

The Problem of the Philosophers.—For a century philosophers like Thales had been struggling to understand these hard, crude factors in human experience—the facts of nature. What was nature? Was it something lowly human—like the human body? Or was it something above the human—animistic, divine? The growth of technical knowledge fostered the belief that there were factors in experience which were not either "human" or "divine." Philosophers were trying to find out what those factors were. Such investigations would have been alarming to the conservative mind. But the philosophers held themselves aloof from current affairs. They were concerned with astronomical and physical facts. They spent their time and energy dealing with problems remote from humanity—in the heavens. They were so impractical that Thales, for example, had fallen into a well while watching the movements of a star. This very impracticality paved the way for a movement which proved profoundly critical to both the conservative mood and the radical pretensions of the Sophists.

The Work of Socrates.—It might have been evident by the middle of the fifth century, B.C., that the conflict between the Sophists and the traditionalists would eventually dramatize the destruction of the city. It was evident to a few that there was no escape from this conflict on any existent basis or in any obvious direction. Breaking to pieces under the impact of diverse critical forces, Athens needed a way of escape, a method of understanding, a means of rediscovering her essential wholeness. In short, Athens—the community—needed a pedagogue!

In the course of this century such a pedagogue appeared—in the person of Socrates. Socrates had grown up as a helper of his father, a potter and a sculptor. That is to say, Socrates had had those realistic experiences with nature which fill the lives of slaves and workers. But he also had a curiosity and an experimental fancy that ranged far beyond the bounds of the usual. He had worked with his father on important tasks. He had come into contact with Phidias, the sculptor and architect, and had often listened to Pericles, the statesman. Hence, he was able to understand both the thinker and the worker. He was also able to understand their deficiencies and to see how those deficiencies should become the basis of social criticism. He found fallacious elements in the programs of both the conservatives and the Sophists. Of course, this displeased both groups; especially, it angered the conservatives. He discovered a way out of the confusions of his age—the way which modern science rediscovered twenty centuries later. But this solution seemed at the time so critically destructive of the received and esteemed ways of the past, that its author was looked upon as a more disturbing element in the community than the Sophists themselves and he was accordingly condemned to death. We must briefly consider his solution of this problem.

The Discovery of Ideas.—The basis of the old folkway life had been habit and custom. Custom had two aspects. It is, first, a bond that holds the whole community together. This is a priceless characteristic; and because, by reason of this characteristic, custom has often proved the salvation of a group, any attack upon it or a weakening of it seemed to be an attack upon or a weakening of the group itself. We have already seen that children can be inured to custom, merely by the process of growing up in such a community. But in the second place, such custom is a mechanical structure, imposed from without, into which children are crowded and by which they are molded. It becomes habit in the individual, and thus tends to suppress all individual nature, originality and initiative. This externality of custom is the characteristic that angered the Sophists in Athens. It is obvious that a habit- and custom-bound community holds within itself the roots of those eventual profound contradictions which the Sophists gave their lives to exposing.

On the other hand, the characteristic of the Sophist's position was his demand that the individual should be permitted to enjoy his own impulses. Now, impulse has also two aspects: In the first place, it is personal and human, the very reality of the inner life of the individual. In his impulses, the individual feels most himself, most free and most effective, even though the final end may be disaster. For, and this is the second aspect of impulse, it often does lead to disaster. Impulse is over-personal, over-individualistic, blind, atomistic, unsocial. It is the enemy of custom, and in the long run, it tears society to pieces.

It must be apparent, therefore, that both the conservative and the Sophist held positions that were alike shot through and through with contradictions, which neither could see in his own position, but which he could easily see in the position of the other. The need of the age was for some one wise enough and detached enough to see both sides and to crack the heads of these contradictions together.

That is, from our present vantage, more than two thousand years later, we can see that each of these contenders enjoyed the possession of a great social good, and this fact tended to make each of them dogmatic; but each also enjoyed the possession of an undesirable trait, and this made them both exceedingly intolerant of each other, and supremely emotional in all their reactions to the situation.

What should a wise man do under these circumstances of social dogmatism and intolerance? Let Socrates answer. Socrates pointed out that what the conservative really wanted was, not so much old custom and habit, but a social orderliness of the sort that habit and custom had always assured. He saw, too, that what the Sophist was really criticizing in the old folkways was not so much that orderliness but the external methods by which it had always been imposed. Maybe, if the conservative could have his orderliness, he wouldn't be so insistent about getting it in any one way. Maybe, if the Sophist could be protected from external impositions, he would not be so much opposed to order.

So, Socrates saw that what the Sophist wanted was recognition of the reality of his own impulses. But he also saw that the conservative sensed a danger in this appeal to impulse just because impulses are so private, so individualistic, so disintegrating. He felt, however, that the positive and personal element in impulse could be saved and used if only the Sophist would undertake critically to examine his impulses and develop their implications. He was sure that any impulse, however private it might be, could, if it had actual reality, be developed beyond itself, and beyond that externalization of itself which we call opinion and which Socrates called a "half thought," even to that complete realization of itself which he called a "whole thought." He argued that if an impulse is carried through to the stage of "whole thought" it often proves to be something which other members of the community may share. In this way impulses may lose their disintegrating quality and become truly social.

That is to say, Socrates showed that any particular impulse may be the germ of a universal principle. Every custom the world knows was once no more than such an impulse. Every impulse of the present may become such a social custom in the near or far future. This is the contribution which Socrates made to men. He discerned a way out of the inertia of the old folkways on the one hand, and out of the disintegrations of the Sophist position on the other. He envisaged the possibility of a third way of living—a life thought through, organized and directed by ideas—the life of intelligence. It is not strange, therefore, that John Stuart Mill should say: "Mankind can hardly be too often reminded that there was once a man named Socrates." But it would even to-day be too much to say that humanity has realized largely upon this discovery of Socrates. Few communities, even to-day, are ready to give up custom—for the sake of ideas.

The Social and Educational Significance of Ideas.— When the pedagogues of Athens led their children through the city streets, helping them to secure and maintain a grasp of the life of the whole community, they were cultivating a psychological element which, though old, had never been apprehended or understood before. They were helping these children, not to develop habits in the old folkway sense, but to get that more comprehensive something which we now call ideas. They did not use the word "idea." They were content with the reality, leaving it unnamed. It remained to Socrates to apprehend this important element in individual and community life, to uncover it, and to discover it to his own age and to the ages.

According to this Socratic approach, ideas grow up, if at all, within the experiences of individuals—in their social difficulties and needs. Ideas are natural products of problematic conditions. They are answers to our efforts to understand and tie together fragments of experience which are more or less contradictory but which must still exist together in the same individual or social world. We all find ourselves involved in such contradictions—facing actual problems. Every one, therefore, at times needs the help of ideas. His own experience properly developed ought to furnish him with the ideas that he needs. Ideas are normal products of experience under certain conditions. Any one may have ideas. Ideas are, therefore, essentially democratic products—all may have them; all may possess them; all may enjoy them; all may organize their lives by means of them.

But ideas are needed in times of contradiction, that is, of crisis. Now, crises are social phenomena. Ideas are, therefore, primarily not individual but social products. That is to say, occasions when ideas are needed are almost always social occasions, crises in community living; and the development of ideas adequate to such crises is a social process. Few individuals can expand their own impulses and criticize and discipline them, in time of crisis. We need social help. The development of an idea within experience is a matter of social give and take: of conversation, communication, the use of language.

Cultivating ideas is supremely the function of the teacher. Socrates conceives a teacher as a member of the community who has skill in drawing out the struggling impulses of members of the community until those impulses have become "whole thoughts," *ideas*, by means of which the individual and the group may organize a more intelligent life. The Socratic method, so called, is just the method of cultivating individual impulses until they become social experiences and thus means of social understanding and bonds of social control.   Thus we may get an intellectual life which does not destroy society, but which makes society more secure.   Society grows not by additions from without, but by division, by birth within the group.   To Socrates, the teacher is a midwife of ideas.

Hence, for Socrates education remains what it was in the primitive folkway community—with one modification: as in the primitive group, children must have experiences with the physical and social world and develop the skills and habits which are real.   Every experience is educative. But in the growing city opportunities of that old folkway sort largely dissolve and disappear.   Hence, Socratic education assumes that in place of many of those old habits and customs, children will be compelled to develop *understanding of life* and to grow adequate crops of their own ideas which will be instruments for the intelligent organization of their developing lives.   Education for Socrates goes on from within as before.   It is still rooted in actual experiences, in skills and habits; but it is not satisfied with skills and habits, only.   It must go on to understandings, to appreciations, to outlooks, to ideas, to a life of organizing intelligence, which will include the whole community, no matter how fragmented that community may be.   The disintegrating community may be kept from destroying individuals by a true "pedagogy."

A disintegrating community needs ideas just as an individual does.   In fact, ideas cannot remain private possessions.   They are rooted in individual experience, it is true, but when fully grown they must become universal and therefore social.   Socrates, as the discoverer of the meaning of ideas in the life of the individual (as this meaning was dramatized in the work of the pedagogues), became inevitably a "pedagogue" to the whole community of Athens. He tried to lead Athens through her own streets to face herself. He recommended to Athens a life of intelligence. He said that an uncriticized life is a brutish life. He hoped Athens would learn how to live on this level of ideas. He hoped the city might become as intelligent as the individual.

In this hope he took a position which no community could endure. He was condemned to death on the ground that he was corrupting youth. He was merely showing youth that Athens preferred complacence to criticism, custom to intelligence: in short, that she preferred the brutish life.

He would probably be a suspicious character in the modern world; for though we spend much for education, we have not yet accepted the doctrine that community life can be intelligent. We fear intelligence as we fear nothing else in the world. This fear is natural: We do not know where intelligence will lead us. Trusting to intelligence makes human life a matter of adventure, with no certain goal. And the race as a whole is not ready to accept that sort of future.

Socrates is, after all these centuries, still too much for us. We want not an intelligent world, but safety and security. We still fly, as did the Greeks, from the adventurous "ideas" of Socrates to the academic security of Plato, if that statement does not get us too far ahead of the story. So, we turn from the poignant figure of the defeated, condemned, but never self-pitying community pedagogue, Socrates, to the substantial and successful academician, the forerunner of all school teachers, as he was first portrayed in the writings and program of Plato. This will look like *history*, but it must feel like personal experience, else the next chapter will be a failure.

CHAPTER VI

THE ESCAPE INTO THE ACADEMIC

At the Egyptian city of Naucratis there was a famous old god, whose name was Theuth . . . and he was the inventor of many arts . . . but his greatest discovery was the use of letters. Now in those days the god Thamus was the king of the whole country of Egypt . . . To him came Theuth and showed his inventions, desiring that the other Egyptians might be allowed to have the benefit of them; he enumerated them and Thamus enquired about their several uses, and praised some of them . . . But when they came to letters, "This," said Theuth, "will make the Egyptians wiser and give them better memories; it is a specific both for the memory and for the wit." Thamus replied: "O most ingenious Theuth, the parent or inventor of an art is not always the best judge of the utility or inutility of his own inventions . . . And in this instance, you who are the father of letters, from a paternal love of your own children, have been led to attribute to them a quality which they cannot have; for this discovery of yours will create forgetfulness in the learners' souls, because they will not use their memories; they will trust the external written characters, and not remember of themselves. The specific you have discovered is not an aid to memory, but only to reminiscence, and you give your disciples not truth, but only the semblance of truth; they will be hearers of many things and will have learned nothing; they will appear to be omniscient and will generally know nothing; they will be tiresome company, having the show of wisdom without the reality."—PLATO, in *Phaedrus*.

We have great aggregations of population, to-day, which are called "cities." In these "cities" men, women and children crowd together, many of them in ways unspeakably primitive. "A great city is a great wilderness." City organization is little but village organization that has broken up and been patched together in a thousand places. City government is mostly village government that has swollen to the bursting point—and then burst. The modern large industrial city is the final wonder of the primitive world.

The Escape from Reality.—Men who are in no sense of the word to be called "citizens" make up the bulk of the population of our cities to-day. The individuals of the aggregates of population who inhabit the areas called "cities" to-day do not, for the most part, know why they are doing it. They are tossed here and there by rapid transit; they do work that has no possible relation to their own personal interests save that it pays them wages; and with these wages, they buy the means to make them sure they will be able to earn more wages next day. "I dig the ditch," said Pat, "so that I can buy food so that I can have strength to dig the ditch." And the fact that the radio and the movie have been injected into this circle does not mean that Pat understands any more about it. It is likely that he understands it even less than before.

The fact is that men, women and children do not live in a real world to-day, though more and more they long for a real world and gnaw their hearts with eagerness for such a world. The city is an artificial world. It has been developed out of the fragments of earlier communities. It is a congeries of primitive villages, carrying reminiscences of primitive emotions and satisfactions, but always promising far more than it can fulfill; and it is bound together by purely physical ties, such as transit lines and the similarity of policemen's uniforms. The big city has little if any reality in the emotions of men and women save when they are away from home in distant parts. Its intellectual reality is purely academic. Art is long and time is endless. The unreality of the city slowly emerges into the consciousness and the conscience of our times. Men, women and children must have a real life or they will vanish from the earth. How did this unreal city ever come to claim so large a share in the lives of men? The question takes us back once more to Socrates and the Greeks.

The Avoidance of Intelligence.—Socrates offered a plan for a way through the confusions of discredited custom and individual ignorance which beset the Greek world in the Fifth Century, B.C. But his plan was not one the Greeks could follow at that time. With disintegrating anarchies closing in upon the age, the counsel of Socrates, that men should critically examine their lives and build up a secure knowledge, was not likely to be taken seriously. The task was too severe, the technic too uncertain, the outcome too remote. Men want finalities at such times, and whatever offers the quickest escape is most likely to be followed.

Moreover, we know now how long and arduous is that task of building up a critical understanding upon which social order can hope to rest. We even wonder at the optimism of Francis Bacon who, only three hundred years ago, catching something of the Socratic method, assumed that the task of developing the knowledge that would make men masters of their destinies would be a comparatively short one. These three centuries since Bacon's time have been filled with thrilling examples of the efforts of scientists to master their methods and to organize their materials. Yet in spite of all these efforts we seem still to be standing with Newton on the shores of the ocean of truth, picking up now and then a pebble of great beauty, but failing to penetrate the unexplored areas stretching infinitely before us. How much more, then, must the Greeks have been lost in the midst of the confusions of the Fifth Century?

The Drift of the Actual World.—The world was on the down grade in Athens from the Fifth into the Fourth Century, B.C. Disintegration threatened the social and political order. Under such conditions social security must rest upon the individual unless some other basis of security, not too difficult to attain, could be found. Plato caught this drift of events and wove of it the fabric of his philosophy, his education, and his remedy for the disintegration of the age.

Plato's remedy, as set forth in *The Republic* (Book IV), accepted the doctrines of Socrates that society must escape from the old controls of custom on the one hand and from the sophistry of impulse and opinion on the other; and that this escape could be achieved by rising above both custom and impulse to the levels of *ideas*. But for Socrates *ideas* are one thing; for Plato they are something very different. Their origin is different; their nature is different; they have a different value and they perform a different function in individual and social living. Socrates taught that ideas develop out of the experience of the individual and the community; and that any one might, out of his own experience, develop and possess ideas. Ideas are social products which arise within experience at need as means of organizing and controlling individual and social living. Ideas are, therefore, important factors in human experience. Men emerge from habit and escape from sophistry alike by developing ideas. The permanence of society depends upon them. Thus, Socrates.

For Plato, ideas are quite as important as they are for Socrates. They are, in fact, far too important to be committed to such lowly and precarious origins as Socrates supposes. Human experience is far too shifting, unstable, temporary, to account for such permanent products as ideas. Ideas must come from more stable and secure sources. They must not share the taint of experience!

Moreover, when we look carefully we can see that the Socratic doctrine that ideas are the products of experience is open to question on another count. Ideas really precede experiences. The craftsman must have the idea of a chair before he can make a chair. Any creator must have ideas as patterns before he can create anything. The conclusion seems inescapable. Ideas come *before* things; that is, ideas *precede* experiences.

This leads to a further conclusion, namely, that ideas are more real than things. Ideas, for Plato, are permanent, pre-existent realities. They are the patterns after which all created things are made. They exist from all eternity to all eternity, in the heaven of ideas that is above, before and beyond all created things. So, Socrates was mistaken: ideas are not products of experiences: they antedate experience; they are gifts to experience; they are the culmination of experience for those exceptional souls who are able to apprehend them and make them a part of their experience.

The Function of Ideas.—We see, therefore, that ideas cannot be social *bonds* as Socrates described them. They do not develop within society; they come down upon society from above. They are social "forms." Society or experience is like the loose staves of a barrel. Platonic ideas are like the barrel hoops which hold the staves together and transform what would otherwise be a mere heap of rubbish into a usable barrel. This is the function of ideas. They come down from eternity upon our masses of experiences and shape them according to fixed and permanent forms and categories. They introduce order into that which is naturally chaotic. Ideas have the form of finished systems. They control experience not by growing up within but by being superimposed upon experience and molding life to their patterns, as a potter molds clay to his chosen pattern.

Now, since ideas are pre-existent and eternal, it is an error to think of them as being developed. Ideas are finalities. Each idea is a distinct entity, changeless from eternity. Hence, ideas cannot become the possession of every one. Any one may have ordinary experiences of life, the appetites and desires, the impulses and passions of the lower human nature. But ideas can be possessed by none but specially gifted natures—the learned. These are they who have golden natures; who are capable of long and severe discipline of mind; and who achieve intellectual detachment from the life of ordinary men. In short, ideas can be secured by intellectuals, alone. And this is well, for ideas are far too precious to be lightly claimed by every one. Ideas are the responsibility and the property of those who are able to appreciate them and to keep them unspotted from the world. Ambitious people belonging to inferior groups may strive to achieve possession of ideas; but these will merely cheapen what they are incapable of understanding and appreciating. One of the sad spectacles of life is the sight of ignorant people attempting to deal with intellectual things! They cannot appreciate, they can only befoul these precious ideas!

For Plato, then, *the race is divided* into levels with varying mental and moral qualifications, and only the intellectual group can have any real share in ideas. Workers have their appetites and their low manual skills; soldiers have their spirit and instinct. Neither of these groups has any sense of organization or control in itself. The intellectual group must furnish controlling ideas; must impose upon these lower orders the forms of organization which will make them useful members of a community. Forms of organization are ideas. Our governments, industries, religions, family arrangements and all such fixed social relationships are ideas. Hence, all our institutional arrangements must be permanent for they are eternal ideas. How evil, how blasphemous, is any revolt against the powers and forms that be!

Ideas in Education.—Any such view as this will, of course, have its definite reflection in education. Education, for Plato, is a different matter from what it was for Socrates. Socrates taught in the market place, urging individual men or groups of men to examine their lives and their experiences, to find out what those experiences meant, and to bring them to the high level of ideas, thus developing intelligence in the very heart of the city.

Plato retreated from the city. He withdrew from the confusions and heats of experience. He found a pleasant spot in the grove of Academus where, surrounded by a few congenial spirits, he could talk about the ideal good, the true and the beautiful, and discover the forms which might be imposed upon experience. In good time his school became known as the Academy; and Plato may rightly be regarded as the first of the academics.

This was, of course, not the first time that men had withdrawn from the world. But for the first time this method was erected into a definite program for experience and for education. Plato's general doctrine is the first formulation of the academic theory of education. This theory has been dominant in education ever since and we must carefully note a few of its implications.

The first of these is the doctrine that reality reveals itself not in experience as a whole, but in the intellectual phase of experience only. Impulses, feelings, and emotions are momentary, ephemeral, unreal; only the intellectual, the realm of ideas, is permanent and real.

Hence, any educational system that cultivates or develops impulses, feelings and emotions must be cultivating unreality, and making confusion still more chaotic. If we are to build education upon reality we must rescue the individual and society as quickly as possible from feelings, impulses, and emotions. The realities of the world are wholly within the realm of the ideal. Life is organized by intellectual forms; therefore, the materials of education must be intellectual materials; i.e., ideas. "Teach Ideas: we build our worlds out of Ideas!"

An intellectual statement of experience is, from this viewpoint, a valid transcript of reality. Hence, the academy with its intellectual materials and its ideas is the treasure house of reality. Children may protest that they are more interested in their own impulses, in feelings, and the day's experiences than in ideas; but that is their lower nature, unreality, overwhelming the real. Education must release them from unreality, and reveal to them the Real!

To be sure, most members of the community cannot do much with these intellectual materials. That is not a valid criticism of the materials or the methods of the school. It merely shows that these individuals have not the qualifications of the philosopher. Such persons must be content to be what they are: they must not aspire to education but be content to do the rough work of the world. On no account may they question or criticize the education that is provided for those whose minds are capable of dealing with Ideas. The Platonist cannot too often repeat: Reality resides in Ideas. Reality is found wherever Ideas are found. Reality is, therefore, at home in the academy. Education is found in schools. The scholar, the philosopher, must be the recognized ruler and guide of society.

For two thousand years this Platonic doctrine has dominated the education of men. It has been and is profoundly influential in social organization, in government, and in religion. It is the essence of school and of the school master. So we must see what it has really meant in practical experience.

The Fate of the Pedagogue.—We have seen (in Chapter IV) the education which the early pedagogues provided in the days when the community was growing out of its primitive unity into its later disorganizing and disintegrating complexity. In the long run, however, the task of helping children develop and maintain an intelligent integrity of experience, even though the city had lost its unity, became too great, and the task had to be given over. The pedagogue failed. Though the story covered a century it can be dramatized in the life of a single pedagogue.

After long years of service to the children and the citizens of the city, the pedagogue came upon the days of his departure. He knew a great deal about his city, historical and contemporaneous—more than any one else. He had known it as a village, and had grown with its growth into the great city. It would never see his like again; for he had labored hard and no one could ever have again the experiences and the rounded outlook he had achieved. His death would mean a vital loss as he well knew. Surely, he thought, something might be saved to his city out of all his intellectual wealth! Therefore, he wrote a book of remembrances of his life and his city, the ancient and the modern ways—the city as he had known it, and also as he still loved it in spite of all its changes. And so he died!

There was none to take his place in the same complete way. Some knew certain aspects of the new city—for their own purposes. But no one knew the whole city in that understanding, historical way which was the pedagogue's; none could reveal its hidden activities to the children as he had done. What should become of education now that he was gone?

Well, though no one knew the city as the pedagogue had known it, there were some who had read his book. One such was found who was practically letter-perfect (say 92¾%) in it. As a substitute, this one must do. But with many children on his conscience and with a book at hand, he found little time to wander about the city. So they built a house for him and the children: a house with windows so high from the floor that the children could not be distracted by outward sights. Here he met the children day by day and assigned them lessons in the book. It was a good book and it was about the city. But it was not the city. And this was the first school!

And here was the first *schoolteacher;* he had taken on the bookish learning of other people and he was devoting himself to passing on this second-hand learning to third parties, namely, little children who have no way of defending themselves against the process. The schoolteacher does not know the materials he is teaching. He finds them in a book. He teaches the book. He does not permit himself to be too closely quizzed about the materials. He can but insist that the children learn what is in the book. They ask him for the city and he gives them bookish irrelevancies. They ask him for problems, and he gives them bookish answers. They ask him for bread and he gives them a stone!

Education Becomes Schooling.—So education gets into a world of its own: it leaves the market place and the city streets, where Socrates walked and talked with his friends; it retreats, with Plato, into the shady groves of Academus, into the suburbs, and becomes "academic"! The teacher in the schoolhouse takes the place of Socrates in the world of experience. The world gets into a book. The book becomes supreme. A book about a city obviates the necessity of experiencing the city! A book becomes more reliable than experience. A book is something inescapable: "It is written!" Which by translation into the Greek becomes: "It is scripture!" From the which there is no escape! Education ceases to be experience in the life of the community and in the growing life of the child. It is something stored up in books, certified by tradition, guaranteed by the learned, treasured in schoolhouses, guarded by schoolteachers, to be taken on in organized fashion by children, willy-nilly, in order that they may become "good citizens."

All this would not be difficult to accept were it not for the fact that the school developed in this way has come to monopolize the word education. Education has come to be something that goes on in schoolhouses, under the supervision of schoolteachers. Nothing else, or at least little else, can be accepted by the schools—"for credit." All else, all the rich and varied experiences of life and the world may be valuable—"for some things"—but not for credit in the schools. School in this fashion achieves a world of its own, with its own standards and rules—the academic world—which is not the real world. Education is discussed not from the standpoint of its bearings on life and active experience, but from the standpoint of its conformity to the tradition. The school is troubled by the fact that a "real world" lies all about it. Teachers are disturbed by the possibility that some pupil will come alive in the midst of a recitation and ask real questions.

For this reason, in most schools to-day, children are not found: only "pupils." A pupil is that part of a child which consents to accept and abide by the rules of the schoolroom. The connection between the schoolroom pupil and the living child that waits at the door for the end of the hour is usually very tenuous, sometimes exceedingly remote. Always this barring-out of a part of the child's personality results in some degree of division of attention; not infrequently it results in a divided personality, with all the pathological after-effects that we now know. But for most children it means their quick elimination from the school. We shall come upon this dividing of personality again.

By Way of Explanation.—This argument seems to be a direct criticism of the schools. It is not. It is likely that history could have developed in no very different way. The story does not justify fault-finding. It is of value as showing us the elements of the academic problem. Education was once of the whole community—the whole of life. That was when the community was small: a perceptual community which all could share.

That community passed away. It broke into fragments and grew large—unwieldy—unintelligible. Borne down with the "weight of all this unintelligible world" men took refuge in institutions: in "government" for social control; in temples and churches for religion; and finally in schools—for education. But just as government does not provide real outlets for the civic needs of men, women and children; and just as temples and churches do not provide reality of religious experiences for men, women and children, so the school does not provide a real education for children, women and men. Why these things are so we must inquire further.

But just as politicians and party headquarters can defend government, however tyrannical and foolish it may be; and just as temples and priests can defend the ritual however barren it may be; so schools and schoolmen can defend schooling however remote from reality it may be. We turn next to some defenses of the academic school, and to some of the pathological results of this institutional defense of much that is personally and socially indefensible.

CHAPTER VII

PLATO'S ROYAL LIE

When the day breaks, the time has arrived for youth to go to their schoolmasters. Now neither sheep nor any other animal can live without a shepherd, nor can children be left without tutors, or slaves without masters. And of all animals the boy is the most unmanageable; inasmuch as he has the fountain of reason in him not yet regulated, he is the most insidious, sharp-witted and insubordinate of animals. Wherefore he must be bound with many bridles; in the first place, when he gets away from mothers and nurses, he must be controlled by teachers, no matter what they teach, and by studies; but he is also a slave, and in that regard any freeman who comes in his way may punish him and his tutor and instructor, if any of them does anything wrong; and he who comes across him and does not inflict upon him the punishment that he deserves shall incur the greatest disgrace; and let the guardian of the law, who is the director of education, see to him who coming in the way of the offences which we have mentioned, does not chastize them when he ought, or chastises them in a way which he ought not; let him keep a sharp lookout, and take especial care of the training of our children, directing their natures, and always turning them to good according to the law.—PLATO, in *The Laws*.

I'll believe anything if ye'll tell it to me often enough. —MR. DOOLEY.

Although most of our school processes are now traditional and habitual, we have a theory of education that

77

more or less adequately rationalizes those processes. This
theory has a long history. It is rooted in primitive practices and logic. It is first found in the writings of Plato,
though Plato merely wrote it down out of current practices. It has been accepted, enlarged, completed and believed with poignant faithfulness, against many vigorous
challenges, with but incidental falterings, by strong minds
and courageous spirits in all the centuries since Plato;
and it flourishes on every campus, to-day.

Civilize the Barbarian!—The basic principle in this Platonic theory of education is the doctrine that children are
natural barbarians. This doctrine has many variations—
moral, religious, esthetic, social, political, intellectual. But
these variations all come to the same thing. Plato wrote:
"If children be insufficiently or ill educated they are the
most savage of earthly creatures." All human institutions
are engaged in an endless battle with the enemies of society, chief of which is the rising generation. Education (in
the more inclusive sense) is a process, or a series of processes, by which these natural savages are brought under
civilization, broken to the harness, taught the discipline,
inured to decency, turned into reasonable beings, fitted
for life here and hereafter. The test of the civilized man
is the possession of certain information and ideas—"the
ideas and information which a reasonable man would
have." The process by which children become reasonable beings is the educative process. Hence, the rational
method of education is the inculcation of reasonable ideas,
and such information as may be useful in the defending
those ideas. That is to say, one becomes educated by
taking on those materials, ideas and facts of which an
"education" is made up. One is educated when he has
achieved this reasonable result. The school is the tool
by which this result is to be secured.

It is a plausible theory. It comes to us out of a long history and with high recommendations.

Plato's Share in Modern Education.—Plato is not responsible for this educational theory in any narrow, personal sense. There are evidences in his writings that, while young and still with his teacher, Socrates, he believed in youth and life, as distinct from knowledge and institutions, and in adventuring beyond the pale. But two developments alienated him from these youthful attitudes. The first was that it was his fate to live and do his work in an age that was headed for political destruction. Few could have kept youth and faith in life under such conditions. In the *Republic*, which was written in his younger years, he expresses some real belief in nature and youth and life. But in *The Laws*, the product of a rather disappointed old age, he teaches that it is the business of education to protect society from the native savagery and anarchism of children. Both those statements are reflexes of the times in which they were written.

The second development was that he early became committed to a System that by its iron logic eventually cut him off from youth, and gave to him a sort of timeless Age. He lost youth, though it took him a long time to grow pessimistically old.

Plato's Social System.—The results of his devotion to System may be set forth briefly. Plato was not a psychologist, primarily; he was a philosopher and an educational statesman. Statesmen of his time were doing what they could to salvage the social order, which was disintegrating in that individual and social anarchy which began in the Persian Wars, was continued in the struggle between Athens and Sparta, and which lasted to the coming of Alexander. These problems of statesmanship were both practical and theoretical. As a part of the theo-

retical task of social reconstruction, Plato dealt with education in both the *The Republic* and *The Laws*. He realized that education had much to do with the stability of
the state. He planned to organize education into the
structure of his Republic. He wanted an education that
would promote, protect and defend his state. Education
should be the state realizing itself in the new generations.
Hence, he had, first, to find out what the state, or the
social order, was.

Working on these lines, Plato found three classes of
people in the state; and happily, the state needed just
those three classes. He found—and found he needed—
workers, who would perform all the ordinary labors of
the community; soldiers, who would protect the state
from foes, within and without; and wise men, or philosophers, who would rule and guard the state—and control
the two lower classes.

Curiously enough, he also found three types of quality,
or spiritual faculty, in men. All men have all these qualities in varying degree; in each man, one of them is dominant and gives the character to the individual. Men who
are dominated by their appetites, who are earthborn, who
have natures of iron and brass, and who have the virtues
of making money, are to be given the rough work of the
world to do—husbandry, trade, the crafts. These are the
workers, and work is all they are fit for or can be fitted
for. A second class, who have what in horses we call
spirit, and who are mixed of silver and have the virtue
of honor, are to be soldiers; these will protect the state
and keep the lower classes in control, under orders from
their superiors. And those who have the ability to become wise, who have golden natures and who are devoted
to the pursuit of philosophy—to these should be given
the guardianship and the ruling of the state, which will

include the control of all who are less wise. The true state, that ideal social order where justice will abound, will be founded in the obedience of workers, in the loyalty of soldiers, and in the wisdom of philosophers. And mostly in the last:

"For until either philosophers govern the state or those who are now called kings and governors become philosophers, and so political power and philosophy unite in one, and most who are now pursuing either of these separately be excluded from both, there will be no end to the miseries of states, or to those of the human race; and not until then will the government we desire come to a positive existence and behold the light of the sun."

Education and the Social Order.—Now it must be obvious that such a social organization will need an education employing exactly the same theory. So Plato believed, and this belief found expression in his famous doctrine of Ideas. The philosopher is the reasonable man— the man of Ideas. In order to produce the philosopher we must know how to get Ideas. As we have seen, Ideas are, for Plato, pre-existent, eternal entities, the true reality, without beginning and without end. The theory is simple. The Idea of a chair must exist before the chair can be. The Idea of the chair has, indeed, existed from all eternity, and will remain long after the material chair has fallen to dust. Ideas are eternal. But Ideas are not easily secured, as most people must admit. The philosopher is just a man who can get hold upon Ideas, bring them into our world, and by their use develop order and system—and so help the world escape from ignorance and unreality, from non-being. Absence of Ideas is chaos, ignorance, emotion, impulse, unreality. Possession of

Ideas is wisdom, order, reality, cosmos, a dependable world!

The search for Ideas is an intellectual process, of course. But philosophers, that is, intellectuals, are not an hereditary class. The children of men of golden natures often turn out to be of silver or of brass; and children of silver, iron, or brass parentage may very well be found to have golden possibilities. No one can claim to be a philosopher by right of birth, or because his ancestors were philosophers. Any one may aspire to be a philosopher. The doctrine seems democratic and human, not far removed from certain modern doctrines. But the argument must be examined further.

If only by securing ideas may one find reality; and if finding ideas means becoming a philosopher; and if the philosopher is the most important person in the community; and if no one can know in advance who the philosophers are to be, if all these things are true, as claimed by Plato, then education becomes a process of selection; the gold natures must be separated from those of silver and brass and given over to long discipline leading up to philosophy and to that intellectual struggle for existence which will select, instruct and discipline them into philosophers. That is to say, if becoming a philosopher is the highest and only true good, then all children must start out to become philosophers, even though few ever achieve the goal. Education must aim to make philosophers; all other hopes or ideals or aims must be of the nature of by-products.

In this kind of selective education, some children will early find that their natures are iron or brass. These will fall by the wayside, to spend their ignorant lives in the common work of the world. Their education is soon complete. That is to say, it is nothing. Others will go farther, but most of these will soon find their homes are of silver, not of gold. These will become soldiers and adventurers of many sorts. These two groups, having spent their childhood and youth in the vain effort to become philosophers, must make what shift they can, uneducated, to fill positions as workers and adventurers. They will have no adequate education for either type or for any other vocation. To be sure, they may have learned a little something useful in their academic days and, anyhow, while trying to become philosophers they were kept out of mischief! They may well be thankful, says a modern Platonist, that they were permitted to be the "mass" from among which the real philosophers emerged!

Those, alone, who become philosophers profit by such a system. But since these are esteemed most important members of the state, their profit is most justifiable. Plato's educational theory, though it offers what looks like democratic and natural opportunities to children, tends to make education wholly an intellectual matter— the taking on of pre-existent materials, a process which only intellectuals can enjoy and profit by. It is an education for intellectuals; it has nothing to offer non-intellectual children, except such joy as they can get in seeing the progress of others.

Historic Developments.—In the age of turbulence which followed the disintegration of the Greek states, and which really continued, with but momentary lulls, for nearly two thousand years, all the hopes of men for a world of permanent social realities gathered round these Ideas, pre-existent, eternal, priceless. Education easily became a technique of inculcating Ideas—and therefore, of defending the abstract world of permanent and ideal reality.

In the realm of method this Platonic attitude was

greatly strengthened when the Greek and Hebrew traditions merged, and the pedagogic methods of the rabbis
were discovered. "It is precept upon precept; line upon
line; rule upon rule; here a little, there a little." When
Roman discipline was added the technique was complete.

Later, in the Christian and Roman traditions, the Eternal City, the fatherland of the soul, was made real by
means of those Ideas. It was no long step from the
Heaven of eternal Ideas to the Heaven of the Christian.
Christianity itself became a system of Ideas instead of a
Way of Life. It was soon identified with authoritative
creeds, which partook of the eternal. Catechisms and
dogmatisms became the accepted instruments of educating men for the eternal world. Life was identified with
intellectual things; *mind* or intellect was the only reality.
All instinct, impulse, feeling, emotion, the red riot in the
blood of youth, was declared to be that undiscipline which
is the body of death. The salvation of the world from
its own casual impulses was to be found in Ideas that are
eternal. The redemption of the Christian world from the
barbarians of the North was achieved by bringing the
barbarians into subjection to these eternal Ideas and into
subordination to the church, which was the embodiment
of eternal Ideas.

So through all the Christian centuries, civilization
saved itself from anarchy and confusion by holding before itself those eternal patterns to which practically all
innovating or revolutionary individuals and forces were
compelled to conform. All adventurings were repressed.
Society became a hard and fast feudalism. Fixed institutions dominated politics, religion, and morality. These
tyrannies were but little challenged until human emotion
emerged once more in the Italian Renaissance and the

earth became once more interesting to men as in the morning of creation.

This modern humanistic movement gradually released the world from the hardnesses of the old intellectualistic and scholastic doctrines which had crystallized through the ages into dogmas. In Italy and in England were men like Vittorino and Milton, who almost rose to that earlier, vivid sense of humanity which Socrates had known. But such humanizing processes could not get far nor be long endured while men still lived under the shadows of the feudal ages. We are afraid of too much of the human, even now. It frightens us. John Locke, voicing the Puritan protest against everything impulsive or instinctive, called the world once more to discipline and order and the long effort to make civilization solid, substantial, impregnable. To him again education became intellectual, unrelenting, and more than Platonic—it became hard, unyielding, moralistic. The Platonic tradition, strengthened and rationalized by Locke, is dominant in the schools of Europe and America to-day, in spite of all the work of the educational reformers. Intellectualism is still the bulwark of civilization against all barbarians, especially those from the north woods of childhood. What gives this harsh intellectualism its perennial hold upon the fears and consciences and loyalties of humanity? Why do parents and teachers who themselves suffered academic wrongs in childhood repeat those wrongs upon children to-day? We must find this out!

Plato's Royal Lie.—According to Plato himself, his doctrine of Ideas and the whole structure of his education was supported on a lie! Always some have suspected that the System has been defended all these centuries by continuous falsifications of the facts of human nature, and kept alive by age-long misinterpretations of history and experience. We are uncovering amazing areas of these old perversions and misrepresentations in anthropology, psychology and psychopathology to-day. The "Freudian" literature is filled with these materials. Was Plato honest in his dealings with educational processes? No. He knew that the foundations of his system were false. He confesses the lie. But he lied, he says, for the good of the race and for the welfare of the state. The words sound familiar.

If we face the matter critically and without prejudice, we shall find that there are two theories of education in Plato: one, a social theory growing out of the teachings of Socrates; the other, his later intellectualistic theory, which was developed in fear and in that remoteness from life which characterized the Academy. This later intellectualism is the first academic educational theory in history.

Plato felt the conflict between his two theories, and felt himself compelled to choose between them. He eventually found himself on the side of the later intellectual theory; and he gave up the social theory of Socrates. The reasons for this result are not mysterious. After the first doubts about intellectualism are stilled, the theory is very plausible. It gives the place of honor to the intellect; it offers the illusion of social stability in an age of social chaos; and it can be held and practiced in the quiet retreats of the academic life, as a social theory cannot. For Plato's age it was probably the only tenable theory. None the less, it was based, as he tells us, on a perversion of the facts—on a deliberate lie. We may escape this lie —by recognizing it!

Facts are not acceptable to Plato and the scared Platonic mind. The doctrine that human experience is the true reality never could have been held by Plato. His

age was too chaotic, human passions too crude and brutal.
To him men were but shadows. Ideas were the only
reality. Men were to be molded and fashioned by Ideas
into the eternal likeness of Ideas. Intellect is the highest
attribute of man; the philosopher, the noblest human
being; and Ideas, increased to wisdom itself, the highest
good. And so Plato became an intellectualist; and, therefore necessarily, he became a liar!

The Excuse for the Lie.—But Plato was enough of a
realistic psychologist to be able to realize that while his
academic interpretation of life and education was essentially false, men still so longed for security that they
could readily be induced to accept it for reality. He
knew that men would believe anything if told it often
enough, and if it offered them something they very much
wanted. But he also realized that his doctrine would not
be favorably received at its first presentation, if it were
too obviously false. Hence, he needed a "cover" that
would hide the most obnoxious aspects of the doctrine,
until such times as the minds of men were inured to it.
As he himself says, he needed a lie—what he calls a
"royal lie"—to give his doctrine a start and a push. He
was engaged in "propaganda," and he accepted the tactics
of the propagandist. Here is his own story of the matter
as set forth in *The Republic,* III, 414.

The Platonic "Socrates" of the Republic (who is of
course, not the real Socrates, but a literary puppet) understands that the educational program indispensable to
the safety of the new state will never be accepted by the
people, since this program proposes to institutionalize
that three-fold classification of people which Plato found
inherent in human nature. If the state needs three levels
of citizens, then education must be organized to provide
those three levels. But how shall such a system be "put

over," if the people do not like it? The problem is deep
—but not too deep for the philosopher: "We must invent
a lie," he says; "a plausible lie, that will turn the trick
and convince the people!"

"How then," asks this puppet "Socrates" of the dialogue, "may we devise one of these needful falsehoods
. . . just one royal lie which may deceive the rulers, if
that be possible, and at any rate the rest of the city?"

The educational plan was of such sort that Glaucon
(the second person of the dialogue) declared: "You had
good reason to be ashamed of the lie you are going to
tell." This charge does not abash the questioner. After
detailing the "lie" in full, the fable of the varied natures
of people, he asks, "Is there any possibility of making our
citizens believe it?" To which Glaucon replies, "Not in
the present generation; there is no way of accomplishing
this; but their sons may be made to believe in the tale,
and their son's sons, and posterity after them." And
"Socrates" makes the very worthy rejoinder: "I see the
difficulty; yet the fostering of such a belief will make
them care more for the city and for one another."

This would seem to be a questionable procedure in lay-
ing the foundations of justice, which was what Plato was
attempting. But justice must be secured even though we
have to lie to get it! Plato recognized the limitations of
lying. He had quite a philosophy of it, in fact. His
"Socrates" suggests in another connection: "Truth should
be highly valued . . . a lie is useless to the gods, and
useful only as a medicine to men . . . the use of such
medicines should be restricted to physicians; private individuals have no business with them. . . . Then if any
one at all is to have the privilege of lying, the rulers of
the state should be the persons; and they in their dealings
with their enemies or with their own citizens, may be

allowed to lie for the public good. . . . If, then, the ruler catches anybody beside himself lying in the State . . . he will punish him for introducing a practice which is subversive and destructive. . . ." The right to lie can of course be deputed to teachers, at times, *if the teachers can be trusted!*

The Philosophy of Lying.—The doctrine that the rulers may and sometimes must lie for the good of the state lingers with Plato. We find it set forth in that later book, *The Laws*. The conversation again turns on the educational process—the content of learning and the method of teaching—and a certain passage is worth reproduction here. The dialogue runs between the Athenian and Cleinias. The Athenian is bent on proving that the good is always rewarded and honored, the evil always defeated and denied, as is still duly proved in all good schools.

Ath. Then the unjust life must not only be more base and depraved but also more unpleasant than the just and holy life?

Cle. That seems to be implied in the present argument.

Ath. And even supposing this were otherwise . . . still the lawgiver worth anything, if he ever ventures to tell a lie to the young for their good, could not invent a more useful lie than this, or one which will have a better effect in making them do what is right, not on compulsion but voluntarily.

Cle. Truth, Stranger, is a noble thing and a lasting, but a thing of which men are hard to be persuaded.

Athe. And yet the story of the Sidonian Cadmus, which is so improbable, has been readily believed, and also innumerable other tales.

Cle. What is that story?

Ath. The story of armed men springing up after the sowing of teeth, which the legislator may take as proof that he can persuade the minds of the young of anything; so that he has only to reflect and find out what belief will be of the greatest public advantage, and then use all his efforts to make the whole community utter one and the same word in their songs and tales and discourses all their life long. But if you do not agree with me, there is no reason why you should not argue on the other side.

Cle. I do not see that any argument can fairly be raised by either of us against what you are now saying.

Education as Lies.—And what was it that this Athenian stranger was saying? His fundamental doctrine was that education must not be determined or controlled by human nature since human nature is undependable and unreliable; as the old prophets said, it is "deceitful above all things and desperately wicked." Education must attempt to do something with human nature which human nature left to itself would not do. Education must dislocate humanity from nature and relocate it on more substantial bases. Education must see to it that civilization is built on more permanent foundations than human nature can furnish. Education must, if necessary, cut the human being in two, suppress one part of him and make a whole new being out of the selected fraction that remains.

A stable state can be built on nothing but honor and justice, says Plato. Human nature in its ordinary types does not know honor or justice. All it knows is appetites and desires. Hence, human nature must be transformed before it can be used in the structure of the state. We must distort it with the "royal lie," and make it want things it does not naturally want. After that, we can build into it the materials that will make it solid and substantial. We can dissect out the native defects in human nature by means of what we may call "compensatory lies," and so find the firm foundations of the good state, and a permanent civilization. This is Platonism, and it has become current, universal institutionalism. It is the doctrine of school to-day. It is based on a lie—but the lie was told that good might come of it!

Some variation of this theory has dominated the history of education since Plato, with the exception of a few revolutionary epochs, such as the Renaissance. This sort of education has been responsible for untold repressions, unnaturalisms, and cruelties. It has rationalized injustice and greed. To it may be traced most of the tyrannies of the centuries, and the dogmatisms, political, educational and religious, which brought the world to chaos in 1914. Institutional religion has been especially vigorous in its support of this doctrine of the depravity of human nature; and school has been everywhere until very recently built on the doctrine that Platonic ideas must displace nature everywhere.

Human Nature Before Plato.—But Plato did not invent repressions and suppressions. These have existed since the beginnings of human institutions. It is a function of all institutions to hold excess individuality in check. The primitive folkways had done this. But in those pre-Platonic days, when Sophist arguments had captured the Greek imagination, human nature had escaped from many of its old fetters. Socrates seems to have believed that a human society could be developed out of the released natures of men. He thought that human common sense, expressed in the form of common ideas and social thoughtfulness, would "hold the fretful

realm in awe." Plato believed no such nonsense. He
knew that nothing but imposed forms—Ideas—would
hold society together. Hence, he would make education
a definite system of discipline and selection, and he
wanted the man of Ideas—the philosopher—to be the
ultimate dictator of the Good Life. He would compress
all living within the bounds of *reason,* just as the primitive group had compressed all living within the bounds of
the folkways of their group.

This fact betrays the Platonic system. It shows us
that Plato, in reality, identified Reason with Custom and
Habit—imported from a distance. Most of his "eternal"
Ideas were just importations from the militaristic folkways of neighboring Sparta. "Eternal Reason" was just
the apotheosis of emotionally acceptable local customs.

Nor should Plato be blamed for all the repressions of
modern education. Much of our modern regimen antedates Plato. It is of the nature of primitive life and
primitive group control. But Plato worked out the first
considerable argument justifying it. He is its intellectual
guarantor. Primitive tendencies toward repression are
supported by the Platonic arguments of the centuries.
They fit the schoolmaster's type of mind; they give him
group assurance and intellectual dignity. Few parents
can resist such a combination. It is true, those qualities
make the schoolmaster hard, rationalistic, unsympathetic
—qualities difficult for youth to understand or endure.
But school years are soon over. A real world waits beyond the academic world. And it is best (we argue) for
youth to be disciplined. And youth itself, having been
soundly inured to these fallacious Platonic disciplines,
habits and ways, turns dogmatic and, in good time, becomes the upholder, above its own children, of the doctrines once abhorred. The royal lie has worked!

CHAPTER VIII

TRIUMPH OF THE ACADEMIC AND THE GREAT DICHOTOMY

As I repeated the line, Miss Amelia sprang to her feet and cried: "Classes, attention! Our Youngest Pupil has just completed her first sentence. This sentence contains a beautiful thought: 'Birds in their little nests agree!' There is a lesson in this for all of us. We are here in our school room like little birds in their nests. Let us all remember the wonderful truth: 'Birds in their little nests agree!'"

In three steps I laid hold of her apron. "Ho, but they don't!" I cried. "They fight like anything. Every day they make the feathers fly!"

In a backward stroke Miss Amelia's fingers, big and bony, struck my cheek a blow that nearly upset me. A red wave crossed her face and her eyes snapped. I was never so surprised in my life. I was only going to tell her the truth. What she said was altogether false. Ever since I could remember I had watched birds fight all over the place . . . There could be no mistake. I was so amazed I forgot the blow and stared. . . .

"I don't see why you slap me!" I cried. "It's the truth! Lots of times old birds pull out bunches of feathers fighting, and young ones in the nests bite each other until they squeal!"

Miss Amelia caught my shoulders and shook me.

"Take your seat!" she cried. "You are a rude, untrained child!"

"They do fight!" I insisted, as I held my head high and walked to my desk.—GENE STRATTON PORTER, in *Laddie*.

93

There is always a loss of truth and power when a man leaves working for himself to work for another . . . The temptation is to patronize Providence, to fall into the accepted ways of talking and acting of the good sort of people . . .—EMERSON, in *The Natural History of Intellect.*

Greek civilization lasted but a tragic moment as a political and social order. It has, of course, lasted more than two thousand years as a humanizing culture. But most men want one thing more than they want culture; they want a sense of security. If culture can give them this, or if it can help give it, or if it can be transformed and organized so as to give them a simulation of security, such culture can remain an interest of men even in days of insecurity. Greek intellectualism, helped by other social factors, such as religion, did bring men this sense of security, and hence it has had a long history.

The Age of Grammar.—After the age of Alexander, the Greek social order disintegrated rapidly and never again made itself effective. Greek knowledge was organized in the Alexandrian period and quickly became material of schooling in other lands. Even the Roman Empire, which had for several centuries a political security of its own and which might have developed a culture of its own, was defrauded of much of that chance by having Greek culture imposed upon it.

Greek culture was carried from land to land by individual scholars. When society disintegrates, the bridge from the old to a possible new social order must be made by individuals. These individuals usually establish themselves in secure hiding places—such as monasteries and castles, where they may realize peace in the midst of universal chaos. There they elaborate the intellectual materials of the old cultures, in true academic fashion.

This intellectual elaboration of culture materials is the most natural thing in the world; but it tends directly to the transformation of any richly social culture into purely academic materials. The humanistic cultures of the Greeks were the natural expression of the life the Greeks had lived. In Greek literature, the imaginative reader can find portrayed much of the essence of the old Greek life. Such a reader will be interested in this literature because it gives him the contagion of a great civilization.

But the scholar, working in quiet, elaborating the materials of culture for school purposes, comes eventually to a prime interest in language. To be sure he studies the language in order that he may more completely appreciate the literature. The transition is simple and natural. Presently he finds that a study of grammar will help him to understand language, and he concentrates his attention upon grammar. In his studies, grammar explains language, language illuminates literature, and literature interprets life. As he puts it the matter is clear and convincing.

But in the outcome, grammar becomes dominant. It becomes the clue to all understanding of life and the essence of education. Language, literature and life are all absorbed into grammar. The academic mind achieves its great triumph. The world is made completely intellectual. The scholar of the Middle Ages is a Grammarian. Plato forever!

The Tragedy of the Formal.—For centuries scholars, assisted by theologians and statesmen, have struggled with the great task of cramming human nature inside grammar; that is, inside the formal interpretation of life and experience. This effort always betrays a troubled mind. Sometimes the scholar holds that the world *is* orderly ("God geometrizes!") and that all that is needed is faith and skill in pedagogy.   But mostly there is doubt and concession.   The world is irrational, human nature the most irrational part of it.   And the task will never be quite complete though it will be nearly enough complete to give the worker the sense of a real victory.   And it is always a moral duty to go on working for this sublime end.

Suso, a German monk of the fourteenth century, gives his own account of an effort to bring his own nature under control of certain formal principles.   He says of himself:

> "He was in his youth of a temperament full of fire and life: and when this began to make itself felt, it was very grievous to him; and he sought by many devices how he might bring his body into subjection.   He wore for a long time a hair shirt and an iron chain, until the blood ran from him, so that he was obliged to leave them off."

But he worked hard at the task and in the long run he brought his body under the control of a moral regimen of extreme severity.   He cut his life in two, suppressing one part of himself ruthlessly.

Effort of this same sort is reflected in all institutions, and quite consciously in schools and universities.   The medieval university was primarily an institution for the examination and certification of knowledge.   All new materials must be certified as acceptable to the old materials, and as being proper stuff for the individual to know.   In this respect the university was like the church.   The church examined all novel doctrines and accepted those only which were in accordance with the faith.   New suggestions had to be subjected to the patterns of the past.   There must never be anything really new in the world.

Triumph of the Formal.—This conflict of the Middle Ages was, of course, one between a great pattern, which included religious, political, moral and intellectual phases, and which was held to be of the nature of reality, and that endless emergence of new materials and new forms of social expression, which has been characteristic of the history of Western Europe, and which eventually resulted in the discovery and settlement of America. On the one side we have ideas, old forms, the folkways of the ages: all the aims of pre-existent civilization woven into a more or less consistent and final pattern for all human society and for all the future. Plato had prefigured it; Aristotle had given the final logic for it; Thomas Aquinas was the genius who gave this pattern its final intellectual form; and Dante was the cosmic artist who wove through that intellectual texture the emotional colorings which made it seem of the very stuff of life and reality.

On the other side were all the stirrings of the new age, the promises of the frontiers, the murmurings of discontent from growing numbers of by-ways of the world, the threats of revolt in the political, the economic, and the religious world; the appearance of rebellious intellects, like Abélard; the recognition of nature, as more imperious than Aristotle, by men like Roger Bacon; the coming in of strange cultures, like the Saracenic.

Some day there would be a Great Battle—but not yet.

Educational Developments.—John Milton had taken note of some of the educational results that had come from the subordination to this Medievalism. He calls that education an "asinine feast of sow-thistles and brambles." Speaking of youths who were lost in it, he writes:

"They do for the most part grow into hatred and contempt of Learning, mockt and deluded all this while with rugged Notions and Babblements, while they expect worthy and delightful knowledge; till poverty or youthful years call them importunely their several ways, and hasten them with the sway of friends either to an ambitious and mercenary, or ignorantly zealous Divinity; some allured to the trade of Law, grounding their purpose not on the prudent and heavenly contemplation of justice and equity which was never taught them, but on the promising and pleasing thoughts of litigious terms, fat contentions and flowing fees; others betake them to State affairs, with souls so unprincipl'd in vertue, and true generous breeding, that flattery, and Court shifts and tyrannous Aphorisms appear to them the highest points of wisdom; instilling their barren hearts with a conscientious slavery, if, as I rather think, it be not fain'd.   Others lastly of a more delicious and airie spirit, retire themselves knowing no better, to the enjoyment of ease and luxury, living out their daies in feasts and jollity; which indeed is the wisest and safest course of all these, unless they were with more integrity undertaken.   And these are the fruits of misspending our prime youth at the Schools and Universities as we do, either in learning mere words or such things chiefly, as were better unlearnt."

It may be assumed that Milton meant his words to be taken seriously.   But they were not then, and they have not been since, as any reader may determine for himself by re-reading them.   It is perfectly obvious that the world has been trying for more than twenty centuries to realize the ends of education set forth by Plato in *The Republic*.   It is not so obvious, but it is quite as true, that the net results of all those tryings is set forth with amazing fidelity, even for our own times, by John Milton in the words quoted above. That is to say, schooling cuts the schooled in two, developing one part of him and ruthlessly denying and suppressing as far as may be, the other part.

None the less, the same ancient academic point of view was restated and justified by John Locke, the philosopher of the Puritan movement, the rationalizer of academic processes to the modern world, and the leading educational theorizer for American schoolmen. His general point of view often quoted may be here briefly repeated:

"As the strength of the Body lies chiefly in being able to endure Hardships, so also does that of the Mind, and the great Principle and Foundation of all Virtue and Worth is placed in this: That a Man is able to deny himself his own desires, cross his own inclinations and purely follow what Reason directs as best, though the appetite lean the other way. . . . It seems plain to me that the Principle of all Virtue and Excellency lies in the power of denying ourselves the satisfactions of our own Desires, where Reason does not authorize them. . . . If, therefore, I might be heard, I would advise that, contrary to the ordinary way, children should be used to submit their Desires and go without their Longings, even from their very Cradles."

Here again the child is cut in two—one part being developed, the other ruthlessly suppressed.

Educational theorizing has made considerable progress since the time of John Locke, but educational practice still everywhere lingers under the burden of his hard maxims. Changes in theory are of no consequence, in themselves, but only as they become organized into changed habits and practices—in the lives of teachers, in the programs of schools, and in the accepted customs of the community.

The nineteenth century made some strenuous efforts to escape from these medieval and academic conceptions of life and the world. The theory of evolution and the psychology of William James were steps in this direction. But the long distance that had to be traversed before education could completely escape is illustrated by a writer of the early nineteenth century, Newham, who, discussing the nature of childhood, says:

"No sooner do children begin to act at all, but we discover how universally sin has pervaded all the sources of intelligence. There is a greater pleasure in reflecting on the images of crime than on the character of piety; the conscience is enfeebled and oppressed; its voice is stifled and its actions perverted; the imagination delights to revel over scenes of iniquity, and is difficultly carried forward to anticipations of future happiness, glory, and praise; the will is enslaved by selfishness; the imitation of all that is wrong is most easy—of all that is right is most onerous—the judgment is prone to perpetual error; the evil passions grow and flourish, while the good are educated with difficulty."

This academic and moralistic outlook upon life had been brought to America by the Puritans and it became the dominant mood of our own American educational and school life. Early American text books for schools were thoroughly moralistic after Puritanical models and academic in temper and materials. The mood of these materials is found in the couplet that was used in probably every primer or first reader:

"In Adam's fall
We sinnèd all!"

Even as late as the fourth quarter of the nineteenth century one of the well-known McGuffey Readers, the *First
Eclectic,* contained a reading lesson on the subject, "The
Dunce," which was accompanied by a picture showing the
master and three or four boys looking commiseratingly
at another boy who was standing in the corner with a
"dunce-cap" on his head. Under the picture was the
legend: "What has he done? He laughs and talks in
school. He loves to be idle. Does he not look bad?"
This last question was a bit "thick" in view of the fact
that the boy was pictured with his hands in his eyes, and
his whole face covered.

The question, "Does he not look bad?" shows the academic temper completely. What it means is, "Does he
not look disobedient?" The picture portrays the dichotomy of the world. The world was cut in two. One part
of the world is orderly, rational, obedient. The rest of
the world is disorderly, irrational, disobedient. The rational must be protected and conserved. The disobedient
must be scourged, flogged, beaten, suppressed and ruthlessly overthrown. There could be no commerce between
the realms of darkness and of light. The "carnal" and
the "spiritual" have no relationships save such as the
"carnal" tries to force upon the "spiritual" for the purpose of corruption.

Current Academic Attitudes.—At the Meeting of the
National Council of Education held in Des Moines, Iowa,
July, 1921, the ten most suggestive "essentials of Democracy" were formulated as an expression of the educational
ideal of that council. After discussing principles of democratic self-assertiveness, equal rights and opportunities,

as distinguished from equal abilities and achievements, and many other similar "essentials," the council came to the tenth "essential," Democratic Compulsion, which it defines as follows:

> "The democratic control of social conduct requires the accustoming of every individual to the compulsion in himself and others, both through public sentiment and law, of every essential of democracy which is not self-acquired. As the essential complement to a stronger individuality or self-assertiveness every individual should be accustomed from the earliest childhood to cheerful submission to superior wisdom and authority, and to ready acquiescence in community standards more exacting than his own."

More recently still, this ideal of the subordination of the individual to institutions has been explicitly set forth by Prof. Charles H. Judd in his book, *The Psychology of Social Institutions*. Professor Judd's argument is interwoven, here and there, with some lingering memories of the modern individual caught in the complexity of the social and industrial order; but, on the whole, his sympathies are with institutions as against the individual. The racial element in experience is so much more substantial than is any individual that the ages have the right to dominate. The individual must give way. He must consent to have his very nervous system taken over by institutions and made over on lines laid down by the "needs of society," and the convenience of the adult world. The standards and judgments of the community are superior to the standards and judgments of the individuals. Education is the process by which individuals are institutionalized—until they conform to the patterns

laid down by society. The school is the social instrument
dominantly at work in this field. The welfare of society
—and of the individual, himself—depends upon the success of the school in this direction. "Education" must
become "scientific": it must set forth the standards and
uniformities demanded by the age, in order that the
teachers and schools of the times may be able to produce
these desired standard and uniform results in all children.

If we may judge by present developments, this sort of
"education"—with all that it implies—is still almost universally dominant in public schools. It is the triumph of
the academic!

The Compulsory School.—All these tendencies have
come to their climax in the modern universal compulsory
school. This school is, as we have pointed out, probably
the most generous gesture ever made by any people for
its children. But to say that it is generous is not to say
that it is wise. The modern compulsory school is, mostly,
just the old intellectual academy of John Locke made
compulsory by legal processes, and imposed upon children whether they are interested in intellectual matters
or not.

The compulsory school does not educate children even
though they do have to attend it. The statistics of war-
time tests show how little compulsory schools between,
say, 1900 and 1910, affected the minds and bodies of the
children. The teacher of a compulsory school does not
have to be an interesting or vital personality: the children have to attend whether they like it or not. The lessons set for the children do not have to be interesting, and
the children do not have to understand them, or relate
them to their experiences. They have merely to memo-
rize them and relate them to the teacher. At the lowest
ebb, the lessons are merely glanced at; at the best they

are merely memorized confusedly by 95 percent of the pupils. These facts are indisputable. The proof is available.

The hopes held out to early America that through the development of the public school system, our citizens would be prepared to assume intelligent shares in the civic and social life of the land, and of the world, have been defeated.[1] Compulsory schooling, resulting at best in the memorizing of academic materials, has not cultivated the *intelligence* of America, but has standardized and defeated that intelligence. This does not have to be proved; it is generally admitted.

The school has triumphed—but education has not. At least not the sort of education needed by a "free" people in an industrial age. We can almost all read: but what do we read? We spend billions of money on schools, yearly; in recent years, one of our most obvious returns for these billions has been increased intolerance, more "fundamentalism," a growing war upon science, a turning to primitive group moralities and a resurgence of a primitive magic. We carry a buckeye to cure our rheumatism, and a "book-list" to cure our ignorance! We know *about* everything: we *know* almost nothing.

The Great Dichotomy.—The fact is that schools are not much interested in furthering knowledge or increasing intelligence either in the individual or in the community. Schools are still most interested in *discipline*. This is sometimes assimilated to "mind," as *mental discipline*, and it is assumed by some that this "mental discipline" really promises intellectual mastery and power. Aside from the dubiousness of the whole matter in the light of

[1] As this is being written, the presidential campaign of 1928 is drawing to a close: a campaign which has released more intolerance, propaganda, "whispering" and bitterness than any other within the memory of the present generation.

psychology, schoolmen and school boards are not much interested in "mastery and power." They are all for "control." As we shall see later (Chapter XXIII) schooling has taken the place of primitive group controls as a means of *developing the minds of children up to the levels of the group folkways and there arresting them!* The school exists to *control* mind. There are more than eight hundred thousand teachers in American schools, of all sorts, including colleges and universities. There are probably not four thousand teachers in the whole number who would "think" of fulfilling the old Greek conception of the teacher's business, namely, to "make himself useless to his pupils." The true academic ideal proposes to "form" the "mind" of the "pupil."

This academic method is continuous with primitive group training: it selects parts of the individual for survival and forming, and it attempts ruthlessly to suppress the rest. That is, it cuts the individual in two. This is the great dichotomy of history and of education. It selects the "mind" of the mutilated individual for shaping according to selected patterns of "social" or "institutional" behavior. It rejects the rest as "lower" and puts it under the orders of the "higher." That is the theory. The *fact* is that it turns the "lower" over to the domination of primitive impulses which, periodically, compensate for the imprisonment of the "higher" by going on emotional or even physical "sprees."

The pattern for much of this can be found in Plato. He got it, not in "eternity" as he claims but in the world around him. He found in his world slaves and freemen; physical laborers and mental leaders; ignoramuses and philosophers; bodies and minds; appetites and thoughts. He assumed that slaves, physical laborers, ignoramuses, bodies and appetites were inimical to the state, and that therefore they were rightly subordinate to freemen, mental leaders, philosophers, minds and thoughts. But if they were subordinate then they must be "lower," and if lower then inferior and to be suppressed at all costs, held in "control" by the higher.

We are still at this point. We *do not know how* to deal with human experience integrally. We must cut it in two, socially and personally, dichotomize it, select one part of it for survival and honor and consign the rest of it to suppression and dishonor.

Because our *aims* are high and holy, having in view the preservation of the state, it is permissible to lie in their service. Nay, more, it is often necessary to lie in their service. The professor of moral education in the great university feels himself perfectly justified in saying: "Here is an interpretation that is so desirable that we ought to believe it whether it's true or not!" The results of this sort of education we have all about us, to-day. It is an education admirably fitted to produce fanatics, who have emotions without control of any sort, and subordinates, without emotions of any sort. If occasionally an intelligent, integrated human being emerges out of the educational years, it will usually be found that he defied the schools, and went his own way to his own education. Of course most of our criminals have been produced in this same way. To the thoroughly institutionalized person, a critically intelligent, integrated personality is always suspect. Socrates was a criminal. Jesus was a criminal—to the ones who put him to death, that is, the authorities. The simplest definition of criminality is nonconformity. To the primitive mind that is practically all it is. But, in the modern world, that is also the simplest definition of "great leadership." Here seems to emerge a great contradiction. Schools wisely avoid such contradictions. They *fear* to produce criminals. They *fail* to produce leaders. There may be some connection between the two facts. Following community standards, they divide the world between the "good" and the "bad," the "rational" and the "irrational," "credits" and "failures." They make their work *academic*, which means "safe and sane," which means, in large measure, sterile. They are caught in the meshings of our interlocking institutionalisms, and can do little else.

And all this is a condition which no amount of intellectualistic schooling, or academic "science," will ever be able to deal with intelligently.

CHAPTER IX

INTERLOCKING INSTITUTIONS IN THE MODERN WORLD

It is evident that the state is a creation of nature, and that man is by nature an institution-building animal. And he who by nature and not by mere accident is without a state, is either above humanity or below it; he is the "Tribeless, lawless, heartless one," whom Homer denounces—the outcast who is a lover of war: he may be compared to a bird which flies alone. . . .

Thus the state is by nature clearly prior to the individual and the family, since the whole is of necessity prior to the part. . . . The proof that the state is a creation of nature and prior to the individual is that the individual, when isolated, is not self-sufficing; therefore he is like a part in relation to the whole. But he who is unable to live in society, or who has no need because he is sufficient for himself, must either be a beast or a god. —ARISTOTLE, in *Politics*.

And Cain said unto Jehovah: "My punishment is greater than I can bear. Behold thou hast driven me out this day from the face of the ground, and from thy face shall I be hid; and I shall be a fugitive and a wanderer in the earth; and it shall come to pass that whosoever findeth me shall slay me."—GENESIS.

Why don't you come into the factories, work with us on the construction of curricula, define the conditions of a progressive training which entitles the employers to use the labor of children and carries this mass forward with a creative ideal of accomplishment in place of the

108

ideals of idleness that you are instilling to-day?—Invitation of National Ass'n of Manufacturers to the Schools, 1928.

When men first came to awareness of life and the world they were already bound hand and foot in the bonds of custom, as we have seen. Aristotle was one of the first to realize this fact; and he accepted it as inevitable. He said, "Man is an institution-building animal." Man secretes institutions as an oyster secretes his shell, and probably he can do no more about it than the oyster can.

Aristotle's Theory.—"The state is by nature prior to the individual," said Aristotle, "since the whole of anything is, of necessity, prior to its parts." According to this doctrine, not only is the whole prior to the part, but any part gets its reality by sharing in that reality which is the whole. The reality of the whole precedes and gives reality to any part. This principle operates in the organization of institutions through all the ages, including our own. We are still subject to it.

This priority of the state or of society finds natural expression in institutions. A great population cannot do all things that need to be done to make life endurable. Special services require special instruments. Our social institutions are instruments of such special import. They are not imposed upon the world. They are implied in the nature of reality and in the growth of society and they are express differentiations of reality and of society.

The state itself, according to Aristotle, is a creation of nature quite as much as mountains or oceans are. The church regards itself as equally the expression of reality and takes its authority from its divine sanctions. The economic system in each specific economic age relies firmly upon the doctrine that it expresses human nature:

that is to say, it is an express creation of reality. Marriage, likewise, holds itself to be above the ordinary vicissitudes of experience—the expression of ultimate reality: "Marriages are made in Heaven!" Should not the school hold quite as exalted an opinion of itself?

The Roots of This Doctrine.—Knowing as we do something more of history than Aristotle knew, we may well ask how such a doctrine ever came to be, and to be held by men. The question takes us back to the roots of social development.

One primitive motive of group and social aggrandizement was fear. Primitive man was afraid. His life was precarious. He was afraid of natural forces. His food supplies were always low and uncertain. He personified the sources of his fears and made them into gods. As Lucretius says, "The gods were born of fear." Not fear of the gods—but fear of the world and of nature.

All primitive customs and organizations, born of life-preserving activities, were nurtured and solidified by fear—fear either of external natural forces, or fear of internal rebellious forces. Primitive customs were useful in curbing individual impulses. The group must present a rigid front to whatever fears or dangers arise. Primitive social organization, which later became the state, held in check rebellious activities on the part of individuals and kept the group ready for external emergencies. Religious ceremonials tended to curb uncontrolled explorations by adventuresome individuals. Industrial activities were early conventionalized and new enterprises were denied. Marriage was expected to keep the irresponsible sex impulses within fixed bounds. No one of these purposes was ever fully realized. But they gave the appearance of order and control; and appearance is enough, in most cases.

The Historic Present.—Over and above all the developments of the centuries, these primitive institutional patterns, born largely of fears, lie very close under the surface of our life to-day, and they break through into action in any critical situation. The modern mob is a primitive group, enjoying primitive fears, and expressing them in some convenient form of sadistic action. We now know that there was an enormous resurgence of these primitive fear patterns in the recent war time. This resurgence is what made the war so enjoyable to large numbers of people. There is little that is so enjoyable as a good fear—at a distance. Under the influence of these war-time fears our institutional patterns reverted to primitive type. They became not instruments of serving social need in the broad civilized sense of the word; they became instruments of repression. The individual initiative that America had long enjoyed in practically all fields of human endeavor was energetically subordinated to standard patterns which got their sanctions in our primitive fears. The state, the church, the industrial organization, the school, the community—all these were filled with fears and they took primitive delight in satisfying those fears by punitive action against individuals who fell under any suspicion. It is the duty of a primitive man to slay the "outlaw."

Many of these aspects of primitive fear, and the institutions and customs that represent the efforts of the group to defend itself against these fears, have been summed up in the modern doctrine of school: it is the general business of school to repress and control and civilize the last of the savages with which civilized man has to contend—namely, the child.

Do Institutions Change?—Contradicting the doctrine of institutions as set forth by Aristotle and as held by practically all conservatives ever since, the course of actual history shows that institutions do continually change. Not all peoples have the same institutions; no one people has the same institutions in different stages of its history. The history of institutions in Europe, for example, from the dawn of the historic period to the present, is an enormous panorama of change: Greece, Rome, Medieval Europe, the modern nations—no two of them alike—no one of them the same for two successive centuries. Even the comparatively short course of American history shows endless institutional shifts and changes. As this is being written, we are in the midst of a stirring debate over the fundamental nature of our whole constitutional system.

However, many who know that institutions have been developed through history still argue that our present institutions should be regarded as permanent, even sacred. Institutions, they say, must *sometime* reach a state of equilibrium. Why not ours at this time? For example, in the Pan-American Conference at Havana in the winter of 1928, it was seriously proposed by delegates from American republics, each one of which was itself the express result of revolution, that the general principle of revolution should be outlawed! Public opinion in the United States was severely tempted to become completely absolutistic in recent war time when, as we can recall, petty patriots generally insisted that no American institution should ever be criticized. "Criticism is unAmerican!" they said, though America was born of criticism!

In actual practice, however, very few of us hold to this absolutistic doctrine. Most of us believe that our institutions can be improved upon even if not substantially modified. The school is held by some to exist for the express purpose of continuous modification of our institutions and customs through the introduction of new knowledge into common practice. But since the school is itself one of our institutions, and since it is almost completely controlled by community opinion, it has become one of the chief bearers of custom; and it seems a bit problematic whether any amount of schooling will ever seriously affect the structure of our other institutions. There is an interlocking of institutional attitudes that makes it increasingly difficult for any one institution to change without parallel changes in all other institutions.[1]

Industry is probably the most powerful of our institutional organizations. Industry holds the power of life and death in its hands: it can heal or destroy by giving or withholding its favors. The state, the church, the school, the family, are dependent upon its moods. But, on the other hand, industry is not stable; it changes with new inventions and the shifts of population and popular interest. The modern world is a great interlocking arrangement, not wholly standardized—yet too nearly complete to permit much individual rebellion. Industry is subject to most changes since it is ever at the mercy of new inventions. In some instances, inventions have been suppressed in the interest of stability. The public is but slightly aware of the extent of these interlockings. Most individuals and institutions consider themselves free.

Can Education Escape?—For this reason some modern educators have rebelled against the submission of education to the control of social institutions, like the school. They hold that children must be protected against the prejudicial institutions of the past until they

[1] Recently the school has been insidiously used by certain financial interests for the purpose of propaganda against "municipal ownership of public utilities." There is not much public indignation against this use of the schools, for most people assume that the school should support current institutions. If the propaganda had been in *favor* of municipal ownership, the outcry would probably have been very great, for that would have implied "undermining our institutions."

have achieved their intellectual, moral and spiritual maturity in a free world. If they can be assured of this chance they will eventually make their own institutions; and in that way create new social orders free from the repressions of the old. Theoretically, this doctrine may have some validity; but practically it presents a difficult program. The generations are not distinct, and there is no possibility of separating them. There is, in fact, no such thing as a "younger generation." The generations are continuous. They interpenetrate. There is no way in which a younger generation can develop free from all contamination of the older generation and its historic institutions. The younger generation inevitably must develop in the same world in which the older generation lives, and it must develop within the shadow of the institutions of the past. The *race* was here before any individual was born.

To-day, perhaps, as never before, the so-called "younger generation" has had the chance to escape the subordination which the older generation holds in trust for them. Some few of them have taken advantage of this chance and have "escaped," via the automobile, etc. But others in larger numbers are flocking to schools and universities, seeking the very controls they might escape. The child cannot avoid the controls of the community and its institutions.

Which Way Shall We Go?—We must consider the whole life of the community, if we are to have any real understanding as to how we are educated and how we can contrive a more adequate or a freer education. Here are some of the factors in the case: Here is the older generation with its institutions handed down from the past, with customs and manners and prejudices and passions and primitive behavior patterns, and, at times, a little bit of critical intelligence. Here are childhood and youth, closely tied to the older generation; under its thumb, in fact. Here are community activities, in moralistic grooves, and with traditional attitudes that induce like attitudes in the young. Here is a bit of knowledge and a few scientific proofs, perhaps, but these are mostly academic and only partially intelligent. Education goes on, and must go on, in the midst of these traditional factors and within the organized life of the community. The effort to segregate children into special houses for the purpose of educating them, as if an outside world did not exist, has not only proved a comparative failure; it will never be anything but a failure. Schools will have some share in the education of children, of course; but it will always be a share, never the whole of that education; and it will always be subject to a last word from the outside world. The school is only *one* of our educational institutions.

Can the World Change?—None the less, there is in the modern world a hint of change. This is partly the result of the clash of irrational forces such as the meeting of many racial groups and cultures; partly the result of the development of science and a method that poses as a technique of deliberate change. Mind, in the active sense of the word, is the instrument of change. *Mind is change that has become aware of itself and undertakes to control its own direction.* What chance has mind of this sort in the modern situation? That is to say, what chance has intelligent, critically guided change in the modern world? In small areas, much, perhaps; in the large, not a great deal. Scientific inventions precipitate changes of enormous import in our physical habits, as e.g., the effect of the automobile on modern modes of life. But we fail or refuse to consider the moral and spiritual implications of those physical changes. We live our primitive lives in the modern world of cosmic machineries.

We may, then, state the fundamental problem of modern education somewhat as follows: we must have communities that will provide breadth, depth and variety of experience to childhood and youth, and institutions which can bring wide ranges of service to the whole community; these institutions must have stability, at least enough to enable the individual and the community to exist; yet they must still have found out how to grow and change, and to offer the chance for evolutionary growth and change to the community and the individual. Education must lead in these antithetic processes.

From one point of view, all human history seems to be a struggle of humanity to get itself completely walled in, with eternal changelessness in habit, custom, and institution. It is typified in the struggle of the Middle Ages to wall itself within great castles which could resist all incursions of change.

On the other hand, much of human history seems to be a continuous struggle to destroy all institutions. In certain ages at least, the mind of man has been extremely restless. No sooner does the Medieval Age get itself safely housed in castles with walls sixteen feet thick, than some restless mind contrives a cannon with powder and balls able to blow holes through walls even sixteen feet thick.

In general, during all the known part of the history of the race, these two agencies—the castle builder and the castle destroyer—have glared at each other and denounced each other and fought each other to the point of extermination. It may be that the real problem of education and of civilization is to recognize the validity of both these principles and agencies in life and the world and to find some means by which they can both be incorporated into educational procedure and thus made a definite part of the technique of civilization. The community and the individual alike need habits and institutions; they alike need changes in habits and institutions. An education that is content with either of these results, either for the community at large or for the individual, is not and will never be a satisfactory education. The academic school may well take notice of this dictum—which seems to be one thing history teaches.

But it is not at all certain that the academic school will take effective account of this need, at least not for some time to come. All casual and practical influences in the community urge to the opposite. Religious leaderships are largely concerned with the maintenance of institutionalisms, and with the type of mind that will not question the finality of the dogmas. Industrial leaderships are still, for the most part, concerned with the maintenance of the *status quo,* which includes the ancient relationships of the employee to the employer, and which assumes that "economic laws," which "govern in all these matters," are eternal. The state, and especially the petty officials who represent the state in local communities, is still greatly concerned with maintaining its authority over the subjects who live in the community. For instance, in many states, school board officials still refuse to permit general public meetings for all sorts of purposes in school houses, on the ground that the school house "belongs to the children," and must not be contaminated. School people, of course, are caught in this distressing dilemma. The school is supposed to be engaged in developing *mind,* but the community is pretty certain that it does not want much of that commodity. Leading educational authorities are equally sure of it. "What we want is habits of

mind," says one authority. "The community, through
the school, must take over the nervous systems of children, and mold them to the uses of the community," says
another; "the community knows more than the individual
what is good for both the individual and the general welfare." "The school's business," says still another, "is to
get children ready to take their places in the institutions
of our times. When they come out of school and youth
into the world and mature responsibilities, they should all
be ready to take jobs in our industrial order; to join some
reputable political party and help carry on the government founded by the sacrifices of the fathers; to share
in the communion of some religious body, and help to
preserve the moralities which, without religious sanctions, would soon disappear altogether; and to get mar-
ried and 'settle down' to the established responsibilities
of men and women."

All these dogmas seem so rational and natural that one
need not wonder much that most people, schooled to the
acceptance of dogma, swallow them whole. The interlocking of institutions in the modern world makes for a
very tight little world, wherein most of us are held to a
stability of career, almost as if our heads were held in
vices. We give somewhat the appearance of those who,
years ago, "sat" for their photographs, with heads held
in a steadying apparatus. The rebellions of the "younger
generation" have tended to make the older generation,
especially all who have any fundamentalist turn of mind,
all the more anxious to reduce life and the world to habits, dogmas, customs and institutions, within which life
can be finally imprisoned, schooled and molded, patterned
and turned to a perfect finish.

It is a noble ideal; too noble for this world.

But now, having followed the course of the history of the academic school from its beginnings in ancient Greece to its present dominant position in schooling, if not in education, we must turn from this aspect of the study, and take up the main line of protest which the modern educational world affords against this complete institutionalization of education. Over against the "old school" which we have been studying there is a "new school," and to that we must turn. We must see what happens when education is regarded, not as something existent to be taken on by the child, but as something to be created by the child's own experience, as the expression of the interest and need of the particular individual. The critical contrast between these two types of school is striking and illuminating. We turn to the "new school" in Part Two.

PART TWO

THE PSYCHOLOGICAL INTERPRETATION
OF EDUCATION

CHAPTER X

THE INDIVIDUAL

Another sign of our times . . . is the new importance given to the single person. Everything that tends to insulate the individual—to surround him with barriers of natural respect, so that each man shall feel the world as his, and man shall treat with man as a sovereign state with a sovereign state—tends to true union as well as greatness. "I learned," says the melancholy Pestalozzi, "that no man in God's wide earth is either willing or able to help any other man." Help must come from the bosom alone. . . . The world is nothing, the man is all; in yourself is the law of all nature, and you know not yet how a globule of sap ascends; in yourself slumbers the whole of Reason; it is for you to know all, it is for you to dare all. . . . Is it not the chief disgrace in the world not to be an unit, not to be reckoned one character; not to yield that peculiar fruit which each man was created to bear, but to be reckoned in the gross, in the hundred or the thousand, of the party, the section, to which we belong; and our opinion predicted geographically, as the north or the south? Not so, brothers and friends, please God, ours shall not be so. We will walk on our own feet; we will work with our own hands; we will speak our own minds. . . . A nation of men will for the first time exist.—EMERSON, in *The American Scholar*.

According to a famous account of origins, the human race began with one individual. Others were added from time to time, and the present millions of the earth's inhabitants are the results of this adding one to one. This theory of the natural history of the race is still, probably,

123

the one most generally held. It has psychological implications and educational implications of the greatest importance; and these implications are accepted by millions
of people who no longer hold to the bald doctrine itself.
"What's the difference?" the supercilious may ask. But
the difference will never be apparent to the supercilious.
We must consider briefly the real nature of the individual.

The Individual and the Race.—Looked at casually the
race seems to be made up of individuals. So many individuals, three, five, eight, make up a family. So many
more make up a neighborhood, a state, a nation, the
world. The population of the earth is some sixteen hundred million individuals.

The census presents America, to the casual student, as
a nation of some hundred and twenty million individuals.
These individuals are classified, and cross-classified in
various ways; but they still remain individuals.

Most of our modern institutions, ignorant of their own
origins, speak quite naïvely about their "members": each
church has so many "members," each school so many
"pupils." This is one of the fundamental weaknesses of
institutions, to-day: they have such an awesome sense
of their own atomic organization, and of the significance
of "members." Some of them issue a bulletin every time
they secure a "new member."

From the beginnings of its modern history, democracy
has definitely stressed the significance and finality of the
individual. There was to be no more subordination of
individuals to the whims of antique institutions. Every
free man is an individual; all men are created equal.
The modern state was to be the creation of free individuals—"we, the people."

Modern religion attempts the same thing. The basis
and the weakness of Protestant religions has been the

theory of the absolute worth of the individual soul. The modern individual is assumed not to get his reality or his value from membership in institutions. He has reality in his own right: frequently he has to turn to and reform old institutions that would, left alone, degrade and destroy him. This theory tends to discredit old institutions.

Morality, likewise, in recent centuries, has stressed more and more the doctrine of individual responsibility above the mere fact of membership in groups. Uncritical membership in archaic groups is regarded by some moralists as the greatest immorality of the age.

The Individual and the Scientific Movement.—The fundamental factor in the modern scientific movement has been the rebellious individual mind that has gone inquiring beyond the bounds set by institutions: Copernicus, Galileo, Bruno, Columbus, Darwin. And that fact has been recognized by the race in according to such men the honor of giving their names to "natural" laws. For instance, we speak of the "Copernican universe," "Newton's law of gravitation," "the Darwinian theory." This means, that in the modern world, the individual is the most important of all factors. Theoretically, institutions are but lightly esteemed, to-day.

Psychology has long held the assumption that mind exists nowhere but in individual minds. The doctrine seems at least plausible. Nothing mental happens save in the mind of some individual. Psychology is the study of individual minds. That which is sometimes spoken of as group mind is nothing more than the sum of a number of individual minds. There is some uneasiness about this doctrine to-day but it is probably still most influential in all psychological procedures.

The Individual and Education.—What wonder, then, if educators should come to the conclusion that the individual is the unit of society and that education must be primarily a matter of individual development? What wonder if, on the one hand, even the academic school man should come to the conclusion that he must study the individual child and build his school around the needs of the individual child as he discovers them? To be sure, the school man will study the child by methods that are of the school. He will use intelligence tests that are academic and standards of measurements that fit into academic routines; and he will translate all his findings into elaborate systems of child accounting which can be made the basis of impressive demonstrations. The institutionalist is compelled to pay some homage to "individual need" to-day; but, at the end, he will see to it that the child is once more the "pupil" and is safely in his place in the lists of the school.

What wonder if, on the other hand, the educator who is not a conservative school man should hold that the child is the unit of society and that education must devote itself whole-heartedly to "individual development"? Such an educator will want a program that will release the initiatives and powers of each individual child and help that child to achieve a creative place in the world.

This school man (or woman) will be so committed to The Individual that he will have little patience with the pretensions, or even the realities, of institutional relationships. He will, probably, not understand institutions at all. He will dwell hopefully upon the doctrine that if the child can be protected from the impacts of antique institutions until he is "habituated to freedom," and has developed his own forms of living, with his own freed emotions and his own "creative mind," he will then be able to create a social order in his own image, that will be able to defend itself and himself from the demands of all the

ancient folkway attitudes; a social order that will, in its
own good time, free all individuals into creative personality, and so give us that kind of social freedom we are
all said to desire "in our highest and best moments."

The assumptions underlying this latter doctrine are so
many, so varied and so revolutionary that, if valid, they
will make the world over. Hence, we must linger to
examine them in concrete detail. We must discover the
occasions that gave rise to this doctrine, the concrete instruments it proposes to use in its realization, and the
many and varied implications of the whole subject. We
must consider the nature of the educational program implied in this doctrine and its assumptions. We must try
to see what would be the nature of a social order made
of "free individuals," who with their "free minds" will
create the conditions that will defend this creative freedom to the end of the ages. We must hear more of these
matters.

CHAPTER XI

THE SOCIAL WASTES OF INSTITUTIONALISM

A curious instance of backwoods Puritanism manifests itself in a mediæval Book of Rules provided every teacher on her arrival (in Big Lick), by the secretary of the School Board. These rules are to be read aloud "at least once a month," as is stated in the preamble. Teachers are forbidden, by this curious collection of prohibitions, to bring any but school texts with them to their work; they are forbidden to do embroidery during the noon or mid-day recess; they may not dance; they may not play cards . . . (They may not have) social engagements of any kind between Monday and Friday of the school week, and on no one of these nights may any teacher be on the public streets after the hour of seven o'clock . . . the twenty teachers ordinarily obey these rules, for infractions, particularly of the one last mentioned, are punished with instant dismissal. This strict guardianship over the morals of the people is seen also in the enforcement of Sunday blue laws. . . . The town for the time being is at an impasse. Divided against itself there cannot be developed a sufficient feeling of unity to bind the people together.—J. F. STEINER, in *The American Community in Action*.

I haven't a diploma or a piece of paper to prove that I ever went to school. I have to summon some old-time witnesses and put them on the stand. They could testify they saw me outside a school, but there is no other evidence. However, I lost nothing by this in the long run, because the educative processes of after life gave it to me better than I would have taken it from books.

128

I got it without reading the books. I got it by looking
around me and by living among people and listening to
them. It has been said of me that I never forget anything I hear, and. in twenty-five years I have heard
plenty.—ALFRED E. SMITH, Governor of New York.

We human beings cling to institutions as the defense
of our precarious lives against the changes inevitable in
natural processes. We have sometimes even been able to
believe that we have completely circumvented natural
processes. But however secure we may have fancied ourselves, we have never been able for long to escape the
uneasy feeling that every institution is more or less temporary in character. The great poetry of the ages, the
great hymns of religion, practically all the great literatures of the world are expressions of this fearfulness of
the human even within institutional bulwarks. Every institution has been much like a precarious sandbar thrown
up in the midst of a treacherous river current. Life on
the sandbar may be cramping but it is a bit more secure
than trying to swim in the current. The human mind
wants stability: men have been quite content to cramp
themselves in all other ways in order to achieve even temporarily this sense of security. In these cramping processes our institutions tend easily to forget and even to
deny their own history and to ignore their own probable
futures.

What Is an Institution?—An institution is a social
structure that has developed in response to social need,
and that has achieved a *vested* existence. But, institutions can be thought of as Ideas that have been embodied
in those structures. Plato held Ideas to be eternal. Medieval institutions built upon this Platonic assumption:
The Church and The State, to mention no others, were
the right and left hands of God. With the forecast of

the scientific movement, Medievalism found itself in a whirlpool of discussion as to whether ideas have this eternal quality ascribed to them by Plato. The question at issue really was—are institutions eternal and sacred, or may rebellious individuals defy them without fear of being punished by the gods? The testimony of the last five or six hundred years seems to be that institutions are neither eternal nor sacred. They change. Concepts change. Ideas change. The Church has come to be many churches. The Empire has come to be many modern nations. The medieval economic system is gone and in its place have come many kinds of organizations of industry, with others yet to be. "Everything flows," said the old Greek philosopher, Heraclitus. Institutionalism must be reminded of this fact, once in a while.

Definitions Change.—The history of words is a story of the transformations of meanings. Many modern scientists, ignorant of history, protest that science needs definitions that will stick. It seems likely, however, that if science cannot get ahead without words that it can nail down, it is doomed to defeat. Definitions refuse to stay put. About the only word that remains changeless is "yard" and similar words, and those words remain stable because the government has expended millions in setting up conditions in the Bureau of Standards which can be *maintained without change* indefinitely.

Humanity Changes.—Nothing is more absurd than the doctrine that human nature is always and everywhere the same. Individual human natures range all the way from the heights of idealism to the depths of materialistic depravity; and social organizations range all the way from the absolute despotisms of the past to the hoped-for democracies of the future. When conditions change, human nature changes to meet them; not completely, not as much as some would like, but it changes.

It seems undeniable, therefore, that institutionalism either ignores or denies many natural and important factors in a possible organization of life. These facts we may set down among the wastes of the world. These wastes are due, in long part, to an uncritical persistence of institutional forms which, however pliable they may have been once upon a time, have long since lost much of their relevance to the needs of our times.

Institutionalism and Youth.—Institutionalism fails to understand growing childhood. It would compress child life into institutions, and make all social relationships conform to standard formulæ. Because of this attitude, great areas of social and personal living are ignored, denied, destroyed. Institutionalism assumes that this repression is necessary to a stable social order. Intolerance of the unformed hopes, the vague feelings and aspirations, the inexpressible longings of youth characterize our schooling, and all other institutions. Education that wants from its pupils "but silence, and mighty little of that" cannot be expected to understand the losses it inflicts upon individuals, and, hence, upon society. Education that is primarily informational, even though that information be scientifically standardized and graded to the levels of the pupils' intelligences can do little but destroy the child; or at best, it can turn him into an automaton which can be set doing some mechanical job in business or industry, without interest or enthusiasm. Institutionalism is responsible for many wastes. Let us note some specific items.

Wasted Promises of Beauty.—Every child comes into the world with something of the glory of the morning in his face.   Many children turn out to be lacking in this glory.   The figures for mental defect and inferior intelligence range all the way from 2 to 30 per cent.   For some of these there is little future; for parents, years of hope wasted.   Even of those who have real capacity, we have been extremely careless.   Any one with native ability in music or the graphic arts may "get his chance."   But for others who are capable, especially in unexpected directions, we recommend "discipline."   We like originality that helps to decorate the walls of our present civilization; but we fear the originality which questions whether these are the walls of the final building of civilization. Schoolrooms have small place for original children.   They are "shades of the prison house" to originality.   As children go "farther toward the west" the glory vanishes completely for most, and life "fades into the light of common day."   They settle down by the time they are forty to more or less commonplace, unimaginative stupid lives, piling up wealth, or prestige, or egotism.   They have a feeling that life really must be stupid and they accept it as inevitable.   They have been educated to such beliefs.

Wasted Energies of Childhood.—Big school systems seem compelled to set up standard types of activity.   In one schoolroom, twenty minutes was given in a certain class to an exercise in paper folding.   The most skillful could finish in eight minutes.   The slowest could not finish in the twenty.   The slow ones were crowded, and the skillful were penalized by being compelled to sit with folded hands until the end of the period.   Is there no escape from such waste?   Why must all pupils start and stop at the same time?   The great immorality of our time is not doing "bad" things, but doing nothing at all.   Immoral education is not training for doing bad things, but for doing nothing at all.

Another wasteful aspect of childhood is the time spent in building habits against which we have to fight all the rest of our days. Undesirable habits built up actively can be cured by further activity. But habits that develop through "inactivity" are almost inescapable. The school helps to develop wasteful attitudes and habits of passivity, with all the evils of repressed, suppressed, and balked personality and "wish fulfillment" which such conditions are now known to generate.

"Wasted Years."—Under present educational practices whole years are wasted for many children. The years from fourteen to eighteen have been called "the wasted years." They are largely wasted by boys and girls who do not go to high school—and in some ways even more so by those who do. These are important years. The child is a biological creature in the pre-adolescent period. He must be transformed into a social and human creature in the adolescent and young adult years. These adolescent years have been too largely wasted in the past, especially in our cities. Adolescent boys and girls try to work at "jobs," but much of their effort fails. They do not know what they want to do. They wander from one job to another, with periods of loafing between—periods which have been estimated to take up about half the time. Out of these experiences of indirection some finally locate work that they like. Others conclude that they do not want to work at all. These years help to supply the wasted men and women that our communities know so well. Society seems little concerned to see so many lives go to waste in these wasted years.

Wasted Lives.—Consider the endless numbers of men and women whose lives do not count: the alcoholics; drug addicts by the millions; criminals; prostitutes; exploiters and gamblers of all kinds—men and women who live by

nefarious, equivocal, anti-social means. They are educated to these careers by the community, not by the
schools, of course, though the schools help by failing to
understand individuals, and by inculcating tastes without
developing the skill to support those tastes. Custom
holds that we have to have some of these wasted people:
criminals, gamblers, prostitutes, etc. The community
would be very uninteresting if it did not have some ruins,
in the way of individuals. American cities haven't many
ruins except this human sort.

But most young people are being trained to-day to be
gamblers. In schools and colleges they develop fine
tastes—they want beautiful and expensive things. We
are careless about helping them to get the skill which will
finance those tastes. The young graduate of a Middle
Western university, when asked what college had meant
to him, replied: "At college I learned a lot of expensive
habits that I am not now able to finance!" The defeated
men and women of our cities are evidence of the lack of
intelligence in our education, in spite of our schools. We
are over-intellectual, but under-intelligent.

Wasted Time.—Consider next the wasted time that
accrues because of preventable diseases, accidents, unem-
ployment, and all the casual drift of our existence. A
committee of engineers has recently published a report on
waste in industry. Among the items is one dealing with
the wastes from sickness. The committee found that on
an average each of the forty-two million persons gainfully
employed in this country loses nine days a year from ill-
ness, an aggregate of 378,000,000 days. Figured at a fair
average wage this represents more than $2,000,000,000,
a large share of which could be saved through proper
attention to disease prevention; through such health guidance as already has revolutionized conditions in some in-

dustrial plants.   Add to this the waste of life and physical
fitness through accidents—many due to carelessness on
the part of the management or labor—which took 23,000
lives and laid up 575,000 workers in 1919.   The total
waste is appalling.

Wasted Emotions and Enthusiasms.—One of the most
destructive of all our social wastes is the waste of emotions and enthusiasms, especially among young people.
Jane Addams said, years ago: "We of America have lost
interest in self-government.   The only hope for democracy is in our immigrants, who bring over with every
ship a new cargo of democratic aspirations." [1]   She said
that we were trying to work out democracy in the most
materialistic age the world has seen—and our only hope,
our only appeal, is to the sense of justice in the hearts
of men and women.

We can see this sense of justice highly developed
among children.   A group of children were playing tag.
One little girl caught another.   A third cried out quickly,
"That isn't fair.   Alice just came and she didn't know the
game."   That is the spirit of justice in the heart "Which
is never so beautiful as when the heart is young."   We
listen to the prudent counsels of age, and we break many
of these children and waste their enthusiasms and hopes.
We break them in our industries, in the machines of commerce, in commercialized social life.   "We break them
in!"   They *must* become good members of institutions!

Our lives become colorless, mechanical, meaningless, if
they become too intellectual, too factual.   Education cannot afford to ignore these facts.   Life is not worth living
when joy and hope and interest are gone.   Intellectualism
does not understand this fact.   It directs the pupil to take
the next ten pages, and often drives him out of school.

[1] This is no longer so certain, to-day.

Wasted Wills.—Consider the wasted energies of men who rage and rail at the ills of the world, but do nothing really helpful. Consider the talk and the emotions of men and women who wish and hope for a Golden Age. Will is the motive power of life. It comes of our native, blind energies. There are blind wills. It may be that, the world being what it is, we need some blind wills—wills that rage and leave the results to chance. Perhaps if Francis Bacon could have foreseen the long centuries that were to pass—the age upon age that was to come and go before the world should get out of the medieval shadows —he would have hesitated to put so much trust in science. Maybe it was just the fact that he could not see the future that enabled him to work freely. One who thinks he is going to make things over in ten years, or in six months, can work with mighty energies and assurance. It may be we need some blind wills. But, as with the automobile it is possible to get farther through the night if we have a headlight, and do not "go it blind" altogether, so it may be not undesirable for men to have foresight for their wills.

How is will to be related to intelligence? Our mature wills are just the integrating of all our impulses and energies. We achieve our wills gradually. We say that children are creatures of many different impulses, momentary impulses that run in a thousand directions. One need of childhood is the gradual integration of these impulses into meaning, intention, purpose. We know people who have never achieved such integration, who "fly off" as easily as when they were children. They are as un-integrated as they were in childhood.

We need impulses. They keep us active and alert all through life. We must organize them, not destroy them. We must integrate them! Education needs a view of will that is in harmony with the facts of experience. Will is like intelligence in this way: it is not there as will at the beginning. We need not only intellectual integrity, but volitional integrity, pointedness of will.

A certain "anatomist" has said that there are two classes of people in the world: those who have backbones and those who have wishbones. Most of us spend our time wishing. We live defeated lives partly at least because intellectualism used the years of our childhood to keep us from developing integrated wills.

At persistent intervals the streets of the city are filled with men and women who have lost all capacity to organize their lives effectively, to do anything positively and constructively. They are the habitually unemployed, the habitually unemployable men and women. They include all those whose wills were broken when they were children—whatever that means. There is room for interesting speculation as to what we could accomplish in this world if all the men and women of the world had wills that were in working order. But intellectualistic education will never know. It can only destroy the wills of children.

Wasted Knowledge.—Two areas of wasted knowledge may be cited. First, the knowledge that exists in books and libraries and in the heads of scholars, but never gets into the world of action. Perhaps it is too much to say that it is all wasted. Some day it may be used, though there is much more interest in piling up knowledge than there is in putting it to any social use. So remote from the world of action are most intellectuals that many of them even decry thinking of knowledge as useful: *useless knowledge* seems so much more distinguished!

In the second place, there are immense amounts of energy wasted by children and young people in taking on knowledge for purely scholastic ends. Most of such knowledge means nothing, either at the time, or later. Students learn, for example, the facts of physiology and hygiene, without ever realizing that those facts have relationship to their own private ways of living and their public activities. It was once held that such learning produced *mental discipline*. That may be true in a few cases. In the vast majority of cases it produces nothing but mental undiscipline—and some school grade. It is a scholastic performance, nothing more. It provides neither learning, nor taste for learning.

This scholasticism develops a kind of "intellect" that was never intended to function in the world of events. Originally, it was meant to be the decoration of a gentleman's life of leisure; to-day, it produces school standings. The only fundamental reason for finishing the eighth grade is that it is necessary for entrance to high school. The chief reason for going to high school is that it prepares for college. At the end of the college course the student is *graduated*, given the stamp of "educated," and sent from this academic, i.e., unreal, world into the "real world." Some hold that four years of visionary, romantic college life is the right of every young man and woman. Others irreverently say that "college-bred means a four years' loaf, with the old man furnishing the dough." Many a college graduate, finished intellectually, leaves the campus with a scholastic intellect and an academic will, the will to talk about life, rather than to enter effectively into life. In some schools, "education" has become a matter of merely mastering a vocabulary, which the student does not always understand. Meanwhile, uncritical habit and unintelligent custom continue to dominate social behavior, and to that extent, if we are to believe Socrates, men's lives continue to be brutish. In spite of all our schooling, impulses of the most primitive sort continue to dictate personal conduct. "Indiana," says Mr. Meredith Nicholson, one of the state's leading writers, "Indiana has spent hundreds of millions of dollars for education in the last fifty years. What has she got for all that expenditure? Three hundred thousand members of the Ku Klux Klan, turning the state into a bedlam of violence and bigotry!"

Some Conclusions.—All of our social institutions feel undercurrents of vitality, to-day, whether they admit it or not. Old habits, customs, folkways, institutionalisms satisfy very few of us. We all want change. Little happens. Why? We all want the other fellow to do the changing. Promising movements are initiated, to reform others. When the movement turns back upon its originators with the suggestion, "Physician, heal thyself!" the thing usually blows up. Religious organizations know these facts. Our political and civic history for the past sixty years could be written in tales of movements that have evaporated.

What is the sum of the matter? We waste, without thought. We waste lives, and knowledge, and emotions, and enthusiasms and will. All about us are the outcomes of this waste. The list is long: the social problems of our local, national and international communities—war, hatred, poverty, disease, crime, slums, mental deficiency and delinquency, and insanity. It is not here suggested that the schools *produce* these evils. But the distinct charge is here made that these evils continue to exist even in an "age of science" because schoolish intellectualism does not know that they exist, is not interested in finding out that they exist, is a bit scandalized that any one should be so lacking in taste as to mention such low things, and would have nothing but more bookishness to offer toward their solution in any case. When one gets through school, he wants the chance to enjoy life, as a gentleman should enjoy it! He doesn't want to be reminded of disagreeable things!

To be sure, not all people are blind to these conditions in school and community. They know, but they ask: "What can we do?" The final indictment of schoolishness is this, that it paralyzes the wills of men, and makes them feel that, when they have "studied" a problem, they have "done" all that could be expected of them. The "academic will" is probably the most sinister disease of the world, to-day.

A schoolish intellectualism cannot meet the problems of our world, to-day. The sort of mind developed in schools cannot be depended upon to deal intelligently with local and world tasks. It will try to apply academic formulæ to these tasks. Education must be free, and it must free the individual into the presence of the problems and tasks of the world. It must leave him at the end not "graduated," but ready to begin. It must spring not primarily out of old learnings and old systems, made out of precedents that have accumulated to the present social impasse. It must spring, primarily, out of the spiritual roots of life; it must well up in individual and social living; it must free the minds of the present to deal vigorously and straightforwardly with the problems of the present. It must give us the *free individual*.

What all this means, we must now ask the New School movement to attempt to make clear to us.

CHAPTER XII

THE NEW SCHOOL IN ACTION

In no other part of the world, outside of America, has modern industrial civilization been carried so far; and, say what one will, this era is the enemy of the child. Life to-day is increasingly urban, increasingly lived in terms of automobiles and apartment houses, under conditions to which children can only passively submit. Even among persons of a considerable degree of wealth, it grows harder and harder for a child to have his own life outside the boundaries of the adult world, as he once could, and still does, at least to a larger extent, in rural communities. There is an amazing parallel between what the most advanced experimental schools try to do for the child, and the life which was lived by the Indian boy or girl in the midst of the tribe, five hundred years ago, before the white man had come. In both cases, the child learns by imitating the activities of the adult, amid a group composed of persons of his own age. The Indian teaching was even more efficient and successful than that of the modern school. It went on constantly, and was taken seriously because on the child's understanding and successful performance of the tasks laid out for him life itself might depend. The reality of this experience, which has existed not only among savages the world over, but to a large degree among peasants in civilized lands, is reproduced inadequately in even the best of the new experimental institutions; and the public schools, through which the rank and file of our future citizens are sifted, have as yet made hardly any use at all of the new techniques which have lately been not so much invented as rediscovered. In them the

141

educational process is, on the whole, still appropriate to the world of 1880—at least as appropriate as it was fifty years ago.—Editorial in *The New Republic*, April 18, 1928.

Some have always rebelled against the academic doctrine that education is something pre-existent, a treasure kept by schools in schoolhouses, libraries and the minds of scholars, which is to be doled out or imposed upon passive children for their discipline and for the safety of civilization. In every century since Plato there have been some few creative minds who have insisted upon interpreting education, not as external, pre-formed materials, but as internal and personal achievement on the part of the individual child, or youth, or adult: achievement which the teacher can do much to help or to hinder, but which no individual can accomplish vicariously. As Mr. Edmond Holmes has said: "The one who is doing the learning must do the learning."

As has already been made clear, this was the point of view of Socrates, as he taught in the Athenian marketplace, and this was the method of work that characterized the Athenian pedagogues as they led their charges through the fragments of the city to that wholeness of understanding that is education. This method also finds an echo in the teachings of Jesus: "The letter kills; it is the spirit that giveth life!" Primitive Christianity also placed special value upon the individual. But this point of view received its first complete expression in modern times in the writings of the French revolutionist, Rousseau, from whose speculations all more recent movements toward a creative education have sprung.

Education not Preparation for Life; It Is Life!— Rousseau wrote in his *Emile:* "Everything is good as it comes from the author of nature, but everything degenerates in the hands of man. . . . The natural man is complete in himself; he is the numerical unit, the absolute whole who is related only to himself or to his fellow man. Civilized man is but a fractional unit that is dependent upon its denominator and whose value consists in its relation to the whole, which is the social organization. . . . Good social institutions are those which are the best able to make man unnatural."

Rousseau's central theme may be paraphrased for clarity: Education is never to be regarded as a preparation for adult living. It is life itself in process. The best preparation for life as an adult is living the most natural life as a child. The child has the right to enjoy his own childhood. Nothing should be done to interfere with his growth; everything should be done to further the complete development of body and mind. The child is father of the man; but he is able to be the best man by being the best sort of child.

The Growth of Cities and the Defeat of Education.— Rousseau speaks of the city as the chief instrument of defeat of all that is human. He says cities are the graves of the human species. After a few generations of city living races perish or degenerate. They must be renewed; and this regeneration is always supplied by the country. Men were not meant to be massed together in herds. The more they herd together the more they corrupt one another.

This doctrine can no longer be completely defended on sociological grounds; but on the educational side there is much to support it. The growth of cities has tended to eliminate much that was educational in the old rural and village community life. The city becomes more and more an educational abstraction within which adults appear as parts of impersonal social mechanisms, such as corporations and "overhead." These impersonal mechanisms have small reality for children. The adult city world is quite unreal to the child. The street and playground are his realities, and streets and playgrounds in cities are not always centers either of wisdom or of beauty. Education in cities has withdrawn more and more into schools; that is, it has become more and more intellectual, academic, bookish.

School and Society.—Because of this trend toward academic schooling in cities, many practical and theoretical movements, looking to the humanizing of the school, have emerged. Rousseau has great theoretical vogue in the modern city. The kindergarten, which is Froebel's interpretation of Rousseau, has done much to defend childhood against the impact of urban barrenness and to provide something of a natural world within which children may grow—even in cities.

But these rebellions against academic ways and in favor of "the child" in some instances ran to ridiculous extremes in the late '90's and in the first decade of the twentieth century. When "the child" becomes the starting point, the center, and the end of all education, the whole movement tends eventually to sterility. One superintendent of schools complained twenty years ago that "our schools are getting easier every day; every child comes to school these days labelled Hands Off, Don't Touch, Handle with Care, Don't Break, Right Side Up; meanwhile our teachers coax, flatter, cajole, wheedle, and bribe great big fellows in silk stockings into doing a little work now and then." This complaining was justified; but it did not justify a return to the methods of the academic school.

That orgy of sentimentalism, or "soft pedagogy" as it

was called, did not last long. Men like Col. Francis W. Parker and John Dewey and women like Mrs. Ella Flagg Young easily diverted the impact of this sentimentalism by serious criticism of the psychology upon which it was based.

One of the first constructive statements of the point of view for the "new education" appeared in 1900 in Dewey's *School and Society*. This book was at once a criticism of the older academic schooling and the then current "soft pedagogy." Its theme, often repeated was, "What the best parents desire for their children, that, the whole community should desire for all children." But this program is more easily stated than put into convincing practice.

Dewey's Elementary School, at the University of Chicago, was an early effort to develop this doctrine in concrete practice. In the short history of that school some very considerable progress was made in the obviously long task of discovering a creative alternative between— to use Dewey's own words—"forcing the child from without and leaving him entirely alone." Thirty years have gone by, and that problem is not yet solved.

Dewey left Chicago in 1904, and in large measure, the experimental program he had begun collapsed with his leaving. It was difficult to find teachers who understood what was meant by the "experimental attitude" in education. It was then, and still is, difficult to maintain an experimental elementary school in a university milieu, as both the University of Chicago and Columbia university could testify. There was little sympathy for "experimental education" among conventional school administrators or teachers. The experimental mood shortly disappeared from the Elementary School. Incidental "experiments" upon gradations, intelligence levels, and special aspects of the curriculum are still to be found; but the school as a whole is without experimental interest.

Contemporary New Schools.—But within the past fifteen years a large number of schools, developed to put into practice various principles of the new education, have come into existence in various parts of the country. Each such school has usually been the creation of some vigorous individual leader who, in most cases, has carried the burden of the new experiment almost unaided through its formative years. The full story of the growth of these various and variant "new schools" may be found in a voluminous growing literature. Space will here permit the consideration of but two or three striking examples. In making this presentation it is likely that a bit of unfairness will be revealed. As in the presentation of the public school movement, the effort was to show what an institutional school may become when given full chance to drift into its most complete expression; so in this instance the effort is frankly made to show what a "new school" may become when the imagination of the organizer is given full sweep.

The Modern School.—One of the most radical and consistent of the new schools, at least until recently, has been the Modern School, at Stelton, New Jersey. The program and theory of that school may be illustrated by brief quotations from one of its publications.

The school was said to have been started for the purpose of "opening wide the avenues of the spiritual life of men." It was to reject "all lesser allegiances in order that it might concentrate on the greatest aim conceived— the building of a Free Society."

"Education must be based on the nature of the child. A child lives in a world of feeling, of imagination, of action. He loves to dance and play. Don't kill the spirit of joy in the child!

"The complaint from most of our parents has been that we have not given as much attention to abstract work as we have to manual or art work and that, therefore, we have not given the children a chance to get it if they wanted it. This in spite of the fact that we have had some classes and that the children were at liberty to ask questions whenever they felt like it or were in need of any information. Sometimes the children would keep themselves to class work for a long time and at other times they would shun the classes as much as possible. What would have been their natural inclination it is hard to say, as there was so much pressure from the adults that the children went to class or asked for abstract work in self-defense. At all events there is no doubt in my mind that most of the time spent in the arithmetic class or English class is lost time, unless the children seem to have some special calling for it. During the time that they spend there they are away from self-activity and in the case of one of our promising boys, when he was made to feel that he would be an ignoramus if he did not get hold of spelling and arithmetic, he dropped all his creative work and seemed to stop in his development.

"We began by throwing shops open to the children, by enlarging the sphere of their activities, by giving them opportunities for developing so much of their natures as they seemed capable of developing. We dared to hope that the mind would be developed by being used, not merely in academic work, but by being used for designing, for planning, for directing the hands. And then the social contacts. Under free-play conditions there would be all kinds of experiences to be met by the children, problems in their play that they would have to solve in their own crude way, but that would call upon their minds for solution, instead of being solved for them by adult minds. This may not seem important to many in view of the fact that so many problems have already been solved by the race and it would seem to be better to use the solutions that have been evolved than to bother with the crude expression of the children, the undeveloped minds. How then would the children, the parents of the new order that is to be, develop the kind of minds that would be able to initiate things different from what they are? How would they be able to solve our present difficulties in the direction of advancement if their minds were attuned merely to copy what has already been done, without the opportunity to solve problems for themselves?

"The Modern School indicts the prevailing system of education, charging that it is an enemy to social progress by destroying initiative and individuality except in the narrow fields where these qualities can increase the efficiency of the capitalist machine. We claim for the Modern School that the hope of the future lies in the ability of the rising generation to think and act independently without regard to the prejudices of the past, and that it therefore encourages its pupils to express their individuality in every direction, without losing sight of the principle that the liberty of others should not be invaded.

"We insisted that it is fundamental with the Modern School to avoid thrusting any opinion on the child, to encourage him to approach all questions with an open mind, accepting nothing merely on authority, but insisting on the right to investigate independently—in

other words, to cultivate what Bertrand Russell calls
an intelligent scepticism."

The Organic School.—The best known of the "new
schools" is probably Mrs. Marietta Johnson's Organic
School at Fairhope, Alabama. A brief statement about
her theory and practice is taken from a recent publica-
tion of the school:

"**What Is Education?**—The schools are engaged in
'raising children' and it is to the best interest of society to produce the finest type of child—strong of
body, intelligent of mind, sweet and sincere of spirit.
To do this requires a study of the development of the
child and the nature and needs of childhood. The integrity of the nervous system must be preserved, the
order of development must be followed. . . .

"**The Child Needs to Create.**—The mind develops
through interest. The supreme question for the schools
to consider is therefore: 'What are the interests of
childhood?' In general, we know that children are
interested in things of sense. They should be allowed
the free use of materials and be permitted to create
things. Using material to express his own thought is a
demand of the child's nature which we dare not ignore.
Judgment and reason are developed through sponta-
neous activity in concrete situations. Personal interest
sharpens the intellect. Therefore we must allow ample
opportunity for meeting situations. . . .

"**True Growth Unselfconscious.**—The moral development of the child requires a life of sincere, unselfconscious experiences. Working for grades, marks,
promotions, etc., tends through false motivation to divide the unity of the being. He should study because
he desires to know or needs the information, not merely

because it is required or because he will receive recognition. This is true growth.

"Fearlessness is a demand of the spirit. Self-consciousness is a kind of fear. The child who is constantly marked and graded and measured develops an inhibiting self-consciousness which may become paralyzing in later life. Or, he may become wholly 'externalized,' depending entirely on outer suggestion, or he may become arrogant and egotistical. No doubt, the anti-social adults of to-day are in large part a product of this standardization of the process of learning.

"**Education Is Growth.**—No child should ever 'fail' in getting an education. All should flourish and succeed. The school process must fit everybody. A sound, accomplished, beautiful body and an intelligent, sympathetic mind, a sweet, reverent spirit—these are the immediate ends in education. In the measure that the school process tends to bring about these results, it is educational. In the measure that it does not, it is not educational, however informational it may be.

"Let us study the development of the child. Let us try to discover the nature of childhood. Let us try to find out the needs of the body, the needs of the mind and the needs of the spirit, and make an effort to provide these needs.

"**Right Conditions for Growth.**—A division of the intellectual and emotional life of the child is very easily attained. This division is wasteful. Too much praise or criticism develops this double motive. Children should be allowed to live their lives straight out. They should not hesitate to expose their ignorance. When children are stimulated to study for fear of failure, to please the teacher or parent, to get a grade or to be promoted, a subtle influence is at work producing double motives. This not only interferes with the co-ordination of the nervous system, often resulting in ill health, but also prevents clear thinking, and most of all interferes with that basic sincerity which is the fundamental condition of a fine moral life. . . . The finest intellectual growth is secured in the course of wholesome experiences where children are constantly meeting situations and mastering problems of their own. All creative work is intellectual. Every home and school should be provided with an unlimited supply of material through which children may develop, not only the creative impulses and thinking power of the highest order, but may also experience social relations of the finer type.

"We are all inclined to think of children as little adults and we often treat them as though childhood were a preparation for adult life. Would it be possible for us to think of childhood as a stage in the development of the individual, very important on its own account? We would then think of chlidren as unique individuals demanding a unique environment suited to their peculiar needs. If we were able to provide the right conditions of growth in every stage of the development of the child the finest maturity would be assured."

The Implicit Philosophy of the New School.—No completely satisfactory statement of the philosophical basis of the new school has yet been made, although many attempts have been made in that direction. The teacher in the new school maintains a considerable freedom of initiative. Hence, practices range over wide variations. Some so-called new schools are but little differentiated from the public school in its more intelligent forms; in other schools teachers are controlled by the most extravagant conceptions of individual freedom. In some cases the teacher refrains from offering any suggestion whatsoever to the children in his group, on the ground that any suggestion from an older person inevitably acts as a control. From this standpoint, the new school exists fundamentally as a means of defending the individual child from any control by the past of the human race.

In principle this *is* the essential philosophy of the new school movement. The child becomes an adult on his own account. He must be protected from existent adults and from historic social influences in order that as a natural child he may grow into a natural man. It is assumed by many that such a discontinuity between the generations can be established and maintained and that, therefore, the present generation of children can be developed into a generation of adults who will be free from the controls of existing institutions. In other words, the present generation of children will develop an adult world wholly of their own construction. In this way all the evils of historic human society will be escaped and a new social order wrought of the native talents of the rising generation will take the place of the undesirable institutions of the past and present generation.

Principles of Progressive Education.—Many special formulations of "progressive principles" have been made in recent years, by specific schools, or groups, or by such organizations as the Progressive Education Association (an American movement) and The World Fellowship for New Education (an international movement). These statements of principles vary a bit, here and there. The following seven principles will serve as a sample of these formulations:

1. The conduct of the pupils shall be governed by

themselves, according to the social needs of their community.

2. Interest shall be the motive for all work.

3. Teachers will inspire a desire for knowledge, and will serve as guides in the investigations undertaken, rather than as task-masters.

4. Scientific study of each pupil's development, physical, mental, social and spiritual, is absolutely essential to the intelligent direction of his development.

5. Greater attention is paid to the child's physical needs, with greater use of the out-of-doors.

6. Cooperation between school and home will fill all needs of the child's development, such as music, dancing, play and other extra-curricular activities.

7. All progressive schools will look upon their work as of the laboratory type, giving freely to the sum of educational knowledge, the results of their experiments in child culture.

It is to be noted that these principles specifically make the child the central figure in education. His conduct is to be his own; his own interest shall motivate his activities; teachers may inspire desire for knowledge, but after that has been done, they shall be guides, and not task-masters; insight into the child's own nature and needs shall determine whatever is done about his growth and development; physical health is fundamental to life, and therefore to education; all social institutions must cooperate in order to maintain an integrated community of living for the sake of the developing child; and whatever any one learns through these methods of dealing with children should be made common knowledge, so that all teachers, everywhere, and therefore all children everywhere, may have the benefits of this enlarging understanding.

Weaknesses and Warnings.—It is not certain that any specific individual working in any "new school" anywhere to-day actually holds to all these doctrines in concrete practice. Many hold them emotionally, and theoretically, or at least they think they hold them. One of the fundamental weaknesses of the whole "new school" movement is revealed in this connection: there is much *emoting* about the *rights* of childhood; but the job of *thinking out and through* what these "rights" actually are, and how they may be secured in this modern world of unstable city living, large-scale industrial organization, and world-wide political and moral reconstructions has scarcely been begun.

But practice is usually more realistic than theory. The concrete practices of the "new schools" are rarely as radical as their theories would suggest. Old habits stand in the way of new practices; old theories, merely emotionally discredited, stand in the way of the development of new habits adequate to new practices justified by new theories. There has been much emotion, but not as much thought, bestowed upon these questions. Many "new school" people hold theories that are found to be, upon examination, full of fallacies. This is one of the reasons why the movement does not find more adequate response in the world at large. Any change in *education* implies a change in concrete living—not in some future generation but in the present. The "new school" has undertaken to make education over. That means that it has undertaken to make the world over. Failure to recognize this fact is proof that the one so failing is more competent in emotion than in realistic thinking. There is place in the world for a "new education." The main defect, as we shall presently see, in the theory and practice of the movement to date, has been that most of its advocates have assumed that they could do their reconstructive work in *schools*. Hence, they talk most about "new schools." But, in this respect, they have not gone much beyond the position of those who still cling to the belief that the public school can be trusted to provide education for the new age. We need a *new education*—not merely a *new school*. And this new education must get in its work in the whole life and structure and functions of the whole community, not merely in the school house.

To the fuller implications of these suggested criticisms we now turn in further chapters of this part of our argument.

CHAPTER XIII

CAN CHILDREN MAKE THE WORLD OVER?

They, to the disappointed earth, shall give
The lives we meant to live! . . . *Anon.*

No man and no mind was ever emancipated merely by being left alone. Removal of formal limitations is but a negative condition; positive freedom is not a state, but an act which involves methods and instrumentalities for control of conditions. Experience shows that sometimes the sense of external oppression, as by censorship, acts as a challenge and arouses intellectual energy and excites courage. But a belief in intellectual freedom where it does not exist contributes only to complacency in virtual enslavement, to sloppiness, superficiality and recourse to sensation as a substitute for ideas: marked traits of our present estate with respect to social knowledge. . . . An experimental social method would probably manifest itself first of all in the surrender of (all preconceived goals). Every care should be taken to surround the young with the physical and social conditions which best conduce, as far as freed knowledge extends, to the release of personal potentialities. The habits thus formed would have entrusted to them the meeting of future social requirements and the development of the future state of society. Then and then only would all social agencies that are available operate as resources in behalf of a bettered community life.—DEWEY, in *The Public and Its Problems.*

They bind heavy burdens and grievous to be borne and lay them on men's shoulders; but they themselves will

not touch them with their fingers.—THE GOSPEL OF
MATTHEW.

Primitive human groups, living precariously in the
midst of both seen and unseen insecurities, long most for
some sort of permanence. They are happiest when most
secure; or at least, when the odds are not too greatly
against them. Most primitive groups, it seems likely,
would rather lose in war than never to have a war; but
the greatest joy of living comes of recounting the events
that led up to a glorious victory. But victory implies the
continuance of the *status quo*. Any persistent threat of
that status implies disintegration, and change, and the
impact of change is always unpleasant. The feeling of a
permanent world—with an occasional victory over the
enemies that threaten that permanence—is the happiest
of conditions. It is the primitive man's dream of Val-
halla, of Paradise.

The Discontented Few.—But since the dawn of civilization, at least, there have always been a few insurgent
spirits in every civilization who have carried the hope of
a better social order, somewhere in the future, even
though such better order must be purchased at the price
of social change. These have always been disturbed by
current conditions, which usually hid beneath a surface
order the hard facts of growing disorder. They have
worked for a better world, more or less consistently.
Among these few are Euripides and Socrates in Athens;
Isaiah and Jeremiah among the Hebrews; the Gracchi in
Rome.

Sometimes these agitators set their hopes upon a future
better world in some non-earthly heaven. This has
usually been the religious solution of the problem. But
within the last four or five centuries, especially since the

discovery of America, which brought the chance of escape from the crowded areas of Europe, the hope of a better world has been increasingly domesticated upon the earth. In some measure, the whole American adventure has, for three centuries, implied the eventual fulfillment of this human hope, to the rest of the world: a land where human beings might at last achieve a really human living.

Freedom in America.—Generation has followed generation, however, and that dream is still unfulfilled, save to those who are content with "prosperity." The pioneer who came, freed as he thought from the tyrannies of Europe, did not succeed in leaving tyranny behind him. He brought tyranny with him, and the arch-friend of tyranny, intolerant ignorance. The weight of the past could not be escaped merely by crossing the ocean. The settler in the wilderness was shortly tied up as tightly in habits and customs as his European ancestors had been. Some of those customs were new; but most of them were brought, more or less intact, from Europe. No generation has found actual freedom here.

But the hope of that better order still persists. "Our children must have a better world!" The result is that Americans have, more or less consciously, bequeathed the hope of creating that freer world to their children. The public school was developed largely by reason of the faith that "education" would bring that better world. For at least three generations, now, we have been assuming that the school would cure all the ancient evils of our community living, by developing new generations of men and women too intelligent to put up with those evils any longer. We have taught our children facts and ideas at school, because we have held the naïve doctrine that, as one superintendent of schools phrased it, "the world is made of facts and ideas."

But the panacea failed in the first generation that tried it, and the failure was charged to the fact that not all the children of the community went to school. Some children remained away from school; they did not become wise and informed; and so the menace of ignorance remained in the community. Thereupon, compulsory attendance laws were passed, gradually, but in the end practically everywhere. All children must be compelled to get ready for their share in this intelligent world of the future. At any rate, no child should be permitted to remain ignorant and thus through sheer inertia provide an obstruction to the coming of that better world.

Now, however, we have had at least one generation, in most of the states, of universal school attendance, and we find not only that that better world still lies beyond the horizon, but that, if we may trust the figures so expensively secured in war time, a very large part of the population is still illiterate and uninstructed. Moreover, most of those who can read, read not the great books and literatures of the ages, but the cheapest and most meretricious stuff that comes from the printing presses. The sale of *inane* magazines outruns the sale of intelligent materials at least a hundred to one. Must we not soon begin to admit that the schooling of a generation of children under the watchful eye of adults who are themselves incapable of producing a better world will not be likely to produce a more intelligent or a more human society?[1] Such an admission may leave us perplexed and discour-

[1] As I was writing these words, a letter from a New England college teacher carried the following unexpected paragraph:
"There is no hope in the colleges for emancipating the minds of men. I say this in a perfectly matter-of-fact way. The institutional grip is too firm, the traditional beliefs and attitudes are too deeply set. Sooner or later, for one reason or another, the colleges accept the status quo and the conventional life and these primary facts determine its values and its methods. In their present form of organization and control the colleges are well-nigh hopeless."

aged. But if it is valid, shall we not be in a better position to undertake the next step?

New Schools and a New World.—But our academic schools do not need, or even imply, a new world. Our public schools are parcel of the world that is. All interest in any sort of "newness," in the past and to date, has come out of the hopes of individuals and groups, not out of schools. But the "new school," the product of insurgent aspiration, does imply a "new world," as its advocates well understand. They have not been hesitant about admitting their responsibility, either. They speak of it frequently, and they assume that they are making real progress in adequately meeting that responsibility. We must here inquire whether they really understand the task they have undertaken.

The New School people make certain assumptions, as we have seen, to-wit: they assume that the social order is made up of *individuals;* that these individuals have been badly educated by our academic schools, in that they have been habituated to things as they are, until all their creative mind has been submerged; but that, if an education can be developed that will lead these individuals out into a life of their own, free from all the contaminations and repressions of the past, these freed individuals will, in their own good time, create their own social order, or make a new world expressive of their own free natures. In this way, the hopes of the race will be fulfilled, and education will make us free. Hence, for two or three decades, now, the new school movement has justified its program of free development of children through "creative learning," or otherwise, by insisting that these free children would create a world in which, as adults, they could freely live.

When it has been argued that too much of such liberating education might mean the development of individuals who might find themselves quite isolated from the contemporary life of the world, and who should, therefore, be compelled to take refuge in some niche or corner or blind alley of the world; or even at length, by revulsion of feeling, in some previously proscribed institutional position, the reply has usually been: "No, the freed individual will create his own place, his own opportunity, his own institution, patterned after his own free spirit and meeting all the needs of that free spirit. In doing this, he will not only save his own free spirit, but he will do most toward displacing the old, repressive institutions, thus helping to bring that new social order so much desired by practically all men."

This doctrine has been so widely expressed, it seems on the whole so plausible, and it is evidently so thoroughly believed by many advocates of the New Schools that it seems necessary to examine the matter more at length.

Can the Individual Create His Own World?—Looked at superficially, this question answers itself. The individual, in America, is a free man in a free land. He is master of his own destiny, the creator of the conditions under which he chooses to live. The theory might be workable *if* a sufficient number of new schools could be developed to assure the existence of something approaching a community. But, of course, that would mean that the conditions of existence were already set up. Always the little "if" interferes with our happiness. . . .

The assumptions of the new school that the world is made of *individuals* is fallacious. The adult generation and the generation of childhood are not separated. They do not exist side by side, or one at a time, as individuals. The generations interpenetrate. Children do not grow up in a vacuum. Children may attend new schools during school hours, but they have to go home through the streets of the city, and they spend their evenings, Saturdays and vacations with the older generation. They do not have to live with the teachers, but they do have to live with their parents. They are educated quite as much by the street as by the school; and when school years are over most of them are still too young to dare the wager of battle against the social world alone.

Some of them, freed from the immediate oversight of the older generation, may establish themselves independently, in some side eddy of the world, in some radical movement, or some "Greenwich Village" of the age. But the theory that any considerable number of them will be concerned to set up a new social order of freedom is a bit fantastic. They will be rebels, heretics, inventors, cynics, "grouches," misanthropes, perhaps; but not many of them will attempt to reorganize the social world. That is to say, they will be *individuals!*

Actually, this is what has happened thus far in the history of new schools. Theoretically, it is about the only thing that can happen. With seven hundred and fifty thousand teachers working in the old schools, with twenty-five million pupils being regimented in the old schools— what can the few hundred teachers, and the few thousand children working in the new schools hope to accomplish? The fact of the matter is that *children cannot make the world over;* and any individual or group that depends upon children for the new world is not only depending upon a rope of sand, but is, probably, rationalizing a personal inertia with respect to the problem. Let no one cry "pessimism." This is not pessimism; this is the most realistic of historic and contemporary facts. The adult generation is always too much for the younger generation.

Education and the New Order.—That new social order desired by all intelligent people will, of course, be achieved—and by education. But it will not be achieved by the education of children. Something of a clue to the process can be found in Denmark, where education has made the social order of the country-side and the village over in less than a century, but it is not the education of children that has turned the trick. That miracle was achieved, and it is being defended by the education of the adult generation, specifically the young adults, from eighteen upwards. Educational reconstruction must begin where education really begins. That is not with children, but with young adults: these are still young enough to learn, and yet old enough to defend their learning and their new outlooks, if any, against the drift and the stupid repressions of the traditional community.

Any new social order must, of course, be eventually established in the understanding and habits of the community. But no community has ever provided, or is ever likely to provide, within itself a special vacuum within which its youth may be carefully defended from all adult pressures while they are being trained to disturb, or destroy, the very social order that is training them. Few communities think so little of themselves, or have so far escaped the control of their primitive patterns of fear, as to be able to undertake, or consent to, their own reconstruction from the ground up. "Progress" is universally the work of minorities.

It may be that social self-criticism will some day become the mark of our more intelligent societies. But that day is not yet. When Professor Dewey writes, as in the quotation at the head of this chapter, that "every care should be taken to surround the young with the physical and social conditions which best conduce to the release of personal potentialities," he is, it must be noted, not assuming that any such "care" will become presently general; and when he adds that "the habits thus formed will have entrusted to them the meeting of future social requirements and the development of the future state of society," it is not to be assumed that he means that the whole drift of the folkway ages will stand and wait while youth, with all "personal potentialities" released, sets up a "future state of society." The "great community" is not yet here. Even the best schools operate only about six or seven hours per day for from 160 to 200 days per year, while *community drift* operates every waking moment at least for 365 days in ordinary years and 366 days in leap years. The world changes. The world can be changed. But those who attempt to change it according to a plan must understand the inertias as well as the "forces" with which they have to make terms.

Pessimism and Realism.—This is not pessimism. It is but honest recognition of realities. The way out of the drift of the times will be an educational way, even though it is primarily economic; but that education will face facts and issues. It will not hope, by means of some *tour de force* or *coup de grace* to take the facts of life by surprise and get them to surrender before they recover. Educational statesmenship in the future will be concerned not with incidentals in the situation, but with a tactical campaign against the whole front of drift. That campaign will not be one of mere violence, or invective. "The kingdom of heaven cometh not by violence." It will be led by statesmen, and its method will be that of psychological and ethical understanding.

The more rational education of children in any considerable numbers will probably follow and not precede the development of that new social world. It will probably be an effect, and not the cause, of the more intelligent social order. At least, the future will not lay its burdens, heavy to be borne, on the backs of its children, and refuse to touch them by so much as the tips of its fingers.

But if this is a valid statement, where does it leave the New Schools? The answer is important for education. We turn to certain obstructions and dilemmas that confront the New School. When educators undertake to make education over, they must enlist not for seven years, or for seventy, but for the duration of the war.

CHAPTER XIV

ACADEMIC BACKFIRES ON THE "NEW" PSYCHOLOGY

If one thinks of education, for example, and attempts to derive a formula for the guidance of the teacher, one finds little that is helpful in the mere recital of individual traits. Even the facts of individual development are comparatively meager in furnishing a basis for a program of instruction. On the other hand, a study of social institutions throws a flood of light on the processes which the schools are engaged in carrying on. Viewed in the light of the psychology of social institutions, education is seen to be an effort to fit the individual into the general plan of social cooperation. Education seeks to give the individual as much as possible of the organized experiences which generations of minds have put together. Education seeks to drill the individual in the use of those instruments of adaptation which have been perfected by earlier generations. . . . In these days we must all become parts of the economic machinery of industry and exchange or we shall go hungry. We must use language and weights and measures. We must learn to be on time. In matters of religion, however, we are allowed a degree of freedom unknown in social units of an earlier day. We talk about tolerance in religion. We practice no tolerance in respect to the Arabic numerals.—C. H. JUDD, in *Psychology of Social Institutions.*

Achievement tests compel the child to aim each educational effort at one object where we are now aiming at a flock. For a certain definite and limited time, each child will attack his own specific difficulty after the application of the test has shown him what his difficulty is. The children will be grouped in such a manner that all who are overcoming a specific obstacle concentrate their efforts upon it at the same time.—POWERS, in *N.E.A. Bulletin of Elementary School Principals* (1923).

The academic school is a logical instrument for the organization and control of education in a logical world. As nearly as may be, it is organized according to logical patterns and it presents a logical front to the world and the child.   Its purpose is to use all the organized accomplishments of the world, the safe learning, the authenticated behavior patterns and the accepted disciplines, in effecting logical organization of the "minds" and conduct of its pupils.   In approaching education in this way, the school must often ignore the vital interests of childhood and youth, and it is, at times, troubled a bit by this fact. But this can be rationalized by arguing that the ultimate result achieved is much more stable and secure: after all, the interests of childhood and youth are ephemeral, unimportant; the interests of "life" are the important matters.

The Psychology of the New School.—The new school, on the other hand, attempts to be a psychological instrument, organized according to current doctrines of child growth and development.   It attempts to discover the developmental interests and needs of children and to follow and supplement those interests through the years.

Approaching education in this way, it must largely ignore the organized culture materials and institutional ways of the world; and it is at times troubled a bit by the fear that its graduates may never find places in the organized world after school is over.   But it rationalizes its failure to take into account these ancient materials by arguing that the freed intelligence of the rising generation will construct its own logical organization of the world in good time; will make its own community, and so provide all needed plans.

Because this point of view offers to many adults and children ways out of the tiresome routines of academic schooling, the "new" school proves a popular innovation wherever it is known. For this reason this new school movement has placed the old school somewhat on the defensive. The old school tries to ignore the threat of the new. None the less it makes some effort to reconstruct its logical processes here and there, and to introduce some "psychology" into its educational programs. This does not mean that the academic school hopes to become a true instrument of child psychology. Rather it tries to develop a psychology which can disprove the criticism that it is behind the times and which will be an effective backfire on the developmental psychology of the new schools at the same time. The present chaos in psychology provides ample cover for such backfire. Academic psychology can get in some deadly shots without betraying its own tactical weakness.

Modern Academic Psychology.—The modern academic school is faced with a very difficult task. It must maintain certain primitive disciplines and subordinations and at the same time inculcate certain necessary knowledges. There is endless danger that a conflict or even a contradiction between this discipline and this knowledge will emerge, since the two belong to two different historic stages of development. Psychology must, therefore, find ways of maintaining these two contradictory areas without permitting them to meet and criticize each other. That is to say, on the side of action, the academic psychology must be naïve and primitive; on the side of knowledge it must be authoritative and at least ostensibly, "scientific." Hence, academic psychology must be a convincing combination of the Platonic doctrine of the subordination of the individual to eternal (Ideal) patterns and the (allegedly) scientific doctrine of the "freedom of the individual" which is to be secured by means of classification based on the intelligence of the individual. This classification provides for the individual need of the particular child. In this way, current academic psychology as it is actually practiced in the schools, secures what society most wants—the subordination of the individual—and at the same time it meets the criticism of the developmental psychologist by showing that it is completely devoted to the interests of the individual. The net results, of course, of this double-faced type of doctrine are to be seen in the products of the schools.

The school, ever since the days of Plato, has been primarily an instrument of intellectual learning. Through all the earlier parts of the modern period, these intellectual processes were practised in the midst of social situations that almost completely hid the fact that they were intellectual. The country and village school of the nineteenth century was entirely devoted to teaching lessons out of books, but because that school was located in the midst of a community in which children worked, played; in which living had the feel of reality, being based on wide social experiences, neighborhood interests and opportunity for out-of-door adventure, the bookishness of the school was not obnoxious. Learning was felt to be legitimate for all who liked it, and the whole process tended under those conditions to the development of an education that had probably never been equalled since the days when Athens was the educational instrument of a nation.

But more recently, with the growth of cities has come the loss of most of that former informal educational op-

portunity in the community. Education has been almost
completely segregated in the school rooms. The learning
processes have been more and more stripped of their
former social and emotional attributes. To-day in most
schools and for most children, the learning process has
become undisguisedly intellectual. It rises out of no
experience of the child but sheerly out of books and out
of school procedures. It answers no need or interest of
the child, but only some need of the system or some fact
or need of the future. The school baldly says to the
child, "Here are lessons that you have got to learn and
the sooner you get to them, the better for all concerned."

In order to make this process as painless as possible,
the school has had to develop a psychology of its own.
This psychology must, of course, rationalize the procedure of the school and yet it must have as good standing
in the community as has the developmental psychology
of the new school. This psychology has two main divisions: it deals first of all with what it calls the laws of
learning, and in the second place, with the classification
of minds. We shall consider both phases of this development.

The Laws of Learning.—This academic psychology is
concerned with processes of learning: "mind" is for this
psychology the instrument by means of which children
learn their lessons. Hence, this psychology finds great
delight in what it calls "The Laws of Learning." These
"laws" tend to achieve the social character of all "laws":
their number grows year by year as the psychologists
"legislate." However, there are *three* such "laws" which
have somewhat the nature of a constitution of the mind.
These will serve as illustrations:

1. The Law of Readiness: when the mind is ready, or
when it can be made ready, learning takes place with

more facility and such learning probably lasts much longer.

2. The Law of Exercise: when the mind is active in the process, learning is much facilitated, and it tends to enter more fully into the experience of the learner.

3. The Law of Effect: when learning has taken place, some sort of result accrues which will later show itself in modified forms of belief, understanding or behavior.

It is to be noted that these are "laws" of *learning*. Children have always learned—when they were *ready,* and when they were *active*—and such learning has always had its *effects*. Of course, outside of schools, *education* is more than learning, learning being but a by-product of living. But in schools, learning is the most important ingredient of education—almost its sole constituent, in fact; hence, learning is very important in schools, and the "laws of learning" form an indispensable phase of the training of teachers. So, teachers learn how to get the "mind" "ready"; how to make the "mind" "active"; and how to test "effects"—in schoolish fashion. This sort of "learning" tends to become the most barren of intellectual exercises; but it is often the only thing the school can provide.

It will be noted that these "laws" all have to do with habit building, or the taking on of knowledge, which is mental habit. School learning may imply the existence of intelligence; but it must not become really intelligent, lest it stir up criticism of the obediences necessary to group life. It must be content to remain on the level of habit. Habit is fundamental, of course. Academic education must state itself in terms of habit. Academic psychology for teachers, since it is the technique of turning out "educated," that is, habituated, people, has no interest in dealing with the rise of intelligence. It uses its inheritance of intelligence to standardize present academic processes on the levels of habit.

Intelligence Tests.—As a foil to the theory of child development that is held by most progressive schools, the academic school has developed a most effective tool of analysis and control of child abilities—the so-called "intelligence tests." These "tests" assume that "intelligence" is some sort of native and fixed quality of the psycho-physical organism—a quality that can be discovered, once for all, by means of scientifically developed instruments. If this native quality can be discovered, the "level" of the child can be ascertained, and his whole human career can be prophesied. Obviously, such foresight, and the "control" that it implies, is far more important than anything the progressive school can claim for its "processes of development." There is little to be wondered at in the fact, therefore, that many progressive schools have deserted "progressive growth" for "intelligence testing."

Discussion in the psychology of education during the past ten years has almost wholly been concerned with the expansion and validity of these tests—in their many forms. They have seemed to offer such conclusive aid to the educator. By their means the children may at last be adequately graded—on a curve of probabilities. At one end of the curve will be found the idiots and imbeciles. Above them, morons of various degrees, and above these the great masses of the mediocre and the average. At the upper end of the curve appear the high grade and the superior; and at the tip, the few who may be called "geniuses." Such a graph gives a cross-section of the "mind" of any generation. It is sufficiently convincing in its "proof" of the nature and statics of "mind," as to win the scholastics, and so to put the doctrine of "mental

development" on the defensive. As compared with the
elaborate "data" of a well-organized academic school, the
vague hopes and expectations of the progressive school
seem pale and vague indeed.

Classification of "Minds."—Offsetting the psychological doctrine that time and growth are of the essence of
child development, the academic school looks forward to
great educational triumphs through the use of various
classificatory schemes. One much in favor now provides
for the segregation of various "levels of intelligence" in
specific groups within each "grade" so that "inferior,"
"average," and "superior" "minds" may all have their
own kind as sharers in the *milieu* of experience. Since
"learning" is a function of a native quality of "mind,"
all who have like levels of this quality should work together, so that group "learning" can get forward at a uniform speed. This is the doctrine and it is regarded as a
very great advance. In some schools, such classification
of pupils on the basis of their "intelligence quotients" is
regarded as an important "educational experiment," definitely putting the school using it in the "progressive"
class. It is assumed that morons should be grouped together, average children together, and the superior ones
together. In this way, teaching is simplified, and each
mind-level is provided with the best surroundings for the
most rapid advancement. It is a further extension of the
general excuse for grading, namely, that children should
learn nothing from each other. The intellectual course of
study is modulated to meet the varying capacities of these
age levels. The academic school is achieving a most convincing complexity of organization. Presently it will take
a bold critic indeed to challenge its perfect mechanisms.

Individual Education.—The boast of the "new school"
is that it provides opportunity for individual growth and

development and that, therefore, it has broken away from all the lockstep methods of the academic school. The academic school retorts by showing that it, also, is now prepared to deal with individual children. It has given the child an intelligence test and, therefore, it can proceed on the basis of that child's actual capacity to do work. The curriculum is adjusted to the abilities of this particular individual. The school is engaged in correlating the materials of learning to the needs and abilities of the specific child. This is what the academic school believes it is doing.

It is true that the recognition that children vary enormously in their abilities to deal with curricular materials has tended in some measure to humanize the school system including the curriculum and methods of instruction. But on the other hand, there has been a finality about these intelligence tests as used by educators which has tended to make this newly achieved classification of minds a more iron-clad arrangement than the old school ever knew. It must be remembered that all this psychology of intelligence measurements and tests is a logical psychology and its results have shown an iron logic that has been intolerably sure of itself. Many schools have been made far more school-ish by the use of these classification tests which profess to enable the teacher to discover the individual.

Efficiency.—The academic school having achieved a certain institutional assurance has been, in many places, captured by the slogan of the business world, "efficiency," and is able to demonstrate its effective processes by an enormous elaboration of administrative and teaching techniques. Not much of this efficiency appears in the ultimate results. It appears only in imposing processes, and its ultimate value has to be taken on faith.

The extent of this development is shown in the following review of a recent book on *Educational Diagnosis:*

"A technique of educational administration and supervision is being rapidly developed that resembles in plan and degree of efficiency the most modern types of industrial management. The raw materials (the pupils) are accurately measured by means of refined instruments and then assorted into homogeneous groups, all units of which are prepared to take the same educational treatment for the same length of time in order to come out with the measured quantity of standardized achievement. Obdurate materials that take the impress slowly can be put through at slow speed; those of extra-impressionability, at high speed; and the great mass, at medium speed. A major task of supervisory officials is to keep the pupils properly assorted so that each is always at the right point of advance for him, and in the group that is moving at the speed to which he is adapted. This task is highly complicated because of the multitude of variable factors. . . . He shows how measurement will discover the needed facts, how they are to be organized to reveal all their significance, and how they are to be used in supervision and administration. The details are worked out with extreme care. Although mathematical and technical, everything is made entirely clear."

Units of Instruction.—As a correlate to the pupil's learning, the teacher's task is, of course, instruction. Instruction is philologically close to construction: and the modern academic teacher comes more and more to be a constructor in mind—whatever that may mean. Since we have come to live in cities, children have been provided with building materials made and cut to order:

"mechano"; "erecto"—and similar short cuts to building fill our apartment houses. Probably, therefore, it was inevitable that the school curriculum should eventually suffer the same fate—in city schools. At any rate, the concept of specific "units of instruction" now expresses the latest step in this complete adjustment of "mind" to "the world."

A school subject is divided into its logical parts, and these logical parts are to be broken up into convenient "units," corresponding, some hold, to specific fractions of the school year, say six week periods; others hold to definite "wholes" in the experience of the learner. Any subject may be taken in six or ten or sixteen units. Ideally, these units should become interchangeable from one institution to another, like the parts of a Ford car.

If there were any way of determining the "wholes" of child experience, such a corresponding determination of the "units of instruction" would be most advantageous. But there is little evidence to support the doctrine that all "minds" operate in terms of the same "wholes"—although there is much evidence for the theory that every mind operates in terms of its own "wholes"—its own integrities. Of course, as long as education is assumed to be identical with "learning" and "instruction," the "materials of learning" will tend to become "units of instruction." What becomes of these "units" in the "mind" of the "learner"? Nobody knows, of course; but all hope that they will somehow naturally assemble into a "whole of learning," some time, somehow, and that they will really affect behavior.

Automatic Schooling.—There is but one further development in this psychology to be hoped for, and that is a complete automatization of instruction. This is on the way. The educational journals are now carrying lengthy descriptions of mechanical contrivances to which the teacher may turn over specific parts of the day's work, and which can either drill a child in some unit of information, or help the child to determine his own mastery of a unit of materials. One such machine, recently described, provides an infallible means for testing the child's facility in any selected drill subject; and, says the description, since the child operates the machine, "the teacher is freed for more important duties elsewhere." It seems likely that we shall presently have an educational set-up which will admit a child at any selected age, say three years, and turn him out at any required age, say eighteen years, fully instructed, infallibly tested, and guaranteed not to deviate from the norm established for him by more than the allowable margin of error. In this way we shall beat Bernard Shaw at his own game!

The Probable Outcome.—There is no automatic escape from these developments. Automatism runs the other way—toward further submergence in them. The public wants efficiency; we all believe in machines. We are afraid of personality and individuality. We seem coming to a social era of standard types. It may be we shall have to await the decisive processes of evolution, and the survival of the *fit*—whoever they may turn out to be. *Providence* does not seem to intend to decide the matter. It is machinery versus understanding—to the end. (This, presumably, is what H. G. Wells meant by the race between catastrophe and education.)

At any rate, there will be no default in the warfare of psychology against psychology. This is the more likely because psychology is not a science in its own right, and can never hope to become one. Psychology is the servant of social and educational programs; and the fate of any specific psychological doctrine will depend in the long run upon the success or failure of the social program to which it is aucillary.

CHAPTER XV

THE DILEMMA OF THE NEW SCHOOL

The child needs intellectual freedom. Free intellectual play for the child is to think about something and wonder how it got there, and what it is for. Every child wants to know a multitude of things that he does not know. It is because adults have so hedged him about by external demands that this desire to want to know has been abolished in our modern schoolrooms. The child must be free to take time to think . . . Thinking is finding out something from an impulse that is within you and that makes a demand upon you. The child must have not only intellectual freedom, but spiritual freedom as well. One of the greatest needs in the world to-day is freedom of spirit.—MRS. MARIETTA L. JOHNSON.

One broad general principle has been evolved out of all concrete efforts to establish justice, namely, the principle that group interests and, in general, group judgments are superior to individual interests and judgments. . . . So important is the racial experience which is deposited within the individual that it becomes a dominant fact. Purely individual experiences and modes of reacting to impressions sink to a level of inferior importance. The individual becomes an embodiment of social tendencies. The individual nervous system is in this way taken over by society and the modes of behavior exhibited by the individual become those which are determined by society's needs. . . . Schools are society's agency for training pupils in the social arts. . . . That process is one of transforming individuals so that they will conform to social institutions.—C. H. JUDD, in *Psychology of Social Institutions*.

A school is a social tool invented and set up by the community for the accomplishment of certain ends. For this reason a school should have no traditions or objectives of its own, just as a handsaw should have no traditions or objectives of its own. A school is a tool of the community just as a handsaw is a tool of the carpenter. Carpenters sometimes misuse their tools, neglect them, allow them to grow dull, to rust and become useless. They sometimes try to use them for purposes for which they were not intended. Under such circumstances, it would not be difficult to imagine a self-respecting tool setting up in business for itself, declaring its freedom from its foolish master and deciding its own future use and destiny.

The Uses of Tools.—On the other hand it would not be difficult to imagine a lazy carpenter saying to his box of tools: "You have helped me build a number of houses in the last ten years. You have seen how it is done. By this time you ought to know how it is done. Why should I have to direct your every motion? You know what a house is: a house is a house! Go to it: build houses! I've got other things to do!" But the carpenter would be mistaken; tools do not know how to build houses. Handsaws can saw; planes can make smooth surfaces; hammers can drive nails. All these things are necessary in the building of a house. But doing them will not result in a house. If the tools are obedient they may saw and plane and hammer away at the materials furnished them, with a sort of blind faith that enough sawing, planing and hammering will produce a house. But the results are not likely to prove satisfactory to the carpenter when he comes back from his other allegedly important business.

Our public schools are in much this same position, to-day. To them has been assigned a job. They saw and plane and hammer away at their materials, with a sort of blind, pathetic hope that enough of such sawing, planing and hammering will produce something that looks like competent individuals, an intelligent community, a desirable social order. But the results are not satisfactory when we take time for critical examination of the product in the light of our social needs. Nothing is more obvious, to-day.

Is the School Nothing But a Tool?—The difficulty arises from the fact that the schools, and the community, too, have come to believe that these schoolish activities, of sawing, planing, and hammering their materials, have conclusive relationships to the ends desired, that is, to an intelligent social order; and that, therefore, the schools can ignore all questions as to their ultimate objectives: they can devote themselves wholly to perfecting their processes. If sawing, planing and hammering their materials are the means of producing desired results, then the schools can forget all about those results; they can spend all their energies improving the techniques of sawing, planing and hammering, sure that the results will naturally follow.

Now, because of such developments, our public schools have largely ceased to be social institutions, devoted to the development of an intelligent social order; they have become pieces of independent machinery, or tools, which just run on, sawing, planing, hammering their materials, and doing these things as worthy ends in themselves, holding to be sure that such processes ought to produce desirable outcomes. That they do not produce desirable outcomes is, of course, deplorable—but school must still be school!

The Social Test of the School.—However, when we stop to consider the matter, this result is not wholly displeasing. Our public school system turns children out rather closely related to present social needs. Forty percent of our children do not finish the sixth grade; these will do the rough work of the world, and they will be happier if they do not know too much. Twenty percent more will not finish the eighth grade. These will be able to fill in the slightly higher grades of work. Forty percent of our children will stick through the eight grades. Twenty percent will go on to high school. Ten percent will graduate from high school. Five percent will go on to college. Two percent will graduate from college. These figures are merely approximate and illustrative. Society is a pyramid of abilities with college graduates at the apex. The school is one of the instruments by means of which society distributes its children at the proper levels of the pyramid. Intelligence tests help the schools do with scientific accuracy what for a century they have done by haphazard, though, at least until recently, with a fair degree of success—namely distribute children through the vocational world with some references to their native abilities. This is the general point of view of the public school—in a world of *laisser faire!*

The Diverse Program of the New School.—Our new schools, as we have seen, have a different sort of program and objective. They emphasize the individual child, his own interests and needs; and they mostly assume that "the community" must be the creation of each new generation in its turn. For purposes of effective contrast let us consider the concrete program of one such school:

"The aim of the school is to prepare each child for a complete life, both as an individual and as member of the social group. Art and craft work; auditorium for music and dancing; science; mechanics; French. All-day plan; hot lunch served; outdoor rest and roof playground for younger children; athletic field; afternoon trips making use of city life in connection with school work. In all fields the school encourages primarily the creative impulse."

The school that publishes this statement means what it says. It undertakes to carry out this program with the children under its care. It is not just sawing, planing, hammering away at its materials. It is more than a tool. It is dealing with its materials with what intelligence it can achieve in the hope that it can make some contribution, of creative minds, to the solution of our common problems. That is to say, this school is a tool directed by intelligence. It is not the tool alone; it is the tool and the carpenter combined.

The Conflict of Aims.—There is a real conflict between this program, especially the implication of the last clause of it, and the practices of most of our public schools. For whatever the wishes of the teacher with respect to the pupils, the public school is the instrument of the community and in the long run it must turn out what the community wants and will pay for. This conflict of attitudes must not be sloughed over. It must be sharpened and defined. The aims of our public schools and of these new schools are essentially different. Our public schools grew out of an attempt to universalize that education which the English tradition had limited to the aristocracy; and no attempt was made to transform the aristocratic psychology and philosophy that underlay that English tradition and justified it. Hence, our public schools have never been democratic in the psychological and ethical sense,

but only in the geographic sense: they have been everywhere—but not for all children "according to their needs."

The "new schools" now claim to be trying to translate
our democratic aspirations into a real educational program. Some of the psychological developments of the
last forty years provide the tools for this transformation.
The "new schools" are, therefore, moving in a different
direction from that which our public schools (and their
sponsor, the National Education Association) are taking.
They propose to be more than geographically democratic;
they propose to be psychologically and ethically democratic: they propose to provide the individual child with
opportunity for development "according to his own need
and nature." This difference of program is the most
hopeful thing in educational procedure, to-day.

The Beginning of the Dilemma.—None the less, these
"new" and "progressive" schools would still like to be
called schools: they want to be counted inside the school
field. Their leaders and teachers want to be thought of
as "school people." They even want still to belong to the
National Education Association. On the other hand,
"regular" school people do not want too close contact
with these experimenters and their programs. Such contacts would probably mean confusion in school practices;
it might even bring down the wrath of the school authorities. Orthodox school people usually dismiss educational
experiments with a shrug. There is a growing sense of
strain between the two groups, whenever they recognize
the fact of each other's existence. The situation is one
that calls for honesty of mind and inquiry. Both sides
are infected with the sense of dilemma!

The Dilemma Grows.—Moreover, as we have seen, a
school of whatever sort needs a community of some sort,
a social world as its background. Children do not grow

in a vacuum. They live in a world. The school must draw its children from some sort of environment. They must go back into some sort of world. If the children are to be kept intact, there should be some sort of continuity through these three aspects of their development —the world out of which they come, the school, and the world into which they go. Does any such continuity exist for the progressive school? If not, what is the justification of the progressive school? Are the elements of such a continuity to be found anywhere in the modern world, to-day? Where and how shall the progressive school find the community backgrounds that can give its work social reality—a community that will provide children for the school, that will support the work of the school even when that work is understood, that will accept and make room for the graduates of the school who finish their preparatory years with individualized and creative minds? Where, on the face of the earth, can such a community be found?

There is, perhaps, one such community, or promise of community; the community of creative artists. But the relationships between the progressive school and the world of art and artists is still very tenuous. The modern world seems not able to assimilate any large number of artists; and a democratic social order needs creative minds in other fields besides that of art. Creativeness and initiative are needed in industry, government, religion, moral relationships, education, as well as in art. Our progressive schools are really interested in general educational outcomes, not merely in developing artists, even though every individual should be an artist in his way. What community support and community outlets can these schools find in these other social directions? If they can find none, then they will find themselves in the inescapable dilemma.

Consider the last sentence of the statement quoted above: "In all fields, the school encourages primarily the creative impulse." Does this proposal—to develop *creative minds*—find a welcome anywhere in the modern world? If we may believe many strident voices, it is echoed from many quarters. "Crucial problems," calling for "creative minds," are said to be all about us. "Creative impulses" are reported to be struggling into existence in industry, politics, religion, and even in many phases of our folkway moralities. Our literatures are reputed to be filled with these "creative trends." In short, all our "arts" are little else than efforts of the "creative impulse" to express itself in variant convincing forms. The current world seems to be groaning and travailing in the pains of creative desire.

Now, if all these things are true, does not this very creative adult world need a very creative type of school as its instrument of assuring the development of this same creative impulse in the next generation? And should not the New School be the accepted educational instrument of this creative anguish of the modern world?

But, if it is to be such an instrument, must it not definitely recognize the logic of its existence, and take its place with all these other creative movements? Must it not reconsider all its bases, and all its relationships in the light of this world-problem? Must it not be willing to lose all standing with conventional academic groups? Must it not lose its life, if it would save its purposes?

Acceptance of such a destiny would give the new school, eventually at least, the community that it needs, both as a sympathetic source of supply of students, and as a world of vocations for its graduates. Of course, such affiliations would tear the souls of many New Schools, teachers, for they want to be "respectable," just as other school people are. Evidently, the modern world is not very simple!

The Other Side of the Dilemma.—Moreover (and this point has been frequently made in recent years) do not all these other "creative" movements need something like the new school? All must admit that every progressive social movement needs a real educational program, both for its adult members and for childhood and youth. Three ways are open to such movements: they can rely on the academic schools for their educational support, and then spend years re-educating their academically minded product to the social task envisaged in the movement they are sponsoring. It is possible, of course, that a bit of adult education will overcome the drag of a conventional schooling in childhood. But it seems an unnecessarily wasteful procedure.

Second, they can set up propagandist schools which will mold the minds of children and youth to "radical" attitudes long before they are aware of what is happening to them, a process that usually ends by turning out minds that are either hardened to the same unyielding qualities that are found in the "reactionaries" they criticise; or that rebound entirely from all molding and revert to a primitive escape from all responsibility. This method, like the conventional one, fails to produce minds that can anticipate the future, or that can assume leadership in "creative enterprises."

In the third place, they can accept the suggestion here set forth. They can make use of the progressive school, the New School, and turn over to this type of education the task of developing in their children the "creative minds" that will make them valuable members of these

minds" they must help them find a world in which "creative minds" will have some chance of survival. They do
not see that, soon or late, they will have to accept the
logic of their positions—affiliation with creative movements in other lines in order to give their graduates a
possible social world; or else they will have to give up
all their talk about "creativeness" and become respectable, even though critical, upholders of the status quo.
Logic is cruel, but a school should not blink it.

The Crux of the Matter.—As a matter of fact, their
prime problem presses upon them all the while. Their
programs of creative development work out fairly well
for children from four to about eleven years of age. After
eleven, everything begins to go wrong. Few of these
schools can hold their children—and their doctrines—
after the children pass the age of twelve or thirteen. The
reason is fairly clear. Up to the age of eleven, creativeness can direct itself to materials and situations that can
be brought into the school room, and to social relationships that can be lived in imagination. After that age,
normal children turn with increasing vehemence toward
the problems of the world. They want the real world,
not a substitute for the world. The effects of their creative training begin to show at home, on the streets, in
relation to social customs and traditions, in questions
about work and money and all the embarrassing problems which a keen mind can readily discover in our present social disorder. Parents of twelve-year-olds begin to
suspect there is more to "creativeness" than they anticipated in the days when their five-year-olds were "creating" pretty little songs and poems.

And teachers begin to find out that after twelve, the
children want a real world. Talk will not satisfy. They
want industry, not talk about it. They want politics, not

a class in bookish civics. They want experience, not moral axioms. The task of the experimental school grows, expands by leaps and bounds after the children are twelve. It escapes from the school house and knows no limits but the world.

As yet, no such school has found out how to give the creative child access to and a share in the real world of industry, politics, and moral struggles. The teacher can cut off selected portions of that real world and bring them into the school. Creative-minded children discover the fragmentary quality of the material very quickly and turn from it in disgust. If, on the other hand, in their search for reality, they go out into the world where real things are, they are likely to find their creativeness of mind a help in understanding the world, but a hindrance to finding or keeping an actual job.

The Larger Task of the New School.—The true experimental school is working out a program that helps children liberate whatever native powers they have into a socially intelligent personality, into a "creative mind." But the school which, under present conditions, treats children in this way and leaves them there, certainly assumes a profound responsibility. Such a school can, of course, try to justify itself by saying that the children must help to make the world over. That may release the school from responsibility, but it rationalizes an impossible position. The public school is justified in much of its present drift because its product does find some access to the vocations of the present social order. No school has any right to put the burden of reforming the world on its pupils. The new school must help its graduates find a world in which the kind of minds they have developed can function; where the knowledge they possess will be accepted as at least provisionally true; where their creative personalities will have at least a fifty-fifty chance of survival.

Old social structures are obviously not meeting the world's needs to-day. New ones are demanded. These new ones must be created. Should not all who talk of creativeness or who really believe in it find a mutual basis of understanding and support? Why should a teacher who talks about "encouraging the creative impulse in children" seek to retain fellowship with teachers who insist upon teaching "cheerful submission to superior wisdom"? Why should not the creative teacher rather seek fellowship with the industrial leader, the political leader, the religious leader, the moral leader who is saying that the industry, the government, the religion and the morality of the future must all be products of the creative social intelligence of the future? A creative school that has no vision of a supporting "creative" community will not long remain creative; just as a "creative" movement in any social direction will not long remain vital unless it can secure the help of a vitally creative education.

One Further Item.—There is one further phase of this logic that must be pointed out. It concerns "science" and the *scientists*. One of the gross humors of our times is found in the way in which "science" accepts its subordination to tradition in the regimen of the school. Of course, this means that what we call "science" is not science at all, but merely organized knowledge about certain aspects of the world which have been more or less gratuitously turned over to become the domain of "science." There is enough fact, or at least implication, in any book of botany, zoology, physics or chemistry, to destroy *in toto* the arrogance of the current public school régime—if any one would care to apply the logic of the case without qualification. There is really no place for *genuine science* in the traditional school; the implications of science are totally at variance to the implications of tradition. Why, then, does science accept its place in current schools? Primarily because most of our "scientists" are not real scientists, but dogmatists teaching materials labelled "science."

The real affiliations of the whole scientific movement and the true scientific spirit are with the progressive school. The spirit of the progressive school is the spirit of science applied to education. At least, that is true in large part—truer for the progressive school than for any other sort of school. But our thinking on these subjects is so feeble, so inconclusive, so unscientific, that we do not recognize these facts. It is even likely that many who call themselves "scientists" will be first to deny and condemn the argument here presented. But such denial will not defeat the argument; it will merely prove what is set forth above, namely, that many who are called "scientists" are merely dogmatists parading under a garb they deny.

Summary.—Our academic public schools fail to develop creative-mindedness in their children. The conservative public is rather glad of this because that public does not care to have much "creativeness of mind" released into the community. On the other hand, creative and reconstructive social movements in all lines are finding progress very difficult because the public does not welcome such movements; because the public schools do not prepare minds to take creative attitudes; and because these movements have no adequate educational enterprises of their own to help find and release such minds. More or less in desperation, many of these movements, particularly in industry, are trying to build their own schools. Naturally enough those schools tend to be tainted with propagandist materials and methods; that is, with dogmatic materials of a radical sort and with emotionalist methods. Such a program must eventually fail, for it does not face the world problems in a realistic fashion.

Somewhere between these extremes, the experimental school is working. But it is only tentatively successful because it has no world into which to send its children when they finish school. It draws its children largely from wealthy homes, or the homes of intellectuals. Its logical outlet would be the creative and reconstructive movements of the social and industrial world. But not all the parents of these children care to think of their children as being educated to leave the class from which they came; or their school as the gateway into revolutionary movements. The experimental school has no other outlet, can have no other outlet. An experimental product must find its place in some sort of an experimental world. The only area of the social world that is experimental is the world of the rebellious arts, of labor unions, of radical political parties, of heretic religions and unconventional moralities. If the graduate of one of these creative schools finds no avenue into the healthful world of social experimentation, he will likely find an outlet in experimenting upon himself, in some individual way. He will become an esthete, a pervert, a fanatic, a cynic, or some other inhabitant of the "lunatic fringe." This is not a profitable goal for the creative school movement.

But this is the dilemma of the experimental school today. The only hope of resolving this dilemma seems to lie in the direction of trying to federate all other creative and reconstructive social movements, for the support and utilization of the work of these progressive schools. In such federating, two difficulties would have to be overcome. First, these creative social and industrial movements would have to learn to accept scientific methods and results, as, on the whole, more advantageous and desirable than propagandist results and methods. And second, teachers in experimental schools would have to accept the fate of being pioneers. They would have to consent to throw in their fortunes with those pioneers in all other social fields who are working for a common end —the creation of a beautiful, humane, and socially intelligent world.

CHAPTER XVI

THE REAL TASK OF PSYCHOLOGY
IN EDUCATION

We appear as selves in our conduct in so far as we ourselves take the attitudes that others take toward us. Perhaps as good an illustration of this as can be found is in
a "right." Over against the protection of our lives or
property, we assume the attitude of assent of all members
of the community. We take the rôle of what may be
called "the generalized other." In doing this we appear
as social objects, as selves. It is interesting to note that
in the development of the individual child there are two
stages which present the two essential steps in attaining
self-consciousness. The first stage is that of play, the
second that of game, where these are distinguished from
each other. In play, in this sense, the child is continually acting as parent, teacher, policeman, preacher,
groceryman, pirate or Indian. It is the period of childish experience which Wordsworth has described as that
of "endless imitation." It is the period of Froebel's
kindergarten plays. In it, as Froebel recognized, the
child is acquiring the rôles of those who belong to his
society. This takes place because the child is continually
exciting in himself the responses to his own social acts.
. . . Having in his own nature the beginnings of parental
response, he calls it out by his own appeals. . . . The
play antedates the game. For in a game there is regulated procedure and rules. The child must not only
take the rôle of the other, as he does in play, but he
must assume the various rôles of all the participants in
the game and govern himself accordingly.—GEORGE H.
MEAD, in *International Journal of Ethics,* Vol. 35.

Psychology, which began as a study of the community and of the social individual, the member of the community, has within the past century largely become a study of an abstraction—the unrelated individual. Psychologists have a theory that *mind* is a function of the individual nervous system, and that its total significance can be discovered by subjecting such "individual mind" to observation. This doctrine assumes that society is but an aggregation of "individuals" who live together; who are held together not by psychological bonds, but by economic and political pressures. Psychologists of this type are able to interpret *education* wholly in terms of *learning,* and this learning takes the form of "conditionings" and "reconditionings," that is, of habits. It is a curious reversion to primitive ways—without recognition of primitive practices.

The One and the Many.—But the world came, and still comes, before the individual. The social group antedates every part of the group. The community, any, every, community, was in existence long before any one now living in it was born. The not wholly dead hand of the past still reaches down through the years to control the present. What we must call "general mind" was in existence ages before "individual mind" emerges. This general mind takes the form of customs, traditions, the folkways and mores of the group. To-day it has been taken over into books, papers, the movies, radio, public opinion, slogans, and all such. This general mind not only antedates individual mind, but always it insists upon becoming the content of individual minds, and the form of such minds. The *many* accept the *one,* almost always, before they find happiness. A psychology that is ignorant of, or ignores, these facts may be very scientific, but it has little of value for education.

Psychology in the School.—Psychology has not only long been the study of abstract individual mind, but as educational psychology it has long been the study of that abstract part of abstract mind, the Intellect. For this psychology, Intellect is the mental correlate of Reality. Knowledge copies the world of things. The essence of things is ideas. An idea is a symbol of reality; hence, for all practical purposes it *is* reality. The academic school deals with ideas as its proper material. "When you give a child ideas, you give him reality." The school has talked much of "training the mind." This means developing the intellect—filling the memory with ideas and facts. The curriculum of the academic school is intellectual: lessons to be learned. The student is supposed to be engaged in intellectual pursuits. It is assumed on all sides that since the intellectual materials which make up the curriculum are the essences of the world of action and social living, they will, when taken on by the individual, give him the reality of the world of action and of social relationships. He will not have to live in the world of action and social relationships; when he gets the ideas of those worlds he gets those worlds.[1]

For the school, therefore, the easiest and most thorough way of reaching an understanding of the world is to master the facts and ideas that represent and symbolize the world. "Education" is such learning; and the laws of such learning are the laws of education.

Hence, psychology becomes, in the academic school, the instrument for interpreting and organizing these intellectual activities. It has to do with processes of learning, and it sometimes purports to be concerned with some-

[1] It is probably demonstrable that to about four persons out of each thousand this has an element of truth in it. But two-fifths of one percent of the population is a narrow basis upon which to build a universal education!

thing called thinking. But in large measure, in the actual programs of schooling, learning becomes memorizing, and thinking becomes reading and copying or imitating the thoughts of others. Schools have much to do with memorizing and with "thoughts," but not much to do with thinking!

These processes, rooted in this schoolish psychology, are so artificial that they have become institutionalized in the contrast or contradiction between the "academic" and the "real" worlds. This "academic" world (excluding the "extra-curricular" aspects of it) is for the most part a flat, dreary world, with length and breadth, but without depth. It is a world of two dimensions, superficial. It cannot bother itself with the experiences of the students, with rich human emotions, or with those roots of life that go deep into the soil of a vital humanity. All such things must be reduced to statistical form and treated as generalized data. Individual instances are distracting: they interfere with "learning." The "academic mind" is a definite problem to-day, even to the academic world. One leading university president insists that this academic mind is becoming increasingly useless even on the campus!

Psychology in the New School.—But "new school people" hold that this academic education is not education at all. It is nothing but "schooling," and they hold that real education never *schools* the individual: it awakens him; it helps him to develop his own individual experience. Hence, the new schools want a psychology that helps them to explore and understand the processes by which children grow and develop into adult members of the community. Such a psychology must be genetic—showing origins and progress.

Such a psychology must also deal with the world of

three dimensions—length and breadth and emotional depth. The child in the new school is not a "pupil"—with merely the abstract intellectual interests of the orthodox school. He is a real child, with interests and emotions of his own, and with all the other concrete characteristics of childhood. For such a child, of course, the best preparation for life is living as a child while he is a child.

The psychology of the new school tries to understand and to dramatize the processes through which the child grows from infancy to maturity. The education that follows the lead of such a psychology undertakes to direct the development of the child through all the various levels of development—not as a process of learning a succession of graded lessons, but as congeries of natural processes involving growth and development, habit building and learning, emotional realization, and the enrichment of personal and social living by means of understanding, imagination and rational participation. The academic teacher is a constructor, or at least, an instructor—the analogy being taken from the inorganic world of the builder. The teacher in the new school is a cultivator—the analogy coming from the world of nature and living things.

Some Contrasts.—The difference between the psychology of the academic school and that of the new school becomes more apparent. Academic psychology tends to assume that an intellectual transcript of experience is identical with experience; that an intellectual statement of the world is identical with the world; that it may even be a better world than the actual world because it has eliminated all factors that are not universal and standard, all factors that are "crude, brutish, immoral." On the other hand, the psychology of the new school tends to assume that the individual child is the unit of the social world, and that a better social world can be secured by developing better individuals—out of these units. Hence, new school people tend to talk rather overmuch about the better social world that is to come by reason of the coming of these better individuals who are to be turned out by the new schools. But, as we have seen, a better social order is not likely to be the product of individual differences.

Academic psychology attempts to reduce the whole of experience to a series of abstract propositions—which individuals may take on, and thereby achieve reality for themselves. New school psychology tends to reduce the whole social world to a number of discreet individuals— who will create order for themselves, and thus give reality to the general doctrines implied. These are extremes, of course, but they are important points of view, and each side of the present educational controversy would be more intelligent and effective if it would candidly recognize its position.

But from the standpoint of normal human experience neither of these extremes standing alone is adequate. The world is more than the abstract propositions of the idealists and the academics. It is all those wide ranges of personal, social, civic, industrial, ideal and emotional experiences within which most of the people of the earth do dwell, and out of which have been crystallized, often with great pain, all the abstract propositions the earth has ever known. But also, the world is something more than individuals described by the new school advocates. Society was in existence before any person now living was born, and presumably it will go on existing after every individual now living has passed into the shadows. Society is more than an aggregate of individuals. Out of the mass of the social "drift," coming down out of the past and pressing on into the future, individuals are sometimes developed—precariously and at great cost. The task of education has been too easily stated by both the academics and the new school people. Both are too much at ease in Zion.

Education and Psychology.—Education must be something more than either the inculcation of a series of abstract propositions or the development of a number of particular individuals. Psychology, if it is to be the guide of teaching, must be something more than either the doctrine of intellect and learning, or the doctrine of individual mind. It must achieve a point of view which reveals both these doctrines as fragments of truth and, like all fragments, distorted a bit in becoming fragments. It must achieve a point of view that sees life steadily and sees it whole—the human story from the primitive into the future; the experience of the individual from birth, or before, through the processes by which he achieves such maturity, or lack of it, as is his destiny; the community, rural and urban, advanced and belated, in the midst of which individual development goes on: all phases and aspects of the story are significant for understanding what the modern world is beginning to mean by "education."

Education begins with an established world. This established social world surrounds every new-born child with elaborate mechanisms of custom and institution. Within a few years of the ordinary drift of group life this new child will, as we have seen, become merely another instance of customary and institutional control. He can avoid such a fate in one way only: by escaping from the group and living as an outlaw or a renegade on the face of the earth all his days. But the fate of the outlaw is, for most of us, harder to bear than is the fate of the group member. Hence, even if we had the chance to choose, we should probably mostly choose to become and remain members of groups.

But modern conceptions of personality deny the finality of this primitive subordination of the new individual to prevailing custom and tradition. Education, in some of its forms, seeks to rescue the individual from this former subordination and to help him achieve "freedom." This problem of education of the individual for freedom has been the concern of some few educators in every age probably since the days of Socrates. What chance has an unsuspecting plastic organism, such as a little child, in the presence of the thoroughly arrogant and monopolistic customs and traditions of the ages? How shall the individual achieve "freedom"?

The problem is universal, complex, obscure. If the folkways of the group absolutely control the destiny of the child, the world becomes stagnant, history repeats itself, and the whole of life turns out, surely, to be "a tale told by an idiot, full of sound and fury, signifying nothing."

If, on the other hand, the child is defended from all impacts of the folkways so that he grows up to be an "individual"—in the sense that everything he is is evolved out of his own native constitution—then the whole history of the race is lost, the experience of the past, whether good or bad, counts for nothing, and the world is turned into absolute anarchy, having no past, and therefore presumably no future—being nothing but an unrelated and therefore perhaps an irrelevant present!

But the past exists, and it refuses to be treated in any such contemptuous way. Just as truly, however, the new individual exists, as an experiment on the part of nature.

This new individual may hold within its latent variabilities new patterns of unsuspected significance for life. At least this has been true of certain individuals in the past. There ought to be some means of defending this possibility of significant variation from defeat and from destruction. This new individual should have the chance to make his contribution to the culture of the world, howsoever reconstructive of ancient cultures that contribution may turn out to be. But if he is to make any such contribution, he must himself come into being as an individual and a member of the human race. He cannot develop in a vacuum. He must have the soils and climates of growth. He must have the chance to use all the materials of the world in his education, without being completely destroyed by the arrogance of the past. One of the problems of education is this of finding ways by which the riches of the past cultures of the world can be made to serve the needs of the new individual without destroying that individual and making him merely another instance of folkway mind. Neither the past nor the present may be denied or ignored in the making of the more admirable future. Both are needed if that future is to be both human and real.

Education for Change.—The problem of educational psychology, therefore, is that of helping to find out how what we may call the "general mind" of the race can help to develop individual mind in the growing child. It is pretty generally admitted, to-day, that the present adult generation, which is pretty much the expression of this "general mind," will never much change, even though there is no reason why it should not change—save the reason of its own inertias. It is not so generally suspected, though probably equally true, that the children of the present, dominated by the academic school and spending all spare time under the general influence of the adult generation, will grow up to copy and repeat patterns of the adult generation and the traditions of the folkway past. Hence, we are in a vicious circle: There is not much chance of change in the adult generation because adults have passed beyond the plastic years; and there is not much chance of change in the coming generation because the children are under the dominance of these changeless adults. How, then, shall we educate for change?

Change does occasionally take place; sometimes by accident, and perhaps now and then by intelligent intention. The real problem of psychology would seem to be, then, that of determining in any specific case how change did actually take place. Change that occurs by accident can be studied and understood and the factors that concurred in accidental change can probably be organized and applied elsewhere. A general program of desired change may eventually be developed and organized for the guidance of teachers and other types of statesmen.

Properly speaking, psychology is the study of the social mind, in its functions and structures, in its historical development, in its contemporary manifestations, and the ways in which it has ever suffered, or been made to suffer change. One important phase of this study is the examination of this mind as it appears in individuals. A psychology that is nothing but the study of the social or folkway mind shortly loses contact with reality and tends to become vague abstractions. A psychology that is wholly a study of individual mind tends to become atomistic, intellectual, academic, unreal. A realistic and useful educational psychology will be a social psychology: it will always see the "individual" as emerging out of the group matrix; but this psychology will also be individualized: it will always see groups and communities as social soils out of which individuals may be developed if we could learn how to cultivate the life that is there.

The Self in Psychology.—The folkway attitude holds children as members of groups, and never permits them to become "individuals," if it has its way. The academic school tends to maintain this same attitude and to argue for the subordination of the individual to the welfare of the group—the submission of the individual to wisdom greater than his own.

The new school tends to over-emphasize the values and the possibilities of "freedom," and to develop "individuals" who have no roots in any actual community.

The world needs neither of these prevailing types in any large measure. It does need men and women who have adventured in both directions, and who are integrating within their growing personalities something of both; who have become, or are becoming, *selves,* with roots in the great folkway past of the race, and with aspirations looking forward into the more individualized future. It is not an abstract nervous system that is important in the world to-day, save for purposes of study and understanding; it is not even an abstract "mind" that is significant. It is the concrete person, the physically energetic and vital being, the social *self;* the member of social groups and the explorer beyond all groups into the emerging community of the world; the keen, logical intellect, and the intelligence that can escape from Plato and Aristotle and share with Darwin and Einstein the discoveries of the age; the emotionally developed personality, whose emotions persist because they have been caught up into a real career; the evolving human being, to whom nothing is lacking in interest, who sees life broadly and sees it whole, and with something of a cosmic sweep can "look before and after."

So, after all the behaviorisms, and the introspection-isms, and the intellectualisms, and the other *isms* that make up the psychological chaos of our times have had their "say," there will remain the social person, concrete, complex and real, who has explored some area of the world, but realizes there are other areas yet unsuspected in detail left to explore; who knows something of him-self, yet realizes there are vast areas still unknown; who is, therefore, the significant *self*, of common sense, of per-sistent tradition, and of the most critical psychology, and who is, beyond all psychologies, the ultimate objective of all educational efforts.

Finale and Transition.—We have searched far and wide, thus far, and we have not found how the complete education of our most creative imagination can achieve itself. We have examined, briefly but realistically, the "old school" and the "new." We have seen them at work, and have weighed their product not in the light of their claims, but in the light of facts and conditions. We admit their contributions, and their limitations. Beyond both of them we see the larger goal of a real education: the development of social selves, rooted in reality, but rising into freedom, with all the attributes of the human. We have met another fact: no one knows, to-day, just how such *integrated selves* can be assured in the midst of the disintegrations of our age. Certainly the schools, either "old" or "new," do not know.

So, leaving the schools, both old and new, we shall turn to the actual world of men and affairs, of institutions and "individuals," and try to find out how *education*, what-ever that may be found to mean, actually goes on, to-day; how human beings are really being educated, to whatever ends they attain. It may be that in this way we shall

learn something of those vital processes through which
selfhood is even now achieved, through which great personalities have emerged at times, precariously, in history.
We must get help and light from every possible source:
from the ancient torch of learning; from the lowly candle
in whose light "self-made" men once studied; from the
windows of the New Schools; from the will-o'-the-wisp,
scorned of the academics. "Nothing human shall be foreign to our interest," though that does not mean that we
shall be able to encompass all that is human.

So, we turn to Part III, and survey the processes of
education going forward under every conceivable condition, to-day. Keeping in mind the work being done or
promised in schools, we turn from the schools for a time
and give our attentions to less formal but, possibly, not
less important matters in education. It takes all sorts
and descriptions of experience and experiences to make
an education!

PART THREE

HOW WE ARE EDUCATED

CHAPTER XVII

EXPERIENCE

There was a child went forth every day,
And the first object he looked upon, that object he be-
came,
And that object became part of him for the day or the
certain part of the day,
Or for many years or stretching cycles of years.
The early lilacs became part of the child,
The grass and white and red morning-glories, and white
and red clover, and the song of the phœbe-bird,
And all the changes of city and country wherever he went.
The family usages, the language, the company, the furni-
ture, the yearning and swelling heart,
Affection that will not be gainsay'd, the sense of what is
real, the thought if after all it should prove unreal,
The doubts of day-time and the doubts of night-time, the
curious whether and how,
Whether that which appears so is so, or is it all flashes
and specks?
Men and women crowding fast in the streets, if they are
not flashes and specks what are they?
The streets themselves and the façades of houses, and
goods in the windows,
Vehicles, teams, the heavy-plank'd wharves, the huge
crossing at the ferries,
The village on the highland seen from afar at sunset, the
river between,
Shadows, aureola and mist, the light falling on roofs and
gables of white and brown two miles off,
The schooner near by sleepily dropping down the tide,

The hurrying tumbling waves, quick-broken crests, slap-
ping,
These became part of that child who went forth every
day, and who now goes forth, and will always go
forth every day.—WALT WHITMAN.

The academic school assumes that "education" is composed of pre-existent treasures of knowledge and stable
patterns of discipline held in trust for the new generations, which children are to accept and be molded by.
Individual experiences are of inferior importance or of
no importance at all. The nervous system of the individual is to be taken over by society, through the school,
and his responses are to be made to conform to the needs
of society. He is to be "socialized"; that is, habituated
to institutional attitudes.

The New School assumes that education is made up of
processes taking place within the individual child's own
"experience"—identifying that experience with the child's
"mind." The culture treasures, the modes of experience,
and the patterns of behavior inherited from the past are
tyrannical: they repress, suppress and defeat the individual and they make the attainment of a better world
impossible. The child must have the chance to realize
his own being, develop his own responses and make his
own creative impact upon the world of nature and society.
In time, he must, out of his own processes, create his own
social world.

The Actual World of Experiences.—Meanwhile, the
fundamental fact about education is that "life" is made
up of experiences and that all experiences educate—in
one way or another. Nothing that ever happens to us is
lost. It leaves its trace in the nervous system.

Hence, a true interpretation of education must begin

with experience, with all experiences, and with the sources of all experiences, i.e., with the community. Education is a matter of experiences and experience, and every experience, wherever achieved, is educational. All experiences are real—each in its own way—and they all leave their own specific impacts upon the individual and the community. They build up and they tear down; they indurate and they soften; they illusion or they disillusion; they enrich personality or they defeat us.

The nervous system of the child must be seen as a part of the world of nature, upon which all the physical forces of the universe play their endless rat-tat-tat. At first, the almost completely helpless victim of these natural forces, the nervous system gradually learns to protect itself a bit, and to select out of the infinitude of stimuli those that are unavoidable, those that are advantageous, and those that are desirable. These processes of selection are enormously complicated and important. Out of their development, organization, and operation will come all that ultimate result which we variously call "education," "personality," "destiny." Experience is, therefore, the fundamental concept in education.

The Import of Experiences.—Not all experiences are of equal importance. Some are ephemeral, some have to do with temporary situations, some are related to matters of life and death—just as some roads turn out to be blind alleys, some to be mere byways, and some to lead to the city of desire. The development of an organized personality or an organized community in the midst of the general chaos of experiences will depend upon our ability to select experiences having real significance and to deal with them in terms of their assured significance. Experiences which first just happen to us must eventually be brought into reflective use and be made to reveal their inner meanings, so that they may be given their normal places in the organic total of our lives. Bit by bit through the ages, experience has organized itself and integrated itself out of the wide ranges of the race's experiences. Bit by bit, through the years, experience organizes itself and integrates itself more or less adequately out of the variant ranges of the individual's experiences. Experiences must have variety and diversity, and experience must be critically integrated.

The Great Educational Problem.—What shall be the criteria of selection and the bases of organization and integration of our experiences into that growing experience which we call education? Shall we permit past custom to dominate present processes of organization? Shall we select and classify current experiences under old, invidious systems of classification? Shall we let certain institutions claiming prerogatives out of the past determine the bounds of present experience and the integration which may be undertaken within experience? Or shall we take all experiences as educational and shall we let the present with its problems and the future with its intimations and needs determine our selections and our organization?

Reflective experience is just as natural as are immediate experiences; reasoning and judgment are as real, if not as common, as seeing and hearing. The difficulty is that our reflective processes are rarely adequate or honest. They are deflected from natural functioning by invidious hangovers from the past. Customary types of attitude and opinion tend to dominate present situations. Previous experiences try to maintain their places in the sun. Former fears and hopes and desires set up prejudicial estimates of the value of present experiences. Sometimes we are too inert to attend to the conflicts that rise within our immediate experiences; unless it is a matter of life and death, we may ignore the whole business. "What's the use?" we ask.

One result of this inertia is that we not only do not integrate our experiences into an experience adequate to our needs, but we often let former types of integration and former categories of interpretation dominate even our very perceptions, until at length we may become able to deny the evidence of our senses, and to rationalize any sort of false judgment. Former experiences, and especially former experience, plays havoc with new experiences that differ from the old.

Experience is the basic factor in education. We are educated by our experiences, whatever they are, and wherever they come from. The task of developing, criticizing, organizing and integrating our experiences into experience, and so into an education is the fundamental task of civilization to-day. The "salvation" of the individual depends upon it. But more. The very existence of civilization depends upon it. Old organizations of experience, whether institutionalized or not, are increasingly failing to convince the younger generations. "No organization at all" is nonsense. We shall have organization of some sort, no fear. What shall it be?

Meanwhile, we are having organization of some sort. We are achieving "educations," i.e., organization of experience, of many sorts, some of them fairly adequate (probably by good luck); most of them of various degrees of inadequacy. We turn first to a view of these various "educations." What has "education" actually become to-day?

CHAPTER XVIII

THE SCHOOL IN A CENTURY OF DRIFT

The professional, or perhaps rather the pedagogic, notion of education appears to be something which is carried on at enormous expense through the years of childhood and adolescence, and then brought to a sharp halt with graduation from some secondary school or possibly with a degree from some institution of college rank. After graduation the individual is thrown upon his own resources in a rapidly changing world and left to keep track of it and to adapt himself to it as best he can. The education of youth is suffering from over-organization, from over-administration, and from hysterical over-emphasis . . . If the formal education of childhood and youth amounts to anything, it gives to those who are privileged to receive it a taste and a zeal for knowledge. It inspires a curiosity which is, or ought to be, a moving force through life. If formal education does not do this, but simply stops against a blank wall of intellectual indifference and lassitude, then it has not been worth a tithe of the amount spent upon it. The formal education of youth and adolescence should pass not abruptly but quite gradually into life occupation. The two should be dovetailed and not separated by a wall. A division of time between school exercises and discipline on the one hand and ordered, useful occupations on the other is a desirable link between the work of the school and the work of life.—PRESIDENT NICHOLAS MURRAY BUTLER, in *Annual Report for 1924.*

One of the first cares of the founders of the republic was to provide a system of public education under which

216

every child should learn reading, writing and arithmetic. That education did not go very far, but it went straight toward the mark.—HADLEY, in *Economic Problems*.

The work of the schools in the first half of the 19th century constitutes the most satisfactory achievement of the American public school system . . .—PRESIDENT H. S. PRITCHETT, in *Annual Report for 1925* (*Carnegie Foundation*).

A glimpse at the fate of our public schools in the past century will help us to get a truer perspective on the present situation in education. Such a glimpse must begin with the rural and the village school, and must follow its development into the big city institution of the present.

The old-time country school was a great institution. It was successful in its own work, and it was the forerunner of many later developments in our education. For generations we have been thrilled by the stories of great men who came up to their fame through that kind of school; and one of the characteristic notes of recent decades has been the lament that we were near the close of a chapter in our educational history—the passing of the country school.

What Was the Older Education?—But not all that has been said about the old country school was true. It is true that here and there, in country and village districts, educational situations that could be called almost ideal did exist. The country school was but one element in the education of the community. Aside from the school the world of nature was at hand, which through the changing seasons offered infinite points of contact and varieties of work of the household and the farm. The school was but one factor in the education of the growing child.

There were some six years of preliminary play, with the beginnings of farm and household activities, before the child went to school at all. These were not always healthy activities, they were not always wise, or wisely directed. But they were largely free, untroubled activities, in the open, with varied stimulations, both natural and social, and with most grown-up people too busy to interfere with their development, except as a last resort. This had its bad sides as well as its good, but it *had* its good sides. There was not much learning of lessons, but there was much growth and development.

After six, there was a maximum, seldom reached, of seven months of school per year for seven or eight years: one hundred and forty seven-hour days, a total of nine hundred and eighty hours in a year. But a year containing fifteen waking hours each to the day, has more than five thousand hours. Therefore that old country school at its best occupied not more than one-fifth the total of the child's waking hours, even in a full school year. There was some school work to be done out of school, but that was offset by the time in school spent in doing "other things" behind the friendly shelter of the big geography, and by the hour and a half of recess each day.

Education Out of School.—Now, if one-fifth of the total was all the time actually spent in the school, will any one argue that the remaining four-fifths had no educational value? As a matter of fact this other time was spent in work and play, doing things, making things, planting things and watching them grow, learning how to care for them and to gather them, how to store them or sell them; making tools and using them; learning the animal and plant life of the farm, the barnyard, field, and woods, in winter and summer; in gatherings and frolics, parties and bees; in church and literary society; in short, in all the thousand interests of the home, the farm, the neighborhood. There were occasional visits to the village or city; long-to-be-remembered times when cousins and uncles and aunts came from far away and told of distant cities or regions in which they lived, or through which they had traveled; and there were the few books, well used and known by heart, and all the legendary lore of country districts that fed the imagination, even though unhealthily.

There were at least four parts of these sorts of things to one part of school, the year round; and as the years passed, and the child grew older and spent less and less time each year in school, the proportion of these outside affairs to the life in school increased. Not many country boys, after the age of twelve, spent more than four months in school each year—about one-tenth of the whole year. Who will contend that the other nine-tenths, spent in outside activities, was time wasted, educationally? As compared with those far-reaching experiences, the work of the school may have been of minor importance.

No contention is here set up that all this out-of-school time was wisely used, or that it yielded the largest educational returns. But the whole problem needs to be fully understood. We need to ask: What was the real value of the country *school* in the life of the child? We have had enough of indiscriminate lauding.

The Value of the Country School.—Few country boys or girls learned much geography or history in school. Most of them learned a little reading and writing, some spelling, and a meager bit of "figuring." This was the total of the school's intellectual service. The school gave them a start, and little else. Most of what the school tried to offer had no meaning to the child. They got their increase in experience, their mastery of themselves, and their experience-controls outside of the school. It is true the farm was not always an ideal educational instrument. It was often too severe in its exactions, wearing out the joy and the patience of youth. It was sometimes too close to the brutal aspects of nature; it failed to provide substance for the finer fancies of the child. Farm life not infrequently defeated its own ends by killing off all interest in rural life, and forcing children away in self-defense.

The real weakness of the country school appears here. There was little *relationship* between what was done in school hours and the out-of-school life. There was little, if any, vital connection between the two phases of the child's experience. Few boys or girls ever found any relationship between the two. School work was unrelated to the farm and home save in the most abstract fashion. The teacher rarely felt the need of showing such relatedness; most children never found any connection.

If the farm and home life had been less exacting, and school life and work had been more concrete, so that both teacher and child could have seen some connection between the two; if they could have seen that farm and home were giving the child those activities and participations that he most needed for the exercise of his senses and his imagination, the calling forth of all his physical prowess and the building of positive habits; and that the school should have been helping him to get the larger bearings and meanings of his life: that geography should make his home and his farm and neighborhood a part of the great world in which men live; that history should make him and his family and his friends and his hopes and ideals a part of the great story of man; that reading and writing and figuring should put him into possession of the tools by which he could open for himself the treasures of man's spiritual past and the resources of the present, so that he too might become a man, "with power on his own life and on the world"—if some one had seen these things, the country school might have so related itself to the community and the community might have so related itself to the spiritual meanings implicit in the lessons of the school, as to have made every country community a completely ideal educational situation for its own age and place.

Exceptional Cases.—This very thing did happen to a degree, here and there. The rare teacher did see just this need of real connection between school and work and was able to supply it in some measure. Such a teacher made himself, along with the husking-bees and the camp-meeting, an integral part of the community life, unobtrusively interpreting by means of his knowledge the meanings of farm and household work, and bringing the world into relation to the community, so that he came to be thought of, not as a teacher to be shunned, but as an oracle to be revered. He opened the two worlds—of work and of books—to each other, so that each found and supplemented the other in the growing experience of youth. A real education was the result.

Here and there, too, was to be found a boy, or girl, of exceptional power to grasp relationships, who could, instinctively and unaided, make these connections in a more or less adequate fashion; who caught glimpses of the meanings of school work in processes and materials of the home and the farm, and who could enrich and ennoble the work of the farm and the home with the understandings gleaned from contact with books in school. Wherever such events happened, real educational processes were going on. Such children became star pupils, devoured books, amazed the teacher, went on to other, better schools—to college, perhaps; became leaders—and their names are probably written among those who for a century have served the republic in more or less notable ways.

What Is Education?—But it needs to be made clear that wherever such education appeared it was brought about by an integration between the out-of-school life and the work of the school, in which work and study became one in the child's experience, mutually interpreting and upbuilding each other. It is not unfair to say that in this educational partnership farm life and work furnished basic experiences, the school interpreting them into and by means of the experience of the race. No proper praise should be taken from the school. All that it has done should be acknowledged, all that it has earned should be paid.

But we shall never get the sort of school needed to-day until we are brave enough to face the facts as to what school actually means. As long as we indiscriminately ascribe to the *school* all the credit for the educational achievements of the community, just that long shall we keep those achievements from being adequately understood, and thus shall we keep education from being organized in the best possible ways. The country school should not have all the credit for that education which, occasionally, was so adequate, for the school did not do all the work. It did an essential part of it, but only a part of it; and often it did that part unwittingly, unintentionally, and often unwillingly. Not infrequently the best service that the school rendered, or could render, a capable country boy was to throw him out, with a little ability to read perhaps, upon his own native, uncramped resources, to be educated by his work and his hope, his despair and his meditations, his observations, his thinking, and his dreaming, and such chance reading as came his way, until, like Lincoln, he emerged through patient years to some audacious purpose, and to some immortal service. We shall never be able to measure, quantitatively, the part which the country school played in such an education—the education which has been the boast of the nation for a century. It did not play nearly as large a part as has been thought. But we must *find out what that education was* before we can hope to reproduce it in any adequate way under the changed conditions of to-day.

One thing is clear: it was not the school in itself; it was the whole community operating upon and within the child that produced these results. The school was but an incident in that community-situation; important in the measure that it connected its work with the life of the community, or gave it oracular finality in academic fashion.

What Has Become of That Community Education?— In the changes of the century, that country school was carried from the village into the city. It was usually, as we have seen, but loosely related to its community in the country. It was too intellectualistic even there where there was much work and play for children and youth. Then, *with the course of study remaining unchanged,* with the same underlying theory of educational processes and the same methods, that country school was torn loose from such community connections as it had, and brought into the city.

The only changes were administrative. Because city population is more dense, more rooms are needed close together. For administrative reasons these rooms are placed side by side or piled one upon the other, making a "school building." Then the children are separated according to the level of their school attainments into "grades," and they are isolated from both the more advanced and the less advanced.

This "grading" of children is in itself a striking proof of a curious misunderstanding of education which has come with the growth of schools. The ideal grade in the city school seems to be a group of children whose experiences are as nearly identical as possible. The less they differ, the more ideal the grade. That is, the less they can learn from one another the more satisfactory the situation for schooling. That is the theory.

In actual practice, however, children learn most from each other. In the country school, with many "grades," children educated each other probably more than they were educated by the teacher. There was the boy who learned fractions by watching the work of an older class. His interest was not killed by drilling; he worked away until he knew fractions, sometimes asking an older boy to help him. Such a school is an educational community, wherein children of all ages educate each other.

But, in the country schools imported into the city, children are cut off from the vital stimulations from those above and below them; and the course of study has even less concreteness of meaning than it had in the country. In intellectual isolation from the social life of the child and the world of natural motivations, the school stands in the city. Rather, we may say that its social rootages were left behind. Cut off from those roots it hangs suspended in intellectualistic and lonely grandeur, the admiration of all who have escaped from it. Teachers and pupils, alike, daily must lay aside the world of vital interests and human joys in living, and climb up through thin ether to those intellectual fastnesses where, cut off from

home and natural doing, and from the stimulus of working with those who are older but not too much older, they
learn lessons and hear recitations.

Is there any wonder that a sober journal said recently,
"The boy who likes to go to school ought to be investi-
gated"?   In order to get them to go, we threaten to
punish or promise to reward; we plead with them to try
to become presidents; we tell them they can live more
easily than their parents have lived; we ask them to go
for the love they bear their teachers or their parents, or
George Washington; we point out how teachers and
others are sacrificing much for them; we show them the
social advantages of graduating.   We do everything except look actual facts of the matter squarely in the face.

The Great Fallacy in Schooling.—The fundamental
fallacy of the school lies in the assumption that "mind"
needs, desires and welcomes knowledge, and that a thirst
for knowledge can be counted upon, at least in a few
instances.   There is little basis for these assumptions in
actual experience, or in observation.   It is mostly romance.
Few people who have safely escaped from school care
anything for more knowledge.   Teachers care for it only
as it furthers their chances in life.   The average adult
demands knowledge only when it has meaning for his personal experience and even then he gets on very well without it.

College "students" call those who are over-much given
to books "grinds" and in spite of themselves most teachers agree that this is proper, since education is not fundamentally a matter of books, even in college.   How
much more is it a matter of activities other than bookish
in the lower schools!   Professor James insisted that
books should not dominate the education of boys and
girls at least until after the fifteenth year.   We know that

the search for knowledge as an end in itself is mostly a myth. Teachers may delude themselves into the belief that students can work for the ends of "pure science," but the fact remains that their ultimate motivation lies deep in some personal or social need. We are not fundamentally *knowing* beings. Most of us want to increase our knowing only in connection with some practical interest, save, it may be, in some pathological condition of mind. Yet even in the old country school the course of study had reference not so much to the personal, civic, or social needs of the child; it was either an inheritance out of a scholastic past, or it had reference to a hypothetical future career in which a lot of knowledge "might come in handy."

Meanwhile we are blind to the facts. Education is not—the school; that is to say, real education is not in the schoolhouse. Many who want diplomas still go to school; but all who want a real education are leaving school as soon as possible and getting out where they can have the experiences that will enable them to live and do some sort of work in the world.

What Is Education Coming to Be?—Some have tried to keep the schools what they were in the past, "wells of English pure and undefiled," etc. They have insisted that vocational subjects should have no place in the schools: such utilitarian concerns were related to the merely physical; schools have to do with the mind! They have tried to save schools from anything merely useful.

All of us have carefully shielded our children from knowledge of political conditions. Yet all these things are in education, in spite of everything. Boys and girls and youth generally are getting their education—whatever it is—where experiences have meaning for them, or where they can get some "kick" out of existence, at any rate.

All these facts show the failure of a country type of school in the industrial city. That school was a good school only because it was set in the midst of industrial and social experiences that were more real than the school itself. But all such experiences were left behind when the school came to the city. That purely intellectual school which devoted itself wholly to "lessons" and recitations from books had some justification for existence—in the rural community where all the out of school life of boys and girls was spent in work and play, in doing things that had meanings for them, and that called out adequate physical and emotional development. There was education there even when the school did little or nothing.

But in the modern city, conditions are almost exactly the reverse of those in the country two or three generations ago. Under those conditions boys and girls had quite enough, often too much, practical activity in farm and household work. Often they longed for other things; for something that would interpret work to them, and open up the larger world for them. Under such conditions they could endure, even enjoy and make meaning out of, the almost barren intellectualisms of the school. There were few books outside the school, few periodicals, no daily papers, no libraries, and the school offered about the only intellectual opportunity, which helps to account for its historic over-exaltation.

How different are city conditions to-day! Homes are full of books, papers and magazines of all sorts. A branch of the public library is a few blocks away. Daily papers cost a few pennies. Children are free to read as much as they want, and they do read immense amounts; if not always wisely, all they read enters into their education. The schools scoff at this reading, and refuse to count it for credit. But every time the schools refuse to recognize the educational value of the things which children do because they like to do them, they but re-emphasize the fact that their allegiance is still to that old ideal of the bookish country school.

The Failure of the Schools.—The failure of the schools comes from their holding to this older intellectualistic conception of education and their refusal to try to offer a real world to childhood and youth. We all live in two unreal worlds to-day—a world of habits that are traditional, and a world of mere knowledge that has no significance. We *know*, and *know*, and KNOW. We are over-intellectualized in our city life. But we are not *educated*. We are stubborn in our habits and wills, and our knowledge makes us, not wise, but cynical. This is one reason why the call for "moral education" has risen so high in the past decade. We have devitalized the child's world, in the city, by taking away from him the chance to work and play and share in civic interests, and by keeping a school that had meaning in a world where work and play were real. We have hoped to make up for that devitalization by concocting some sort of "moral education" that would fill in artificially what we have taken away from the natural processes of education.

But it seems to be true that life cannot be moralized by injecting into it such extraneous materials as are usually included under "moral education"; or made civic by "civics." The flabbiness of our wills comes not from lack of facts; nor from lack of "feelings"; nor from lack of "motives" (certainly no age ever had more facts or "feelings" or "motives" than has this one). No. The roots of our difficulties are to be found much deeper than popular psychology has ever penetrated. City children suffer to-day a lack of convincing contacts with those natural and social realities which give experience its feel

of reality and which result in habits that make and mold
the world. We have deprived them of meaningful work
and creative play; we have given them months of study
and "learning their lessons"; *the results we have all
about us.*

The school of the city is the old district school, with
some of its intellectualistic evils multiplied. But, this
city school is rooted, not as was the rural school, in actual
work and play and social life in a neighborhood, but amid
artificialities of the same sort as itself. Hence, city children get an oversupply of artificiality and intellectuality.
Since they are not intellectual beings, normal children
soon become satiated, and they want to get away from it
all as soon as possible. They do not understand their
"lessons"; they do not know what they are reading;
teachers talk to children in a language that belongs to
what the philosophers would call a different "universe of
discourse."

This is true all through the grades and in the high
school, although the "great migration" has taken place
before the high school is reached. In no less than 60 percent of the cases of all children in the elementary grades
the service of the schools, beyond the rudiments of the
old three R's, which are drilled in by merciless repetition,
is practically nil. They carry nothing away with them—
nothing of those great treasures of culture which statesmen and educators talk so wisely about; their lives are
intellectually barren to the end. Sixty percent of our
boys and girls never finish the eighth grade.

Why the School Fails.—The reason for all this lies in
the irrelevance of what they are required to do. Meaning is lacking! Yet, the only real reason why school
should exist at all is to be found in the social need of
helping children build worlds that shall be full of mean-

ing for themselves, in which they can find life that shall
be real to themselves.

In the practice of the country school, education con-
sisted of learning lessons made up of "facts." This varied
somewhat, of course. There were teachers who dreamed
of something else, and even tried to realize something
else. But sooner or later, almost universally school work
comes back to a drill upon *facts;* in classrooms of grades
and high school, and on into college, the endless round
of memorizing facts goes on. Facts are not interesting.
We have been forced to hunt for "motives" to get the
child "moving" in the direction of those facts. The child,
the fact or facts, and an adequate motive between them
—that was and is the school. Children and facts seem
objective and real. The "motive" is the obscure thing.

Children do not want *facts*. Hence "motives" have to
be thoroughgoing. In practice they all reduce to some
form of the maxim of the Hoosier schoolmaster: "Lickin'
and larnin' go together." They are all either physical or
mental violences.

On the other hand children do want meanings. Meaning is, for the child, the realization of its own implicit
activities, its own self. Hence, it is not "motive" in the
invidious sense of the word. It is not a sort of engine
outside the child which pushes him into learning. Meanings need no "motives." The child is already "moving"
in the direction of the meaning, and he takes that meaning as he takes his breath or his food.

The city school has long been uneasy; but school men
hesitate to look for the real cause of this uneasiness; they
prefer to depend upon assumptions. One of those assumptions has long been that the school child has a mind;
that minds are capable of knowing; that minds are made
to be trained and filled; and the proper material for this

training and filling is knowledge.   Hence, the endless round of assigning lessons, hearing recitations, giving examinations on facts, and passing or flunking children.

Such schooling has been, at its best, a failure, even with the majority of children, and at its worst, it has been a merciless torture to all but a few.   Children have not always wanted to learn their lessons; and even when they have been "motived" to learn them and recite them glibly, they do not practice the memory gems lodged in their expanding "minds."

In other affairs, men say that failure in results is due to some defect in the instrument.   But school men seem never to have learned this first lesson in logic.   Instead of facing the fact of failure, and trying to account for that failure by examining the whole situation, the schools have contented themselves with two traditional solutions, one of which is pseudo-psychological, the other theological. The latter explanation tells us that the child does not practice what he has been taught because he is "naturally depraved" and "the imitation of all that is wrong is most easy—of all that is right is most onerous."

The pseudo-psychological explanation—an explanation that has taken the place of the theological with many—is as follows: the connecting link between knowledge—that is, facts of a lesson—and will—that is, doing the thing learned—is found in the feelings: if the feelings can be stirred in the right direction that is a "motive."   Properly stirred, a child will first sit for hours drinking at the fountain of wisdom, and then spend other hours practicing all the virtues that wisdom dictates.   The great problem in education is that of finding proper motives. If we could just find the secret we should be able to turn on, in the child, some sort of forty horsepower "motive," set him on the beaten track that leads to knowledge, and turn our valuable attentions to something else.

There is much folly in all this talk of motives. The real lack in our schooling has not been lack of feelings. City children, as a rule, have plenty of the mere froth of feeling and emotion. They lack depth of feeling and emotion, just as they lack depth of knowledge, and for exactly the same reason. Their whole experience lacks essential elements. They lack, especially, what was left behind when the district school was brought to the city. They lack *real* chances to *make* and to *handle,* to *observe* and *manipulate,* to *care for* and *feel responsibility for;* they lack intimate contact with nature in all its infinite variety; they lack rootage in natural experience and activities like the work of the household and the farm; they lack participation in the life of the larger neighborhood with its interest in them, its criticisms, and its supports. These, not the things learned in the schoolroom, are the fundamental things in education. The city child misses most of these things, save as he finds fragments of them. It is lack of depth in life at its fountain-head that keeps the city child from depth of feeling and understanding and will. He "knows" everything—but nothing worth dying for!

A Point of View.— Some assume the school to be a center of intelligence. But there is no realm of human endeavor where unintelligence is more deeply intrenched than in the field of educational theory and practice. But in the fields of biology, psychology, logic, ethics, and sociology, and in the practical demands of modern industry and the civic life, there is gathering such a massive array of arguments, still only dimly perceived, as to startle us by their radical implications for education. The so-called pragmatic philosophy has long portended a revolution in the point of view of all our educational processes. And pragmatic philosophy is but the generalized statement of the scientific method. The "Gestalt" psychology is an interpretation of the same movement in psychological terms. Its educational implications may be summed up as follows: Education implies the activity of the whole being, physical, emotional, moral, and the intellect is the tool by which all the conflicting factors in experience are integrated and brought into order. "Intellect" has long usurped the "spot-light." But life is not intellect. Life is more than facts. The intellect must be disciplined and put back where it belongs in the general stream of experience as a tool of life and not the master. Life itself is bigger than intellect will ever know. We must take some of life on faith—though nothing is unknowable. The vital foundations of education are not in facts but in living, developing experiences—in action and emotion. We care for facts just in so far as they help experiences grow into more comprehensive and self-contained experience.

Even in city schools we are giving up our worship of facts and "lessons," and are developing education on activity foundations, supplying children as many as possible of those elements which the city world does not now provide them, helping them to get something that can be really called community.

But the city problem is very complex. The city school will have to learn how to provide what the farm and the country home formerly provided since no other social provision is made in the city for those phases of education; and since much of the intellectual training attempted by that older country school is now being done by other agencies in the city, the city school may find itself with an entire change of program on its hands.

A Reversal of Theory.—The implicit theory that underlay the old district-school teaching was that the comprehension of a subject is a function of the intellect, and that an intellectual presentation of any subject is sufficient. This theory was not wholly impossible then because the life and work of the community provided experience with which to comprehend the things in the books. But that same theory is still implicit in school work. It is an anachronism, to-day, because the community offers small content of actual experience with which to make intelligible things in books. The failure of the country school in the modern city comes of this transplacement of community experience.

Following the lead of the country school, where, owing to the active life of the community, a certain over-emphasis of the intellectual element was natural, and permissible, the city school has gone on doing the same thing, with little thought as to an ultimate integrity of experience in the personality of the child. City schools have over-emphasized the intellectual until real learning has come almost to a standstill. Our schools have become hives of bookish activity from which most children escape as quickly as possible, taking with them few permanent interests, not even intellectual ones. Nor is the great increase in high school and college enrollment evidence to the contrary. No one assumes that these hordes of "students" want "learning": all they want is "graduation." The school has drifted for a century, from the country to the city. What is to stop its drifting? *Nothing*—except understanding and a program based on understanding.[1]

[1] Most of the material in this chapter has been taken from an article by the author on "The Failure of the Country School in the Modern City," in the *American Journal of Sociology,* July, 1912.

CHAPTER XIX

OUR EDUCATIONAL ACHIEVEMENTS

The American educational system spends its best efforts in the cultivation of "middle class virtues." One of our greatest needs to-day is the establishment of *club colleges* which will help free the regular colleges of the questionable materials now clogging them up. These club colleges, as a matter of course, will have no libraries and no class rooms. They will offer close contact with bootleggers, lots of ash trays and easy chairs, all the advantages of fraternities and sororities, and plenty of opportunity for social recreation.—News report of an address by President J. Edgar Park of Wheaton College.

The American mania for popularizing everything under the sun, the wholesale "dumbing up" of the arts, sciences, philosophies, literatures and music, is found implicit in a political system wherein offices from the presidency down are filled by competitive experts in the art of "dumbing up" the greatest number of abstract political and social principles for the greatest number of noodle-noddles. . . . There is absolutely no place in American life, political or literary, for the man who refuses to "dumb up" his principles, his character and the things he has to offer . . . The written word in its multitudinous printable forms is the gigantic mill that is "dumbing up" the English language and all the ideas it can express to its lowest possible terms. There is funnelled into our skulls by day and by night through books, magazines, newspapers, tabloids and radio the pulverized debris of all the arts and sciences . . . The champion dumbing machine, however, is the moving picture. It falsifies the plainest facts about life and is moronizing the world.—BENJAMIN DE CASSERES.

For three centuries *in situ* Americans have been in process of becoming educated. For nearly a century we have known the work of the public schools. We should be able to show some definite results from these long efforts. Further progress depends upon our finding out where we are to-day.

What Has Been Accomplished?—We have developed a profound, almost a pathetic, faith in education, though we are not sure what education is. To some of us it means schooling and subordination; to others it means something entirely different. This faith has led us to expect some impossible, even some undesirable, results from the schools. Most of us are proud of our schools though few seem satisfied with what they are turning out. But we keep our essential faith in the value of education.

We have undertaken, and in large measure accomplished, a universal school program—a school for every child, and every child, within certain age limits, in school. The curriculum of the schools is not universal, it does not offer opportunities suited to the interests and abilities of the children at every age level and in every sort of community; the work of the schools is still arbitrary and bookish; but they have been on the whole democratically inclusive, making no distinction of sex or class and in the North, at least, very little of color. Some provision has been made for mentally defective children, for the crippled, the blind and the deaf, and for the retarded children of belated neighborhoods and immigrant groups. The schools have been largely free from militaristic and theological influences, though these influences have grown in recent years. In the main, we have been exceedingly sensitive about the character of the political controls of the schools, at least on the surface, though here, too, recent years have shown disquieting trends. The community has wanted *good schools,* though we have never known what a good school is. We have gladly paid the bills, whatever the product, perhaps hoping that our good will would somehow count for ultimate intelligence.

We have developed a rather general ability to handle the simpler tools of education—reading, writing, spelling, and arithmetic, though the army tests showed that our success has not been as complete as we had thought. Elementary education has been too bookish and formal: but until within recent years we had felt that in ability to read and write we were accomplishing what such a program promised. The nation was severely shocked by the discovery that the actual results were nothing to be proud of even from the standpoint of purely formal methods.

We have done a little in the teaching of citizenship; and much for social control through the transmission of customs, tradition and ideals. The latter process has been far more effective than the former—and at present, popular attitudes toward citizenship are not such as are likely to be taught in schools. The school is in a difficult position. About all it can do is to accept the general educational "drift."

In the last forty years, under the influence of the Herbartian and Froebelian movements, we have tried to develop richer ranges of materials and activities for school uses. We have not always understood how to use such materials and activities; and most of them have degenerated either into "fads" or into just a bit more academic material to be taught. For the most part the schools stick to the "good old materials." The new materials have usually become "supplementary."

We have smuggled into the schools opportunities for some of that education which is the product of action and interest. In the old rural community much education went on outside the schools, and, hence, was of that active and interested sort. In the city we have provided some substitutes for those former constructive activities which were so vital in the education of rural boys and girls.

We have made a little provision, here and there, for the proper nutrition of children by means of school lunches; and for school nurses with their instruction in diet and hygiene and health habits.

We have made some progress in practical civics in the school community. In some places the children take part in school government, selecting their own leaders and making their own rules. But these experiments are generally controlled by the teachers in paternalistic fashion. Where the children have a real share, the experiment is usually carried on at the teacher's own risk and is likely to be sporadic and impulsive rather than intelligent and decisive. Usually the experiment breaks down just when something important is about to be decided.

We have done a little toward helping children find employment after school is over. This vocational guidance and placement has not been carried very far, and some of it has been very short-sighted; but it shows the beginnings of interest on the part of school people in making schooling have some bearing on life. Some day this work may have some retroactive effect upon the school itself.

We have some evidence that the school has helped a bit in the promotion of reform and social progress. It is true that the school is usually regarded as a conservative institution; but intelligence compels change whenever it comes face to face with old and indefensible abuses. For example, compulsory education has been generally accompanied by restrictions upon child labor, prohibition of certain types of industry for children, care for children in destitute circumstances, and provision for subnormal children.

We have seen the school gradually extend itself in recent years by taking up extension work, evening schools, and community center development, including a wider program of adult education. Education cannot much longer be kept inside the school house.

We have made some progress in the selection and training of teachers. The public begins to feel the value of teaching and, perhaps, the need of more adequate compensation for teachers. It becomes evident that schools have taken a real hold upon the appreciations of the community. This does not mean that the public understands what is meant by democracy in education, or even that educators understand what it means. A long uphill struggle is ahead for educational leaders who want an American education rooted in the realities of social living, but that rises out of old custom and habit and becomes the social intelligence of the age.

Finally, we have witnessed, since the war, the most remarkable of educational phenomena: the appearance of millions of young people in high schools and scarcely fewer than these in colleges and universities. Few people pretend that these millions are in high schools and colleges for *intellectual* purposes. Few agree either as to what they want or as to what they are getting or likely to get. But all agree that "education" is our most popular present diversion; and it seems obvious that, for the masses of people, "going to school or college" is synonymous with "getting an education." Current criticisms of this recent development seem to mean that we are all going to have to face some years of bitter give-

and-take, and probably some still more bitter disillusion-
ment. It is fair time for us to try to find out what "education" really means.

The Tides of Criticism.—More than thirty years ago
criticisms of American education and of the schools began
to roll up like a tide. For example, Edward Everett Hale
declared that our public schools failed to develop anything properly to be called morality. President Eliot said
that the intelligence produced was ineffective and not
worth the time spent on it. Edison suggested that the
knowledge inculcated in the schools dulled minds that
might naturally have been inventive.

In England the same sort of criticism made its appearance, the educational philosophies of the two countries
being almost identical. Arthur C. Benson and Frederick
Harrison agreed that English education was successful
only in turning out uniformly stupid types, devoid of
initiative. In both England and America prominent individuals went so far as to suggest that all schools should
be abolished.

One English writer, dipping his pen in gall, wrote of
"The Curse of Education," developing such topics as:
Flourishing Mediocrity; Square Pegs in Round Holes;
The Destruction of Genius; Human Factories; The
Greatest Misery of the Greatest Number; The Output
of Prigs; Boy Degeneration; Youth and Crime; Mental
Breakdown; The Apotheosis of Cram; The Great Fal-
lacy.

More recently, Bernard Shaw has been turning his
shafts of criticism upon the schools. He declares that
the schools are prisons. He says:

". . . no progress is possible until we face the fact
that our school system is a hypocritical fraud, cruel,

unnatural, and so incapable of educating us that the voters from the elementary schools and the governing classes from the public schools and universities have between them half wrecked civilization, and seem in a fair way to finish the job."

Without accepting such drastic criticisms, we do need to face the facts. Here are some of them. Census returns before 1918 had indicated a national illiteracy of not to exceed 10 percent of our adult population, and we had naïvely assumed that these illiterates were Negroes, poor whites of the South, and foreigners in our population. However, the most backward county in the country in 1910 was in New York State. The selective service statistics of war time showed an actual illiteracy of from 25 to 33⅓ per cent which was pretty uniformly spread over the whole population;—at least no part of the country was exceptionally free from this condition. In addition we found that about 30 percent of the men were physically deficient. We may assume that parallel statistics for women would show similar conditions.

We have long known that only 40 percent of our children were graduating from the eighth grade; but we had been complacent because we assumed that in these 40 percent we should find all the individuals needed for the higher vocations and learned professions. Now we know that not to exceed 20 percent go beyond the eighth grade; and the 80 percent who do not go beyond the eighth grade are really so scantily educated that one of our leading school superintendents felt justified, a few years ago, in saying that "we are a nation of sixth graders." Recent political manifestations show how superficial is the intellectual culture of our times, how persistent the primitive fears and the behavior patterns that are our inheritance from the ten thousand generations that antedated the coming of schools.

One of the hangovers from our early agricultural civilization is the assumption that preparation for life vocations will take care of itself; that, save in the case of the learned professions for which special schools exist, such education naturally happens in childhood and youth, even now just as it did on the farm; or, if it doesn't, the defrauded individual is, somehow, to blame for his own misfortune. This assumption was rather valid seventy-five, or even fifty, years ago. But it has no validity to-day, not even on the farm. Still it persists, and with it our verbal tradition of a universal "liberal" education. These twain, of one bone, are responsible for the fact that millions of our young people come into their vocational years without the slightest conception of the world of vocations, or any manual or mental training for anything real in the world of work. Hence, they must live either by their wits, or take some incidental employment at low wages. The industrial world is equally responsible with the schools for this situation, of course. Our whole social order has *drifted* into an amazingly complicated industrial chaos; but both industry and the school have studiously avoided taking any responsibility for helping young people find their ways into real work. Voluntary organizations have done practically all that has been done to save youth from complete disintegration in the presence of these bewildering facts. In the main, most young people *drift* into work, or no-work, as the case may turn out. The results are two-fold: industry devours youth because we do not know how to make work educative as it once was; and industry is being handicapped because young people come into it with their minds only partly developed, to say the least.

Our wisest leaders have held that democracy could not succeed unless all citizens were to have real shares in the responsibilities of civic control. But enormous numbers of our population feel no responsibility about even so concrete a thing as voting. Comparison of voters with registration lists shows that anywhere from 5 to 60 percent of the qualified voters fail to register as a regular thing; and but from 40 to 90 percent of those who register take the trouble to vote. Yet voting is but a small part of the whole range of civic responsibility. It is obvious that our present education does not develop a citizenship interested in real participation in democratic government. So great is this failure of interest that many are asking whether "popular" government can be maintained.

Our democratic theory holds that all children should have equal opportunity; and that within the limits of natural ability all shall be helped to achieve intelligent shares in common social tasks and privileges. Yet in spite of this theory many do not accept democracy as a really desirable ideal. An English writer sums up the undemocratic developments of English education in terms that are at least partly applicable to our own conditions. He says that English education is characterized by "perverted ideals, debased standards, contracted horizons, externalized aims, self-centered activities, weakened will power, lowered vitality, restricted and distorted growth, and (crowning and summarizing the rest) a profound misconception of the meaning and value of life."

In general confirmation of this as to America, is it not true that our American school graduates are generally characterized by a lack of any individuality of taste or personal discrimination? Culture exists for them not as an enrichment of their inner, spiritual lives, but as exhibits in museums, art galleries, libraries, and the like. And their attitudes toward particular items, when they take the trouble to observe those exhibits, are determined for them by comments in the museum catalogues or the guide books.

In like manner our school graduates almost universally lack any compelling conception of any individual share in democratic society. Most of them fail to achieve any moral initiative of their own. Their morality is either wholly conventional and traditional, intolerant of change or criticism, and to that extent obstructive of democracy; or it is wholly unconventional, intolerant of the past and obstructive of personal and social growth. Lack of moral initiative may be charged to biological defects, of course. But some of it is due to the uniformitarian results of our mechanical education. And the same may be said of the rebellion against all conventions.

All this means that in spite of the fact that our children have come into contact in the schools with some of the great literatures of the world, have stood face to face with many of the great moral heroes of the ages, and have spent time in science laboratories, they show persistent thoughtlessness as to the values of life and have no interest in the problems of civilization. Multitudes are still dominated by medieval attitudes in morality and religion and have committed their destinies to the keeping of antiquarian institutions, and these have no time to waste on the evils of the world. Other multitudes, freed in a sophisticated way from all faith in anything more than ten years old, are inclined to deny all value to civilization, and are ready for anything that offers a momentary sensation. Thus do extremes meet. There is small difference under the skin between the over-religious and the under-religious; between the too-moral and the immoral;

between scholastics and illiterates. Habitués of all sorts of schools learn to mouth vocabularies that have no real meaning for them, just as ignorant Negroes when they became free, wanted to learn Latin and Greek in order to prove they were educated. The (alleged) human race behaves at times like a cartoon of its own self in infancy.

Finally, multitudes of people still rest in knowledges and ideals which, though antiquated, still persist because they are the bearers of emotional values. We cling to creeds, dogmas and rituals that we do not understand, because they have a reputation for sanctity. We all prefer half-gods to no gods, not being quite brave enough to believe with Emerson that if we could get rid of all half-gods, we might find some real gods. We toy with the idea that we live in an "age of science," but as a recent writer has shown, we mostly think of science as a new form of magic which will eventually save us without effort on our own part. So little do we appreciate the true spirit of science that we find no incongruity in using the radio for the purpose of denouncing evolution. Our minds are so departmentalized that we have little critical integrity left. To that has Schooling brought us! Or, at any rate, Schooling has not saved us from this fate!

CHAPTER XX

HOW WE ARE EDUCATED

Every object in nature is a word to signify some fact to the mind. But when that fact is not yet put into English words, when I look at the tree or the river and have not yet definitely made out what they would say to me, they are by no means unimpressive. I wait for them, I enjoy them before they yet speak. I feel as if I stood by an ambassador with the message of his king, which he does not deliver because the hour when he should say it is not yet arrived.—EMERSON, in *Natural History of The Intellect.*

The improvement of education cannot be made secure merely by better training of teachers. Parents, school officials, taxpayers have the last word, and the character of that word is dependent upon *their* education. They may and do block or deflect the best laid plans. That is the circle in which education moves. Those who received education are those who give it; habits already engendered deeply influence its course. It is as if no one could be educated in the full sense until every one is developed beyond the reach of prejudice, stupidity and apathy. There is no possibility of complete escape from this circle. Education returns upon itself in such a multitude of ways as to render out of the question any short-cut solution. It is a matter of accelerating momentum in the right direction, and of increasing the effective energy within the movement of the factors that make for removing obstacles.—DEWEY, in *Body and Mind,* an address.

246

We have seen (Chapter XVIII) the long drift of the school and (Chapter XIX) the actual achievements in education and schooling in this century of drift from the country to the city. We turn now, with such facts as we can collect and such imagination as we can muster to the inclusive problem of education to-day: How are we educated as a matter of realistic fact? We can never hope to have any critically valid notion as to what a *school* should be these days until we have found out what *education* actually is. The real task of the school, as already pointed out, is a function of the community's total educational responsibility.

When we escape from the narrow concept of school, we find ourselves in the presence of an enormously rich world of educational possibilities stretching away to the dawn of time and reaching to the bounds of the infinite. Schooling, of course, has some part to play in education and there is here no desire to minimize the facts in the case. But we must face *all the facts;* those dealing with the world outside the school as well as those having to do with school.

Education Before School.—As we have noted, the education of the individual begins with birth, or even before birth, and continues throughout life. The school provides a fraction of this totality of experience. Children live two, three, four, five, six years before they start to school. They live in the home, in the neighborhood, on the street, in the country village. They come and go with their parents, older brothers and sisters and friends; they take on language, habits, customs, attitudes. They lose themselves and begin to find themselves in their emotions. Their bodies are coordinated and the emotional patterns of their lives are incipiently developed. If we may believe modern psychology, the patterns of their lives are established before they ever enter a school house. They learn the rudiments of living, and though every such child is subject to the limitations of his own home and neighborhood, he has entered into and been subjected to enormous ranges of experiences before he ever starts to school. Education does not begin with schooling. Schooling takes up the task long after it is well begun.

Education During School Years.—Assuming that the school day lasts seven hours and that the school year is ten months long, we find the child in school 1,400 hours in a single year. (This has probably never been true of a single child.) At the same time if we assume that the child's waking day is fifteen hours long, he has 5,400 waking hours in a year. That means that he has 4,000 hours outside of school; or nearly three times as much time outside as in school. Some will argue that an hour spent in school is more effective in education than an hour spent out of school. This may be true of an occasional hour, but in general it can be argued that hour for hour, out-of-school experience is quite as influential in determining the ultimate outcome of the lives of most children as the hours spent in school. School may be more influential in the case of a few children—of an intellectual type.

If we add together the hours spent out of school in the first six years of life, the hours spent outside of school during the school years up to fourteen or eighteen, and then all the hours of life beyond the years of schooling, we shall see more vividly how slight a part of the individual's experience is the time actually spent in schooling. For most people school life represents no more than one-twentieth of their actual waking hours. The other nineteen-twentieths is "real" life, not academic. It seems preposterous that *education* should get no credit for these out-of-school hours!

The Nature of Community Education.—We must attempt to get at least a bird's-eye view of what happens in these out-of-school hours. If it would be possible to schedule all the experiences of life and reduce them to system and order and present the results in statistical form, this presentation might be more convincing to the academic mind. But children do not live according to statistics. Personal and community experiences do not happen in regular order. They come as they come, like a stream, like the years; and they leave what they leave. One writer, dealing with this aspect of education, argues in normal haphazard fashion: "Every child should have mud-pies, grasshoppers, water bugs, tadpoles, frogs, mud turtles, elderberries, wild strawberries, acorns, chestnuts, trees to climb, brooks to wade in, water lilies, woodchucks, bats, bees, butterflies, animals to pet, hayfields to play in, pine cones, woods to roam, snakes, huckleberries, and hornets." In such a list there is not much order. In this way it is like actual experience. It is certain that many a country or village boy has had just such a panorama of experiences in the course of many a day. It is the failure of this in the city that has precipitated the "present problem of the school."

The Cosmos was developed out of chaos. That method of creation seems the most valid. Education, likewise, requires chaos for development. This chapter will present wide areas of what will seem to be chaos. Let no one quarrel with the facts. The effort will be made to present as nearly as may be on the pages of a book, the enormous ranges and variety of experiences which have their share in the education not only of children but of

young people and adults as well. Lest the reader feel that
this chaos of experiences is presented in this way merely
because the task of introducing order into the chaos was
too great, a minimum of organization will be allowed.
But the emphasis is upon the chaos, not upon the organization. The child who is presented with a ready-made
world by the school is usually not only not pleased or
thankful, but he has every right to feel resentful. He
must organize his own world if he is ever to be a free
individual.

Types of Community Experiences.—Children, young
people and adults alike are continually being educated,
one way or another, by their contacts with each other,
with social institutions and with objects, materials and
events in their environment. Some of this education
tends to compel more complete habituation to things as
they are; some of it breaks through old attitudes, dissolves old habits and understandings, and compels reconstruction of habit and outlook upon the world. No effort
is here made, in presenting these elements of chaos, to
differentiate these two aspects of education.

1. Individuals are educated by the home and family
relationships, and all that gathers about the home, including visits to and from distant relatives, the tales of
other days in the family and family festivals, such as
Thanksgiving or Christmas. The home is still the most
powerful single factor in education. Where the home has
broken down, there education has largely broken down,
and "schooling" has taken its place.

2. The neighborhood, whether real, fragmentary or
merely a series of memories, educates us all. The varied
homes, conflicting family customs, neighborhood gatherings, if any; neighborhood centers of interest, neighborhood play and social groups, neighborhood feuds—all

these enter into and call out our more or less active responses. We are educated by the ways in which we respond to the stimulations of the world about us.

3. The playground, whatever its character, with its play and its games, both informal and organized, educates all who have any share in it, either actively or passively. Here may be found patterned activities and creative plays; crowded conditions which make actual play difficult or impossible, or such generous provision of space, equipment and leadership as may make play the most joyful thing in the world; large chance for participation under conditions that develop spirit, standards, "character," or the reverse. The youth of early Athens were educated in playgrounds, not in schools.

4. Nature educates us when we have access to it. The continuous variety of natural things;—plants, animals, birds, growing crops, trees, soils, the contrasts of day and night, the procession of the seasons, the infinite variety of weather and climate, the starry heavens. Fire burns, bees sting, poison ivy must be avoided; the world of nature is inexhaustible: to some it leads on to the endless vistas of science; others find in it those "elevated thoughts" which Wordsworth celebrates; still others may be destroyed by its "natural" brutishness. The banishment of nature from the modern city is the greatest loss to education the human race has ever suffered.

5. Religious institutions and activities educate. The church, the Sunday school, religious festivities, religious rivalries, religious antagonisms and hatreds, sacred music, celebrations, and many other phases of religious interest have had in the past and still have educative influence in the lives of millions of people. Even those who "have no interests" in religion are educated by their denials.

6. Work educates—work in the family, in the neigh-

borhood, and in the community at large. Work was once
more available to children and therefore it educated far
more than it does to-day; many children grow up without
much actual contact with work, to-day. But whether
children work, or get out of work, work has its educative
significance. (This phase of experience and education is
so important that a later whole chapter must be devoted
to it.)

7. Civic conditions of all kinds educate. The policeman, elections, Fourth of July, political parties, political
rivalries, political and civic conversations and rumors—
all have their share. Politics makes us burn with political
ardor, or with sham enthusiasms, or turns us into cynics.
Courses in civics in the schools may even have some bearing on the subject.

8. The street educates. The endless panorama of the
crowd has inescapable effects upon us. Shop windows,
showing materials and goods from all parts of the earth,
and flaunting objects that we desire and cannot afford—
all this educates us. The casual experiences of the street,
accidental meetings, the sordid objects and activities; the
traffic and the feelings of danger, order, security and
triumph so often sensed—these too contribute. The back
alley has its no less important influence upon us.

9. Travel educates. Early visits to other neighborhoods, to other parts of the city, and later visits to other
cities and other parts of the country or to other lands—
the sense of the world grows by what it feeds upon.

10. Beauty and ugliness all about us educate us. Our
homes, our streets, our communities show us beauty or
sordidness and tend to make us long for beauty or to be
satisfied with the sordid. The countryside, with its billboards shutting out the views, might give us beauty,

though often it gives us little but echoes of the sordid city street.

11. Our group memberships educate us. When we belong to a group we grow into its being; when we belong to many groups we become rich with their offerings to us and filled with the conflicts engendered by them. When we are excluded from groups we suffer and compensate in more or less healthful ways; and we find happiness when we achieve memberships in social classes, racial groups and other stratifications and fracturings of the community. We are largely products of our group relationship. This aspect of our problem is so important, too, that we shall go into it at much greater length later.

12. We are educated by our experiences with authority or lack of it; by our dealings with arbitrary individuals; by orders imposed upon us, by efforts to control us, to break us, or to teach us; by our compliances and our resistances. Our responses to all these matters have large part in our final character.

13. We are educated by sicknesses, accidents, poverty, wealth, pains, defeats—and by all experiences that compel us to consider the conditions under which we live. Under such compulsions we may even, at long odds, learn how to think a bit.

14. We are educated by punishments, rewards, temptations, vices, crimes, inventions, lies, fairy tales: by the suppressions and repressions enforced upon us by parents, brothers and sisters, teachers, institutions, the community. These educations are not always what we expect or what they purport to be; but education is there just the same.

15. We are educated by our longings, our friendships, our aspirations, our reverence, our satisfied and unsatis-

fied desires. Infinite distances and lonelinesses, as well
as sheltered hours and real friendships, help to mold the
ultimate patterns of our being.

16. We are educated by our reading: by newspapers,
magazines, books, libraries, the wisdom and the filth of
the printed page. We may think we escape, but *whatever
touches us, educates us,* if we respond in any way to it.

These are a few of the many factors that enter into our
real education. Schools play some part in all these matters—but never as much as school men would like *to
believe.*

The Chaos of Community Experiences.—Coming and
going through the highways and byways of our cities, individuals of all ages are compelled to suffer or enjoy a
continuous bombardment of chaotic impressions which
sometimes involve them more or less deeply in actual experiences. The street is filled with people of all ages
engaged in their more or less mysterious types of seem-
ingly random activities. Work goes on before our eyes.
We sometimes linger to watch it go on. Business, industry, transportation, pleasure—these fill the street with
color and mystery, and sometimes meaning.

Theater and moving-picture advertisements attract us.
The streets are littered with newspapers and handbills,
pamphlets, books, magazines, each one of which is
planned specifically to catch the eye. Public opinion of
various kinds presses through all this printed material.
"Salesmanship" is after us always. Public opinion is
sometimes sordid, cheap, vulgar, filthy; sometimes respectable and bourgeois; sometimes stirring and idealistic.
We linger by stores and shops and yield ourselves to desire, temptations, hope, expectation, loss or gain. We
want things we cannot have, we have things we do not
want. We are beset by patterns of action which are

respectable and moral; we are solicited into recreations and amusements that promise much and pay little. We are astounded by the contradictions between the doctrines and the practices of religious people. We see schoolish principles of arithmetic denied in the market, and doctrines of truth ignored before our very eyes. We are "cut" on the street by the people whom we should like to admire, and we are denied a place in the group life that we most long for. We have what we have, and are often sick of it. And we destroy our spiritual lives trying to achieve things that are worthless when secured. School itself is filled with both teachers and pupils who long for prestige, position, admiration, conquest more than they long for "truth," or information. The most cherished places in school are rarely those achieved by "scholarship."

We are held in check by herd instinct, and compelled to do the things we do not want to do because we cannot resist the pressures of our groups. We must be "100 percent." We are dressed up in fancy uniforms of fraternal organizations in order to carry through rituals and ceremonials which we do not understand when we are not in uniform. But we enjoy the shows and trappings of the gaudy hour, largely, however, because these carry us back to pre-school days and to primitive experiences.

We share the feuds and antagonisms of the community; we follow the trail of old warfares; and we make ourselves sublime or ridiculous for great or petty things. We accept social activities and become part of the community, and we betray our natures by assisting some corrupt procedure or engaging in some crusade in which we do not really believe. We deny vice and crime theoretically and accept them both practically. We are hurt by misunderstandings of other people and we misinterpret other people glibly. We share the lies and deceits of the community. We are for the government or against the government, depending upon whose ox is gored. We take part in social gatherings, mobs, and mass programs; we are caught in popular processes; we are convinced by what we read on billboards; we attend lecture courses and Chautauquas; we fight as Fundamentalists or as Modernists, in religious conflicts we do not understand; we go to church and enjoy the sermons; we share the violences and the hatreds of the community; we secretly idealize Buffalo Bill and Jesse James.

We accept poverty in the life of one part of the community and riches in another part without question. "It's the way the world was made." We accept corruption in political life as inevitable, but want the schools to teach children the "principles of good citizenship"; we join organizations whose program it is to prove that it is vicious and unpatriotic for others to belong to antagonistic organizations.

Finally (though this is not all), we are all profoundly educated one way or another, by sex, by marriage, by birth and by death. These things are specially true of young people from fifteen to thirty years of age. Adolescence laughs at the schools, having something far more important to concern itself with than logic-chopping in lessons. Sex interests, courtship, display, high aspiration, bleak and sordid despair, marriage, adaptations, the sense of high achievement, the flowering of all the hopes of youth and the creative sense of sharing the cosmic life of the race; the making of a family, the care of children, the disciplines of social responsibility, the gradual transfer of duty to a younger generation; the longing for security, the building of a property, the share in the task of social protection, the interests in education, the fear of sickness, the certainty of death—all these and a thousand other items enter into that total process of experience of which education is the total precipitate.

In all these matters, the schools both cheer us—and let us down. We expect much from them—and lay on them responsibilities they cannot fulfill. We praise them unduly—led on by our hopes—for praise is merely pay in advance for work we secretly fear cannot be done. Then we scold them, equally thoughtlessly, because they are unable to do the things we have expected them to do. In almost no case do we honestly ask, either ourselves or the schools, what they *can* really do. That would be trouble, and it might involve us in real thought!

In short, we are human beings—with the infinite variety of the human race—privately proud to be what we are, but publicly always trying to prove we are something else.

And because we want, publicly, to appear to be something other than we are, we freely support schools whose prime duty is to teach our children to "do as we say, not as we do"!

But of course, schools controlled by us will in the long run do what we are, not what we say. And our children will be educated not by our advice, but by our acts; not by the "lessons" we set them, but by their own responses; not by the schools but by the community.

CHAPTER XXI

EXTRA-CURRICULAR

Poetic, creative, original fancy is not a secondary form of sensibility, but its first and only form. . . . Fine art is older than servile labor, and the poetic quality of experience is more fundamental than its scientific value. Existence may revert at any moment to play, or may run down in idleness; but it is impossible that any work or discovery should ever come about without the accompaniment of pure contemplation, if there is consciousness at all; so that the inherent freedom of the spirit can never be stamped out, as long as spirit endures. . . . Facts for a living creature are only instruments; his play life is his true life. On his working days, when he is attentive to matter, he is only his own servant, preparing the feast. He becomes his own master in his holidays and in his sportive passions.—SANTAYANA, in *The Realm of Essence.*

You have certainly made a fine "mess" of the education of my daughter! I sent her to you because I thought you would be able to protect her from the nonsense and folly going round the world these days. But what have you done? Last week you let her go downtown, here in her senior year, and while standing on the street corner waiting for a car, she overheard some wild orator prating about the "wrongs of the poor." Did your attendant tear her away and take her home? She did not! She let my daughter stand there for a half hour listening to that street-corner rubbish, and with what result? Why, the girl's head is turned. She writes me she's through with my hopes for her. She's going in for some sort of "economics," and plans to "make her own way in the world." You may say that you are not to blame. Well, all I have to say is, my daughter has been ruined, and *somebody must be to blame!*—From a father's letter to the headmistress of a "finishing school."

One of the striking facts about school and college development in recent decades has been the emphasis placed by students upon their own extra-curricular activities, which have, according to certain disgruntled critics, become "the main show," the college and school courses having come to take the position of "side shows." Another equally striking fact appears also, namely, that large numbers of the faculties and administrative officials of the schools have seized upon these outside activities as a means of justifying the existence of schools at all. "The courses taken in classrooms may not amount to much, but students do certainly learn the ways of the world and the roads to success in these outside activities." Well, the fact is obvious, but the logic is not so very clear.

The Extra-curricular in the Past.—As has already been pointed out, the school was never, until within the last century, the main reliance of the community in individual and group education. Always the life and work of the community, the industrial, the civic, the social and religious activities, and the inflow of interests from the larger world have been fundamental factors in individual education. The work of the school has been ancillary, supplementary, providing elements not obviously present in the common life. That is to say, always in the past education has been *predominantly extra-curricular.*

Present absorption in extra-curricular activities merely means that youth at least realizes that education, for most of us, is not primarily a matter of *lessons,* in the academic sense, but of becoming acquainted with and adjusted to the world of men and affairs. Since, however, the school does not know how to provide these important outside activities, they must be provided by the students, themselves, or by commercial agencies of the world. At all costs, youth must be served; youth must have education. Whether school keeps or not is of no great importance, except to teachers, as long as *education* goes on.

The Extra-curricular To-day.—There has been an enormous growth of the extra-curricular in recent years. "Students" of the matter, accustomed to taking "one thing at a time," have tried to find the explanation of this phenomenon in the "decrease of intellectual interest" in the modern young person, or in some equally facile phrase. It has not seemed to occur to these "students" that these "outside activities" may be the perfectly normal efforts of normal young people to organize a world that shall have as much breadth of social interest as the old-time rural and village world had at least. The fact is that, the more industrial and standard the modern world becomes, the more youth will demand means of escape from such a barren world into this world of broadly varied and significant education. Finding in the classroom an equally standard form of intellectual activity, youth has no recourse but to make for itself a world of interests suited to its normal social and moral growth. The extra-curricular is proof of the broadly social normality of youth to-day.

Once these outside activities were athletic and recreational. Young men coming from the farm and the village with abundant physical vitality had to find means of maintaining, developing and exhibiting that vitality. To-day, these activities have become, in addition, social, vocational, civic, literary, religious and intellectual, in the widest profusion. The extra-curricular programs of many high schools and colleges take far more of the time of the students and seem to all concerned far more important than do the "regular" programs. The facetious contrasts between "college studies" and "college work," or between "studious activities" and "student activities" are far more important than the bantering tone in which they are described would seem to indicate. If there are not so many extra-curricular activities in the elementary schools that is because children of those years are still able to find interesting activities at home and in the round of neighborhood life and play, as in former times.

This recent enormous growth seems to be due to the following three main causes: First, the failure or decay of the old-time community, with its provision for interesting ranges of activities outside of school. Second, the failure of the school itself to provide, in its regular "activities" of the classroom, for this failure or decay of the community. Third, the emergence in recent years of a freer and more energetic younger generation that refuses to be convinced by the offerings schools provide for them. Youth, to-day, refuses to accept scholastic chaff as a substitute for education. When youth asks for bread, it wants bread! And when offered a stone, these days, it is irreverent enough to retort, "That ain't bread, that's a stone! Get organized!"

The Psychology of the Extra-curricular.—No complete psychology of these outside activities can be offered here. The subject is too vast. But a few considerations must be introduced, to connect the subject with our main argument. In general, then, there are two kinds of educational procedure: one, education by interest and the participation of the one being educated; two, education by imposition and external pressure. The former method accounts for Darwin and Einstein, the latter for uneducated graduates of schools. Our compulsory schools are almost entirely committed to education by external compulsion, or what is but another name for the same thing, external direction.

Extra-curricular activities are, on the other hand, almost entirely of the former sort. Youth participates in them, after their kind, because they find therein wide possibilities for self-expression and self-realization. They are free to choose, for the most part, and they mostly choose such activities as offer them interest and congenial expression. School and college organization, in the classroom sense, leaves out of account the most interesting ranges of interest—for the vast majority of young people. The student must "go out" for these if he would find them. Of course, to-day, as never before, youth must get its education in its own way—or go without. This fact is not pleasing to institutions, and it is a bit disconcerting to many young people; but it is inescapable, and it is significant of the future.

The Curricular Versus the Extra-curricular.—Now, it is never the wish of any institution to see any considerable area of *free initiative* developing in its neighborhood, or within its traditional domain. Free initiative is always inimical to institutional stability. Hence, while all schools to-day look with favor upon so much of these outside activities as tend to keep the individual "interested in school," few of them view with equanimity the enormous developments that are taking place. It is difficult to outlaw them; that would prove unpopular. What, then, can be done about them?

They can be brought under the control of the institution—in one way or another. Of course, this involves the authorities in various difficulties. To control is really to authorize, and some of these activities are scarcely "academic." Moreover, schools scarcely know what to do with an activity the "product" of which cannot be carefully measured, and for which a definite scholastic credit cannot be set down. "Control" can be established in some cases, for example, in football, by making "grades" in other work a condition to participation. Non-academic "brawn" is thus made subordinate to the more highly academic "brain." But many types of outside activity are too unformed as yet to be subjected to such respectable controls. Other methods of treatment must be worked out.

The most popular method at present is that of trying to find some excuse for making the activity yield credits toward graduation, and thus subjecting it to the fixed rules of the institution. When one of these activities shows sufficient "content" so that something resembling a "credit" can be safely assigned to it, it may be safely even though awkwardly taken into the curriculum, standardized and "finished." Some justification for this taking over of these free activities may be found in that complacent old doctrine that says that all new activities are initiated by inventive individuals, but as soon as the activity gets well established, it is rightly to be taken over by some institution and made available to all the public. This is thought to be a desirable, even virtuous, arrangement. What it mostly means is that what intelligent individuals initiate the public or some scared institution later "takes over" and organizes out of existence. The real interest of institutions, that is, of schools, in these extra-institutional activities does not run to an interest in free individuals and free areas of social activity, but only to the maintenance of institutional prestige.

Values of the Extra-curricular.—The amount of education achieved by students in these extra-curricular activities cannot, of course, be estimated. This should be reason for congratulation, for education should always have a large margin of unmeasurable freedom. But neither schools nor the public is quite able, officially, to look at education in this free way. The old group fear that something may be learned that is not according to the pattern keeps the college dean awake too much nights. "Possible evils" ought to be squeezed out of all these activities by organization and control!

Schools and colleges ought really to learn from these outside activities what is wrong with their inside activities. They will, too—in time.

Now and then, doubtless, a teacher or dean does learn something from these facts. But in general the attitude of the campus is that established ways are right, and that all extra-curricular ways are on the defensive. They are guilty until they prove themselves innocent—and "co-operative"!

Education by Accident.—We come to one final phase of the argument. The main trend of all organized schooling, to-day, is more and more in the direction of rejecting everything that has not been passed upon by some board of educational censors, of refusing to countenance any area of experience within which *something unexpected* might happen. Scholastics seem to feel that the unexpected, the novel, the individual exception is more or less of a scandal. Education must be compact of organized patterns. By the time a child is two years old, his whole future ought to be an open book to the educational tester and measurer. In such ways we should be able to decide upon, and *control* the future of society. It is a noble plan—and deadly!

In all the modern period, down to our own time, education, in the sense of the large outlook upon life achieved by the individual, has been often a matter of accident. The most creative minds of the past four centuries have been, in large measure, non-institutionalized minds, and their "futures" were never predictable until they were past. Even to-day, in spite of all efforts, there are wide areas of action within which anything may happen; within which free minds may be educated by the disciplines of their own efforts to understand the world. This fact is held by most schoolmen to be reprehensible. Most schools long to see the areas of individual freedom and personal initiative in education narrowed. "If I could shake all the personal initiative out of you," said a professor of languages to a college class, "I could then get somewhere in educating you!" Educational psychologists want to find the means by which individual behavior can be predicted, determined, charted and controlled. Scholastic ideals of education, from the kindergarten to the Ph.D. degree, move steadily in this direction. Even graduate studies in our large universities tend more and more to be modelled upon the patterns of stupid pre-war European pedantries.

None the less education by accident is likely to increase rather than decrease in extent and value, even as the world of industry becomes more complicated, as facilities for travel develop, and the automobile and airplane become universal. All such means of travel promise that, in the future, any energetic individual any time after the age of twelve, will be able to escape from institutional control more easily than in the past. The older generation may continue to ask: "What's the world coming to?" Schools may protest and threaten and promise. But the world is big, and waste places still abound, and the automobile enables any one who wants liberty to escape from the Middle Ages in short order. Our highways are filled all summer long with the "buggies" of the "gasoline gypsies." The life of young people to-day tends to become more and more extra-institutional, extra-curricular. Education is likely to be increasingly of that sort. In many universities, the fire-side discussion grows at the expense of the classroom lecture; a fire-place is a great liberator.

Schools must also *learn:* they cannot forever merely *teach!*

CHAPTER XXII

EDUCATION THROUGH GROUP MEMBERSHIPS

"Faith comes by hearing": a man will be a Buddhist in China, and a Quaker in Pennsylvania by virtue of traditional and not racial heredity. He will, on principle, be a polygamist in Persia and a monogamist in modern Europe. In the Congo he will "think cannibal thoughts." As it was not the individual who made society in the first place, but society which created the individual, so the mind of every human being is the product of the society in the midst of which he is born and the age in which he lives. "Men," says the Arab proverb, "men resemble the time in which they live more than they resemble their fathers."—BRIFFAULT, in *The Mothers.*

Always and everywhere customs supply the standards for personal activities. They are the pattern into which the individual activity must weave itself. This is as true to-day as it ever was . . . Customs constitute moral standards. They are active demands for certain ways of acting . . . It is the essence of routine to insist upon its own continuation. Breach of it is violation of right. Deviation from it is transgression.—DEWEY, in *Human Nature and Conduct.*

The primitive child was born into a group. So is the child of to-day. The birth of the child increases the membership of the group, but not by addition. He is the product of division, rather. (All biological increase is by division.) He is product of the group. Just as his physical body is a product of the physical life of the group, so his emotional and moral being and, in large measure, his intellectual life, or lack of it, will be the product of the group's emotional, moral and intellectual life, or lack of it. Society creates the individual. That is, society begins the process, but rarely carries it to completion.

The Nature of Groups.—Groups are of two general sorts, historical or biological, and self-initiated. Most of the groups with which we, even to-day, have to deal are ancient, historical, natural, biological in character. They antedate the existence of their present individual members. The member was born into the group, or he slipped into it in some natural fashion. With self-initiated groups we shall not be greatly concerned in this chapter.

Every natural, historical group has a feeling of its own reality. It exists. It *is!* It has always existed. It is of the nature of things. It has a sense of completeness and power when *all* its members are present or accounted for: it has a sense of precariousness when its membership is depleted in any way. It has its own group-ways, or folkways, and it always feels that those ways are *right!*

These feelings of its own reality and rightness are not usually flaunted to the world. They are implicit, but final. The individual is submerged in the ways of the group and does not boast, save in moments of crisis. Most of the group's processes are customary, and carried on by habit, not self-consciously. This fact makes them the more real, and therefore, the more natural, right, sacred.

The group lives and acts on reflex levels, not on reflective levels. Its acts are impulsive rather than intelligent and, though these impulses run in channels of habit and custom usually, they are subject to momentary diversions that result in irritations and sometimes in explosions. Group impulses may be generous or vindictive; they may be humane or cruel, or they may *just be.* In general, no one can tell in advance just what they will be.

The group has a sense of its own power, which often becomes magnified to omnipotence. Under the "head" of this power, it may run wild and lay waste its surrounding world; it may even destroy itself. But even in its self-destruction it will demonstrate its own rightness.

The group is exceedingly credulous. It will follow its own leaders blindly, into any excess. It has no critical faculty, and when fooled, as it most often is, it is usually not disgruntled or disillusioned. "Theirs not to reason why, theirs not to make reply, theirs but to do and die." When a group begins to doubt its own finality or its rightness, it begins to fail and to disintegrate.

The group is entirely conservative. It holds strictly to the behavior patterns selected and approved in its past; it is averse to all innovations, and has unbounded reverence for its own traditions. The most contradictory opinions can be held side by side in the group-mind, provided those opinions are old, just as they can be held side by side in the mind of the child, or by a neurotic person.[1] The group is controlled by slogans, phrases, words, signs, banners, flags, tokens, symbols of any sort. A flag can sway a group to tempests of passion, and the appearance of a sacred symbol can still such passions almost in a moment.

The group has no interest in what the scientist calls *facts,* or in truth of a disinterested sort. The group prefers its own illusions to anything that can be called objective truth. In fact, the objective truth of modern science is particularly obnoxious to most natural groups, whose roots are deep in old prejudicial traditions and whose mentality is wrought of their own illusions. Dis-

---

[1] Most groups are neurotic in temper, owing to the existence of these contradictions in their structures.

illusionment is not only most painful to men; it is also destructive and blasphemous.

In short, the organization and control of groups, even to-day, is almost wholly on the level of primitive behavior patterns. They incorporate and express not the behaviors and outlooks of critical intelligence, but the behaviors and outlooks of the primitive world. Their own world is *the* world. Their reflexes are right; their prejudices are ultimate facts of the world; their emotions carry the sanctions of reality and finality; and they are "never able to understand" how any one can do otherwise than they do, or hold opinions that traverse their own. All these things make a group very effective in getting things done and in education. They also often make the group an obnoxious factor in the community.

Group Influences in Education.—Groups have profound influences upon their individual members, molding them to fixed patterns, lifting them out of their particularistic ways, shaping them to group standards, opinions and rules. A child growing up in such an atmosphere takes on just the patterns of action and emotion which are the group's. He becomes "socialized," or civilized up to the level of the group's achievements. The group's members are his kin. The group's ways become his ways. The group's enemies are his enemies. What is right to the group is right to him; what is wrong to the group is wrong to him. The gods of the group are his gods, and all other gods are no gods at all.

These results are not merely "mental" in some ethereal sense. They are structural. They are in the reflexes. They are patterns in the nervous system. They are felt in the viscera, and when those patterns of behavior are violated in any way the violator even feels the "conscience" of that violation in the pulse of his heart and his breath and in the "pit of his stomach."   In comparison with these deep-lying reflexes, the later learning of lessons in schools is of little substance.   The child may be able to "recite" the lessons learned in school; but he *lives* the reflexes wrought into his spinal cord by the experiences of group life.

Such education, wrought moment by moment in the processes of group living, is the most substantial matter in the world.   It is so substantial and so natural that it has been generally passed over as not education at all. The "mind" thus produced by the patternings of the group has been generally set down by students as being, not the product of experience at all, but as an innate mentality rooted in instincts.   Slowly, however, it becomes clear that much that has been attributed to "instinct" is the product not of biological heredity but of the inescapable inculcations of the primitive group life.   The enormous importance of this group training is obvious when we see that it is so very effective that students in the past have been led to believe that it is a natural inheritance and wrought of the biological structure of the race.   Our more recent light on this aspect of education makes it not less important but more important: it is so important that it may no longer be left to chance, to the "sacred rights" of groups.   It must now be dealt with intelligently. Group absolutisms can no longer be tolerated—even in the name of biology.   We must consider the absolutism of the family as a factor in this group education.

The Family and the Child.—The family is an historical group.   Its controls are now biological, habitual, of the folkways.   Its dominant interest is in its own survival, no matter what its actual influences in child-care and education may be.   The family has achieved the status of a "sacred" group, and discussion of sacred things is always precarious.   But the child's future is still more sacred than are the prerogatives of any group.

The child's earliest education is in the behavior patterns of the family group.   These patterns differ enormously, round the world, but that fact does not interfere with the further fact that in every variant form the patterns are still sacred.   "Our ways of doing things are right ways."

But the family is related to the neighborhood or the community and the world.   The family has vocational interests: it must have economic security; it has social relationships with other people in the community; it has racial and personal interests which reveal its biological and social heredity; it has moral interests which express its faith in its own right to survive.   The child is early molded to the patterns of these family interests and relationships.   Its first stabilizations gather about the responses to these family patterns.   In most instances the child spends from ten to twenty years in close apprenticeship to these group patterns of the family.   Few ever escape the permanent moldings of those years.   Says one college president: "As young people come to college some of their most difficult problems relate to traits fixed in their earliest years.   Poor health, from the effects of bad physical habits; irritability, selfishness, disorderliness, solitariness, or extreme dependence on others—these often are attributed to inborn traits when they are but the result of early influences.   The extreme effort necessary to correct such defects, even during adolescence, makes us regret the more the absence of that skill and wisdom which would have established wholesome habits, almost as second nature, during infancy."

Other Groups in the Child's World.—The child is born into a family; but as soon as he begins to run about he also begins to feel the formative influences of other groupings. The children of the neighborhood probably play together, openly or furtively, with or without adult interference. He may begin to share, periodically, the meetings of some Sunday-school group. At six, the groups ordained of the adult world for his shaping begin to operate regularly. He goes to school. The passing life of the street will grip him, and he may join a gang.

As he grows older he will dip into other groups: school groups, clubs, gangs, teams, scouts. Furtive groups with awful secrets will appeal to him, holding an exaggerated importance in his imagination, and maybe in his habits. All these groups will call to him, and his responses to these calls, the shapings he will get by the way in which he acts toward them, or within them, the patterns of behavior and emotion that he will incorporate in his being by these experiences will be about the most real things in his life-long education. Few school "lessons" will ever sink as deep into his reflexes.

Educational Processes in Group Membership.—Most groups have been closely knit by processes of selection and survival. They are compact of customs, attitudes, traditions and current opinions so that every part of each group is bound closely in with every other part in a compactness that makes the group a real social tool of education. So real is this solidarity of the group that members are outraged beyond measure when any one acts as if the group were not all that it thinks itself to be.

Group behavior becomes the pattern of action for the child or any other new member of the group. Life for the child is made up of responses to group situations. Proper responses are provided him, if he fails to hit upon them without help. His habits must, as quickly as possible, become replicas of group custom, if he is to be happy in the group. His speech must echo group opinion if he is to escape the heavy hand of group discipline.

Along with habits must go acceptable attitudes. He must be at ease, as one to the manner born. If he cannot find this complete ease in group living, he is either broken to it by severe initiations and "hazings" or he is thrown out as an incapable, or as an outlaw.

For every group the individual later joins in any permanent way, he achieves effective membership by assimilating himself to the habits and attitudes of the group. In the modern world, where the child comes into contact with and probably joins many groups through the years, and within each of which he must develop adequate patterns of response suitable to the group, the ultimate result is likely to be increasing decentralization and even disintegration. Later childhood and the adolescent years are marked by these incipient disintegrations. When we face the fact that each specific set of these habits and attitudes is arrogant and even insolent, we can see what a youth of eighteen is often like: he is made up of any considerable number of non-cooperative habit-groupings, each of which will fight to the end for its right to be and to dominate.

It is to be noted that these various habit-groupings are rarely consistent with one another. They are arrogant and insolent. Eventually they develop incipient clashes and antagonisms, and soon or late, they break out into actual personal conflicts within the individual's own personality. This unsuspected world of "personality difficulties" has come within the knowledge of psychologists and psychiatrists with startling suddenness in recent years.

These difficulties do not ordinarily become known to the individual concerned until the conflicting habits and attitudes rise into consciousness as specific bits of knowl-edge. Not all such conflicts are pathological. Many of them are desirable and necessary to his fuller develop-ment. When a boy becomes aware of the fact that "my family does things *this way*," while "my gang does things *this other way*," he has become aware of such a conflict, and soon or late he will either have to come to intellec-tual grips with this conflict, or else he will have to sup-press one member of it and ignore its existence more or less continuously. If he is ever to have an intellectual life of his own, he must develop it out of coming to grips with his conflicts in habits and attitudes. Memberships in diverse groups always means that such conflicting areas of experience will develop. How shall he learn to deal with these experiences of conflict healthfully?

Group Methods of Handling Conflicts.—These con-flicts and contradictions in experience are natural in a social world made of diverse groups. They cannot be avoided, and they should not be avoided. They are necessary to the future development of anything that can be properly described as the individual's *own* intellectual life. Not to have them is to fail to have the *soils* out of which a diverse and many-sided personality can develop. To ignore them is to fail to understand the natural his-tory of personality, especially on its emotional and intel-lectual sides.

But adult group opinion deprecates the appearance of such conflicts. The group mind never understood such things in the primitive ages; adult minds do not under-stand them to-day, and do not know what to do about them or with them. In the primitive group, they were ruthlessly repressed, and banned, with no understanding of, and less care for, the hygienic effects of such repres-sions upon the child. It should be the function of education, to-day, to deal intelligently with such conflicts and contradictions, but our philosophies of education are, as yet, almost totally unaware of the existence of these conflicts, and our psychologies of education are interested in much more schoolish matters. The Greek pedagogues and Socrates dealt with these matters rather intelligently, without being aware of the problem in any acute way; but Plato dismissed it with the remark (see Chapter VII) that if you tell a child a sufficient number of lies he'll eventually take them for the truth. Mr. Dooley, modern American philosopher, puts the matter admirably: "I'll believe anything, Hinnessy, if ye'll tell it to me often enough!"

Hence, as most any psychiatrist could tell us to-day, the net effect of memberships in conflicting groups in the modern world has been disintegrative rather than integrative. In scme cases the effect has been completely dissociative: the individual has built up his personality in separate compartments, not letting one side of his being know what the rest was doing, until in the end he turns out to be two "alternating" personalities instead of an integrated being. The full story of this type of development is just now being told. But the group never wants its members to face these facts intelligently and thus achieve integration; for intelligence implies emergence from group levels and group conflicts to community levels and cooperations; and no group ever willingly permitted that to happen. As we shall see later, the implication of "intelligence" is *emergence from the primitive group*.

In our older community civilizations, the structure of the community gave the child help toward integration as over against the variant pulls of his group experiences within the community. So he got the advantages of group memberships, but was saved from disintegration. Under the best circumstances his memberships in groups brought him richness and variety of experiences, by affording him many patterns of action and emotion; and the community brought him integration by affording him the support of an organized background larger than and inclusive of all these variant groups. So he secured an education that was, at its best, characterized by richness and variety in details, with all the round of human interests represented more or less; and at the same time by a growing integration of all these details, bringing to him the growing sense of wholeness and real accomplishment, and a tentative place in the whole life of the community.

Where the School Has Failed.—Most of that old community life is gone to-day. Its boundaries have all been broken down, and little remains of it but some fragments of the old institutional structures. These fragments still offer some valuable education, at least to adults. Groups we have in increasing numbers, far-flung along the highways where the automobile takes us, and in the distant villages and cities, now drawn so near. What is fifty miles after dinner to a car that can make sixty miles an hour? We get plenty of variety and "richness" of experience, and so do our children. But since we have no organized community living, we have no way of determining what group experiences are important, or necessary, or desirable, or profitable. We cannot tell, beforehand, whether a proposed experience will bring enrichment, profit, variation in desirable directions, or merely disintegration and dissociation. We have no means of testing the experiences as they come and go, or of using them in actual organization of our lives. We get what we get; we miss what we miss; and the ultimate result is on the laps of the gods—of laughter, or of fear!

One instrument of social integration we have, although we rarely think of it in this light, and still more rarely does it look at itself in this light.   The Greek pedagogue, the antecedent of the modern school, fulfilled the purpose and need of the social integrator in those Athenian days which were so curiously like our own.   The intellectual materials which the school has conserved in its curriculum is stuff that has come out of historical processes of disintegration and integration.   Its ultimate social significance is the *interpretation* of the *whole of life* to the *needy individual*.   Theoretically, the course of study is sufficient for all the integrative needs of individual education.   It is made up of the "humanities," and the "sciences" and other highly recommended materials of personality-integration developed in past civilizations for those very purposes.

But in general the materials of the curriculum are not envisaged in the perspectives of experience.   They are not seen as factors in the experience of the race, every item of them having historical connection with some moment of variation or of integration of individual or racial experience.   They come as *knowledge,* not as *interpretations;* as facts, not as meanings; as matters of information and instruction, not as means of understanding and integration.   This makes them exchangeable end-products of processes, not living intermediate phases of development; the hard grains of ripe and threshed wheat, not stages in the processes by which wheat comes to be. They are finished, not growing, aspects of experience. They are aspects of completeness, not aspects of growth. Hence, they cannot and they do not enter, in any great degree, into the growing processes of experience or of mind.   About the only thing the average child can do with them is to commit them to memory for safe keeping, as the farmer commits his threshed wheat to the granary for safe keeping. They may come in handy some time!

But if schooling tends to end in masses of information committed to memory (and one authority insists that ninety-five percent of school work consists of memorizing) this very fact impels, even compels, the child to think lightly of, or ignore, all his underlying conflicts of habit and attitude. The teacher does not know what the child is talking about—any more than the child does. So, in the long run, he trains with the herd, and suppresses his conflicts, isolates and rationalizes those that refuse to be suppressed, keeps them as remote from one another as possible, and compensates for these isolations and rationalizations by an occasional "fling" which gives expression to what cannot be controlled or forever repressed.

The "educated person" of to-day is, accordingly, one who has taken on, largely in the forms of information, the materials that are called "cultural"; but whose underlying habit and emotion patterns have been, generally, untouched by those "culture processes" of the schools and present, therefore, either a number of "water-tight compartments" of habit and emotion complexes, each absolute in its own domain (so that, for example, a teacher of science can be at the same time a fundamentalist in religion and a member of the Ku Klux Klan); or else they are the sort of wilderness of impulse and desire described so vividly by some of the Freudians. So, the "great dichotomy" praised by Plato persists unhealthily into the modern world.

Of course, teachers are not primarily to blame for these things, nor the schools too much so. All this has been in the drifts of history, quite undiscoverable until modern anthropology and social psychology had uncovered the roots of human experience in the primitive group life, and found the clues to history in the processes of folk psychology, especially in the rationalizations of the existent. The past is not to blame. Even Plato is not to blame; he but "rationalized the existent" like the rest. But the present will be to blame, and the future surely, if we fail to see history and education in this more realistic psychological interpretation.

As for the "uneducated person," whether of the schools, or self-made in his own uneducation, he is usually the final product of the training of some dominant social group—a church, a political party, a job; or of such a combination of groups as have learned how to work together in harmony to the production of a more complex result. The "underworld" turns out some complex graduates, not infrequently having the help of friends in the "upperworld." They are patterned, and "proud" of their patterns. They are not so much "educated," as "arrested." Hence we must pause for a chapter to consider the significance of that type of education, of which we have so much to-day, which has been called "arrested development." Group living and group education are essential to the adequate development of the individual, to-day as always. But "arrested development" is one of the natural results of group education, probably the result that has most often appeared in the history of education. But it is not the only possible result. We must examine it—in order to learn how to avoid it!

In later chapters we shall consider other implications of the argument of this chapter.

CHAPTER XXIII

ARRESTED DEVELOPMENT

Man has existed in much the same state of organic development for fifty thousand years or more; and yet during much of the greater part of that time he has remained a miserable savage. During the five or six thousand years that he has enjoyed some measure of civilized organization, all his arrangements have remained to a great extent primitive, his thoughts have been for the most part delusions, and he is still at the present day in every aspect of his existence the victim of self-imposed conditions which his thought, whenever it is even in the slightest degree rationally applied, utterly condemns and repudiates. . . .

Man has had much to learn, but he has had even more to unlearn. It is not so much with the riddles posted by the Sphinx of life that thought has had to deal, as with the answers and solutions already established in possession and strenuously proclaiming their validity. Man's chief task has not been to build but to destroy . . . Freedom is not, as it has become the fashion to consider, an empty shibboleth, but the condition of human development.—BRIFFAULT, in *The Making of Humanity*.

The concept of *development* is one of the real achievements of the modern mind. In general, such a concept was quite foreign to the ancient and medieval mind. *Growth* they could understand—the growth of the individual. But the development of a species, for example, was something not imagined.

What Is Development?—The implications of this concept, which is borrowed from the biological sciences, have

slowly penetrated into our social and psychological attitudes. Development implies a preliminary balancing of
internal and external factors in the life of an organism,
or in the life of a social group. This is what is usually
meant by the term "adjustment" or "adaptation." Environmental stimulations play upon an organism endlessly.
It responds in ways provided in its response mechanisms.
Sometimes it is unable to make adequate response and
in consequence it is either driven away from its habitat,
or it perishes. Sometimes it makes the new response and
its life habits are greatly changed; for example, in the
life history of the whale, which changed from a land
animal to a sea animal.

The life history of most social groups shows endless
developments of this sort. The human race is characterized by this capacity to readjust itself, i.e., to develop.

Education and Development.—Education is in general
a series of processes intended to promote the more adequate adaptation of the individual to its environment.
The individual is stimulated by factors in the situation.
He responds; and he develops those responses into habits,
skills, attitudes, understandings.

Environmental situations offer an infinite array of
stimulations. Hence, education and adaptation are presumably endless. But no organism is capable of an
equivalent infinitude of responses. At any rate, no educational program that the race has ever developed has set
up endless responsiveness as its goal. In practically all
groups and communities the race has ever known, the
educational process has been surrounded with definite
limitations. Always the individual "graduates" become
adult—a finished member of a finished world.

The community within which that process goes on has
been usually a definitely organized world with its own

finished patterns and molds. Education has been a process of making a "member," a "citizen," who can satisfactorily fit into those patterns and molds. If any particular individual felt the need of going beyond existing patterns and molds, he was either definitely suppressed and brought into conformity, or he was expelled from the country. For ten thousand generations groups were able to defeat rebellious individuals and to hold all who remained members to a fixed level of achievement. This has been and generally still is everywhere regarded as desirable and good. *Arrested development* has been the universal goal of community life and education. The exceptions to this rule have been few. (But, of course, those exceptions have been the most important facts in history.)

What Is Arrested Development?—Arrested development is always a function of a finished physical and social environment. Any social group is, of course, conditioned by its physical environment. The Greeks were stirred by the sea and the mountains. America has been pushed ahead by great natural resources. Every social group in its lifetime builds up or accumulates patterns of action that more or less adequately adjust it to its sources of supplies. Civilization becomes for any group the patterns of adjustment which make for the kinds of security its history, its fears, and its physical and social environments make possible. These patterns become sacred. The one who respects them the most uncritically is a hundred percent good citizen.

That is, when any such secure structure of group life has been achieved, that structure takes on a sacred form and stubbornly resists innovations of every sort, even innovations that are demanded by changes in the environment itself. New ways may offer themselves, but they are ignored; the old ways are the good ways! Groups have probably perished through their sheer inability to change their habits when environmental changes made such reconstructions of habit absolutely necessary to survival. "People would rather die than change!"

Old ways achieve religious sanctions. Superstitions of many sorts gather about old practices. The places in which people live, the highways, the names of individuals and objects take on sacred character. Every such sacred character tends to strengthen the hold of the old ways, to defeat new ways, and to preserve intact existent levels of mental and moral development. Any level of culture or mentality that has achieved finality must be described as arrested. This includes most of the cultures the world has known.

Advantages of Arrested Development.—Such finalities have obvious advantages. A community that has reduced all its living to final and fixed ways escapes much waste and worry. There is no experimentation, no loss of time or energy or materials. Everything is organized in habitual ways, and habit enables the group and the individual to perform all functions more easily, more skillfully. This great ease and skill tend to deepen the impression that this is the right way.

There have been few civilizations that have avoided this finality. Athens is a conspicuous exception. Yet even Athens suffered from momentary arrests. For example, Socrates was put to death as an expression of the fear of change. There can be no doubt that men long for security as for nothing else. "Heaven" is the idealization of this longing.

Disadvantages of Arrested Development.—But any such complete habituation of life is only one side of the problem of human living. A satisfactory life is not possible without habit, but a *human* life is not possible without occasional emergences from old habits. An education that expresses itself entirely in terms of "acquiring habits" inevitably ends on a level of arrested development. The customs of the community become bounds beyond which individual action may not go. The habits of the individual become organized in brain tracts and neural pathways. When these have been formed, they resist all change. Most present schooling ends in arrested development. The individual becomes "finished." He graduates. He *has* his education. In a stagnant world this is a great desideratum. But modern America is not stagnant. Hence, much of our schooling is not wholly satisfactory. It trains for a finished world—and the world is unfinished!

Primitive Arrested Development.—The primitive father trains his son to follow the accepted patterns of the group in all his occupations and also in his ordinary beliefs. These patterns become wrought into the centers of the nervous system. Fear tends to keep the youth from questioning customary ways. Industry and the arts remain static. Religious forms and beliefs are protected against all criticism and change. Youth copies: it does not create. All the sanctions of group life operate to arrest development. When a stable stage of culture has been reached; when finished patterns of group life have been achieved; when the "inner" and the "outer" are evenly balanced, then everything conspires to hold life at this level. Religion, education, morality, social order—all are concerned in maintaining this static level. Arrested development, that is, security and permanency, is the normal objective of education in a static community or group. Whatever threatens this permanency is regarded as a menace.

Modern Arrested Development.—This same tendency is found almost everywhere in our modern world as well. The ubiquity of machinery illustrates the process and dominates the situation. A young man learns a mechanical job: the machine he is to operate compels him to learn the processes of the operation; it also tends to keep him from learning anything more. Adapted to a machine process, he is usually arrested in his further mental development. The adding machine, the bookkeeping machine, the cash register—all provide mathematical accuracy in business, and they arrest the development of the individuals who operate them. A bank president recently said that he would never think of looking among his bookkeepers or adding machine operators for men for responsible managerial positions.

The school, as organized to-day, tends to the same direction. It has standard results and standard tests. It stimulates some individuals to do more than they might otherwise have done; but the average school room does not know what to do with the unusual individual. The tendency, therefore, is to repress unusual ability and to bring it into line with the average.

The Production of Morons.—At this point we find an explanation of one of the curious developments of the modern world which current educational psychology has obviously misinterpreted. The use of intelligence tests and measurements has made us all familiar with the concept of the "moron." Much effort has been expended in recent years to show that feeble-mindedness is a biological trait. It is now beginning to dawn upon us that the modern world with its standardized academic and industrial processes and patterns may be responsible for turning large numbers of young people into morons. Many inefficient people are not the victims of bad ancestry, but of bad education. They were not born to be morons; they have been made morons by an education, whether of the schools or of life, that has resulted in an arrest of their development. Their "stupidity" is the result of repressive methods which made them feel "inferior"—until they actually became inferior.

This does not mean that there are no naturally "retarded" or "feeble-minded" children. It means that the results of questionable educational processes should not be made absolute and then justified by imputing these results to ancestral deficiencies. Here, as nowhere else in education, teachers should have the facts before they play the rôle of Jehovah! The dogmatic arguments and conclusions of all such writers as Stoddard, Grant, MacDougall, Brigham, and Wiggam and the intelligence measurers generally should be put definitely on the *shelf of doubt*. As matters now stand, teachers accept those doctrines at their own risk, and at the peril of their pupils. There is enough arrested development in the world at the best, without arbitrary additions based on a "science" that is too much the rationalization of our racial, economic or social prejudices.

CHAPTER XXIV

EDUCATION ON THE JOB

Sir, it is a favorite phrase of those who boast of what is called "the march of intellect" that things are thus changed because the "schoolmaster is abroad." But I tell you that something far more effective than the schoolmaster, a mightier than Solomon, is abroad. It is the *steam-engine.—Hugh Swinton Legare* (cir. 1840), quoted by Parrington, in *Main Currents of American Thought*.

The biological point of view commits us to the conviction that mind, whatever else it may be, is at least an organ of service for the control of environment in relation to the ends of life. If we search in any social group for the special functions to which mind is thus relative, occupations at once suggest themselves. Occupations determine the fundamental modes of activity, and hence control the formation and use of habits . . . The occupations determine the chief modes of satisfaction, the standards of success and failure . . . they decide the sets of objects and relations that are important, and thereby provide the content or material of attention . . . The directions given to mental life thereby extend to emotional and intellectual characteristics. So fundamental and pervasive is the group of occupational activities that it affords the scheme or pattern of the structural organization of mental traits. Occupations integrate special elements into a functioning whole.—DEWEY, in "Interpretations of Savage Mind," *Psychological Review* (Vol. 9).

Practically all education was originally on the job in the inclusive sense of the phrase. Professor Dewey has

shown that vocational interests have been largely responsible for the forms which the human mind has taken in
its evolution.   There is a primitive hunter type of mind;
there is an agricultural type of mind; there is a skilled
worker's type of mind; mind is not *one*—it is many and
diverse, and mind of one type has much difficulty in understanding another and diverse type.

What Is Work?—A job is generally looked upon to-
day as a means of making a living, and its drive is largely
this economic interest.   That is legitimate; but it is a
partial view of what is implicit in work.

Originally, the rural or village worker got most of his
education as he worked.   He began as a child.   He
learned materials and relationships and processes, as a
by-product of growing up in a community of workers,
and in the later responsibilities of earning a living; and
he frequently became not only a skilled craftsman but an
intelligent citizen through these processes of sharing and
mastering his work and its social implications, such as
the sources of his materials and the run of the market.

Often under former conditions, and occasionally even
to-day, the worker forgets that he is *employed* and he
develops free play of hand and mind in the sheer enjoyment of creative action.   Under such circumstances his
job comes to be real experience.   His brain becomes alive
to the many stimulations of the world and his muscles
grow tired gratefully.   His materials are real.   He feels
the differences between wood and steel and clay; he
reaches sensitive appreciations of the differences among
various kinds of woods.   The world is not made of dead
materials, but things come alive to his touch.   So his job
gives him sensitivity to processes, growths, developments,
qualities of reality, actual goings on in the cosmos itself;
and his being responds to all those goings on—with the

artisan's pride, or the artist's joy. The worker shapes himself and his materials in the same processes.

Sometimes the job becomes manifold, complex, and ranges through the uses of many materials, processes, and activities, through days and seasons, through changes and decisions. To be sure, when his job is nothing more than putting on a Ford nut, it pares down to meager materials, a single process, a repetitious activity that wears out a specific function of his body, denying all the rest of the body, and at the same time over-emphasizes a specific bit of the world, denying all the rest of the world.

Such a job may bring the worker nothing but the counters by means of which he can secure the things that interest him, many of which, though important, lie outside his experience, and which he therefore but dimly understands. Industrial tendencies of the last century and a half have been largely of this sort. They have stripped work of many of its old emotional, social, educational factors, and made it too often simply a job—a means of earning a livelihood. A "job" of this sort is educationally very different from "work."

Modern Industry and Education.—As a consequence of this stripping off of the emotional and educational aspects of work, and its reduction to mere processes in a mechanical order, it has been necessary to legislate children out of the industrial world. It is not here contended that all children were properly protected emotionally and educationally under the old conditions of rural and village industry. Many children suffered great wrongs under those old conditions; but much of the work in which they shared before the coming of the steam engine was deeply rooted in emotional and educational values, both material and social, and out of it they got their real education. In other words, children in rural and village

days achieved most of their actual education by participating in the work and life of the community.

Children in the modern city have small chance to participate in any such life and work. The community has
been stripped of its old-time family types of work; work
is now segregated in factories; and a factory is no place
for a child. Practically all that is left to children to-day
is chores that irritate, and do not educate—very much!
It is true that, here and there, a child has a few tools or
even a work bench, and he can do interesting stunts with
radio and the like. These incidental opportunities which
a few of the children of the community enjoy have value,
but they have not the old emotional and educational
values. The industrial activities of their elders are shut
away from the knowledge of children, and in many cases
children do not even know what their parents are doing.
The real work of the community once so much a part of
childhood that all their games, even, were imitations of
work processes has ceased to play any large part in the
education of children. The specific process must have a
background if it is to be truly educational.

All that is left to children in general in the way of community education through work is that which comes of
watching the casual activities of the street, and that which
is called "work" in the school house. In none of these
does he find the motivation that children used to find in
participating with parents and older brothers and sisters
in real activities. These substitute activities offer him
little that is continuous, cumulative, constructive, disciplinary. He does not really share in them. They stimulate impulses, but they dissipate energy. They do not
provide continuous purposes and programs. Few city
boys and girls ever have the kind of continuous, progressive, disciplinary activity that was the privilege of the

country boy or girl who raised a plot of corn which took him six or eight months, or who cared for a pet animal, which would absorb and discipline the interest and thought of a child for two or three years. The street stimulates, but we are *educated* by our responses!

The academic school makes slight provision for the part of the child that is not mind. Most of his hunger of muscle and nerve, most of his longing for achievement, most of the things that were so vital a part of the life of the rural and village child never come within the realizations of the city child. The city child at sixteen may know many casual, momentary, sophisticated things, but he has slight appreciation of what work, in the sense of shaping materials of the world to social and personal uses, means or may mean. City experiences may make him superficially clever, but depth and reality of experience may be sadly lacking.

The Divorce Between Industry and Education.—The gulf between industry and education appears most tragic just at this point. His job is, for the city man, his most real chance of contact with real things, his one chance of becoming an effective agent of achieved results in the world. He wants this because he is the descendant of generations of men and women who wrought their impress on the world and on him; and he can never quite escape the tingle of nerve which comes with the achievement of real results, even though he may never quite understand what it is that gives him the thrill. But because we have made his job primarily a matter of economics, we have stripped it more and more of all its capacity to enrich experience and to release the creative intelligence of the worker. Work is just a job; and instead of offering the worker intellectual and emotional enjoyment, he early finds that he performs its regimented processes the better the more fully it reduces to completely unconscious habit. At the lowest levels of work the best type of worker is the completely automatic moron.

How Shall Children Have Their Chance?—How then, under city conditions to-day, can we provide children some sense of participation in community and work activities that will call out all their latent capacities? Must educators not learn how to underwrite the years of childhood with some of the old-time work opportunities adjusted to the age levels of childhood? Children must still have chances for real and effective experiences—which will release their wills into the processes of the world; which will unshackle their imaginations and leave them free to develop projects; which will train their senses into ever finer sensitivity and discrimination. These results will be realized only as they have materials of life and the world upon which to test and discipline their powers. They can find such opportunities neither in the academic schools nor in organized industry to-day. The academic school has substituted books about industry for actual work, and talk about the experiences of other times and places for personal experience, itself. The intellectualisms of the schools are remote echoes of actual processes—they tell of the skills, the imagination, the careful discriminations of the good worker on the job in the medieval gild or in pioneer America. All such tales are vaguely real to children; but a child who has had no experience with real things and with creative processes can get little meaning out of mere talk about them.

On the other hand, a child who is forced into the factory world too early is almost certain to be mentally broken before his mind has strength to grapple understandingly with the processes and materials of the job. To prevent this breaking, and at the same time to make sure that children shall have something of the education that can be found nowhere but in work, the community must learn how to provide the individual child, even in the modern city, with the materials of experiences that will release and organize and integrate all his native hungers for sensing, creating, and willing things into being. Such "materials" are primarily opportunities for action upon things—shaping, organizing, relating things, and, bit by bit, coming through to understanding of the world of things, and things in process.

The world of the factory and the world of school are *too much* with us. What goes on inside the experience of a child or a worker is not of sufficient importance to us. The natural world can be depended upon; but the individual experience of the child and the creative activities of the worker do not usually come into being save as the world wants them and makes room for them and gives them the stuff upon which to work. Our schools, our educations, our industries, our communities, must provide particularly for these profound realizations, if all that finer education which is suggested by the phrase "skilled workmanship" is not to be lost to the world, and with it, all those infinite reaches and sensitivities of mind and spirit which have always been the joyous by-products of good work.

It may be said, of course, that the world becomes increasingly mechanical and that therefore all talk of education through work and for work is anachronistic nonsense. Well, economically this may be so. But educationally it cannot be so. The personality of a child is not an existent thing which can be depended upon to develop *inevitably* even in an automatic city apartment, in the sterile formalisms of a residence street, and in the bookish barrenness of an academic school room. Not for economic, but for educational, i.e., for social, moral and spiritual reasons, the modern child needs the chance to handle the world as materials and to share the world as industrial processes. Education by work is not for the sake of the job, but for the sake of the humanity of the worker. The present drift of industrial organization may be fully justified on economic grounds; but the *educational* bearings of industry cannot be entirely ignored.

CHAPTER XXV

RECONSTRUCTIVE MOVEMENTS

The annual return of the epidemic of criticism of schools, no matter how contradictory, is a symptom of unrest. The causes lie in the changing conditions in our economic, industrial and social life. The increase in wealth in itself constitutes a perplexing problem. Children to-day possess material things in far greater measure than even a decade ago. Industrial processes are gradually cutting off the outlets for the creative energies of the people. Speeding-up processes give rise to more leisure, and present another problem.

Educational authorities are questioning educational procedures at every point. In total, however, their strictures are inconsistent, conflicting and self-destructive. . . .

Many of the more recent extensions of public school education answer the needs of the changing world. In music the cultivation of a creative or expressive art becomes the safety valve for the pent up emotional energy resulting from our industrial situation. The analysis of child problems and the diagnosis of individual problems are just beginning. The development of wholesome recreation projects itself into adult life. The development of recreatory reading to occupy some of the future leisure hours of the children is an illustration of the way in which the school is attempting to meet the demands of the changing world.—News Report of an address by a superintendent of schools, Oct., 1928.

The morning newspaper (the date is of no consequence because the story appears practically every morning) tells

of addresses made by two well-known educators before
the State Teacher's Association in an important mid-
western state.   The first of these addresses declares that
American schools are the best in the world, and that the
American citizen and teacher desire to give the individual
child a square deal and an equal chance.   School facilities
of every kind are being widened.   Whereas, all students
were treated exactly alike some years ago, now each pupil
is treated differently in order to bring out the best that
is in him.   The speaker declared that society needs and
uses all kinds of talents and the schools are attempting to
train every pupil according to his interests, in order to
meet society's needs.   He went on to say that underload-
ing brilliant pupils is just as bad as overloading backward
pupils.   The latest trend is to group all pupils according
to their abilities rather than their ages.

The second speaker criticized what he called the current tendency to standardize the schools.   Educated persons, he insisted, could not be turned out by quantity
production methods.

Can Both Speakers Be Discussing Realities?—The
teachers who listened to both of these addresses must
have been a bit bewildered.   Superficially, they could not
both be true.   If the schools are treating all children according to their individual abilities, all this talk about
standardized schools and mass production must be merely
reminiscent of an age that is gone.   What's the answer?

The answer seems to be that the first speaker has fallen
into one of the current fallacies of the school administrator which has been handed to him by the educational
psychologist.   It is assumed by practically all school administrators to-day that when children have been tested
and measured their native abilities have been discovered;
and when forty children all having the same I. Q.'s, say

95, are put in the same class, those children are then grouped according to their abilities and any teacher charged with instructing them will treat each of them according to his needs. Since they are demonstrably all alike, treating them alike will be treating each one individually.

This makes it possible to have "individual education" and "standard mass education" in the same school. So both those speakers were dealing with "facts," each according to his lights. The former was dealing with what ought to be facts, by all the theories. The latter was dealing with actual facts.

Discussion of school reconstruction over the country is in general lost in this same confusion. Mass education is not only inevitable but also desirable under present conditions of education; it secures that development of a common mind through our common heritage, which seems to be the significance of democracy to the school man.

On the other hand, attention to individual need is dominant in modern social thought. How can we have *individual* education and *mass* education at the same time in the same school? This problem is easy to the present-day schoolman. We can classify all children according to their abilities and probabilities; and then we can deal effectively with each such group of identical atoms. A great many schools in all parts of the country are victims of this latest of the "schoolmaster's fallacies."

The Fate of the Compulsory School.—The history of institutions should have taught the world the danger of making or permitting any institution to become absolute in its own field. None the less, America, rather thoughtlessly but with a generous gesture, eventually made her public school system compulsory and to that extent, absolute. The result has been what might have been predicted. The compulsory school has arrogated to itself not only the general task of educating children and young people, but in recent years, like the medieval church, it has argued its moral and legal right to the time of these children and young people. It has achieved the right to prosecute parents for keeping their children out of school. Its absolutism is contingent in but one respect. Parents still have the right to choose the school to which their children shall go.

The school has secured and is happy in this legal absolutism with occasional moments of uneasiness. In the last thirty years, the drift from the country to the city and from the farm home to the city apartment has stripped away most of the old-time educational influences of community life, revealing the compulsory school for what it always was, an intellectual abstraction. That fact was not apparent as long as the school worked in the midst of a real community of all sorts of human interests. "Schooling" was a good thing then.

But it is not so good in the barren community life of to-day. Having taken charge of all the children of all the people, it has little to offer this age, barren of social education, except its almost completely intellectual program, which all must take, intellectuals and non-intellectuals alike.

One result has been that the intellectual materials of the curriculum have been, step by step, diluted down to the level of this bare "intelligence," until at present they are little more than formal exercises; and the "intelligence" of the individual child has come to mean almost nothing but the ability to get by in schools and pile up credits. The utter irrelevance of most school material and most schoolish results is admitted. But we all hope that "something good will come of it all."

Compensatory Activities.—Feeling the unreality of much city schooling, reformers have been remaking the school for many years. One of these reforms has attempted to supply in the school what was lost from the community. For example, manual training and "domestic economy" came into the schools in the last decade of the nineteenth century as definite compensation for the passing of the old-time rural home with its household and farm activities in which the free use of tools, implements and utensils had so large a share. It was thought for a time that these activities would save the city school from complete intellectualization.

But manual training became a *school* subject. Hence it had to be organized like all school subjects; and soon it had eliminated freedom of creative action as effectually as had the most completely organized lesson in Latin.

To provide a new area of free activity in certain schools, so-called "industrial courses" were organized. The plan was set up in the seventh and eighth grades. Three teachers were provided for these two grades—a "regular" teacher, a manual training teacher, and a household arts teacher. It was assumed that these two latter teachers, since they were interested in "activities," would be able to hold their own against the intellectual insistence of the regular teacher. But there is a subtle compulsion in schools which undermines the non-conformity of teachers of "activities" and compels them, sooner or later, to justify their work by their ability to show that their material can be as highly organized as any other material, old or new. Soon these industrial courses went the way of manual training and became "regular."

Other "activities" had to be looked for to save the school from intellectual dry-rot. A series of such "discoveries" has been passing in review in the last two decades. The series began with the "problem method" of twenty years ago. Soon the *problems* became *examples*. Then the "project" method was devised. Soon the projects of the children gave way to the projects of teachers. Then the "challenge" method was introduced. But "challenges" grow stale. Even Falstaff gets fed up at last. So the "contract plan" came in.

We are now in the midst of "contracts." This has been variously stated. In general, the subject matter of any course is to be organized on perhaps three levels of complexity called, let us say, A, B, and C levels, corresponding to three "levels of ability" of children! The materials of these levels are then cut up into units of instruction. Any pupil, taking counsel with himself as to the amount of energy, time and inclination he can command, may contract with the teacher to do such and such units of instruction on A, B, or C levels or on all of them put together, taking his pay in grades. "If a laborer works for *pay,* why should not a child work for *grades?*" An interesting outcome of this is found in what may be called the "calculus of desire." "To get or not to get 90 percent" by getting both A and B levels of instruction comes to be one of the indoor sports of school children in the long winter evenings, under this plan.

If now, we add to all these things the so-called Dalton plan, under which the pupil is free to do all his arithmetic for a month the first week, his history the second week, his geography the third week, and his incidentals the fourth, we have a fairly good picture of the efforts that have been made by honest school people to get around the indisputable indifference of the great majority of school children to the lessons which the generous adults of the community have so kindly paid for for them. Each of these "methods" has brought us to a vision of the Promised Land. But we've never really been able to get inside.

Certain schools have promised a great deal in recent years in the way of individual instruction. The so-called Winnetka system has won a world reputation in this direction. There is however little in the Winnetka system that was not introduced by Col. Francis W. Parker into the Quincy, Mass., schools forty years ago. The Gary school system (at Gary, Ind.) was for a long time looked upon as the leader in public schools in America. Developed in a rapidly growing city, it had too few school rooms for the number of its children; so the superintendent arranged the children in platoons, and work, study, and play could be alternated in a continuous round of these activities. But Gary has now caught up with its school-building program and most of its original fame has deservedly evaporated. It is "in step" again.

In the high school field the Junior High School movement has been highly developed and much praised. These schools, usually including in their membership the seventh and eighth grades of the elementary school and the first year of the old four-year high school, have been thought to be organized in such a way as to mediate the change from the elementary school to the high school; to help young students find their way into the more exacting intellectual life of the senior high school without loss; or to come to the decision that the intellectual life was not for them, and so to be guided sympathetically into some congenial vocation. Just what the junior high school is going to do to the American public school system still remains a question. It can be pretty safely predicted that as long as it remains a school it will do little.

In the college field the quarrel with old methods and attitudes has been on for twenty years or more, but it has gathered momentum in the years since the World War. Certain colleges have solved their difficulties, temporarily at any rate, by revamping their curricula. Swarthmore has done this, following the English models more or less; Dartmouth has also done something, though not as much as newspaper headlines imply. Other colleges have been attempting to reorganize in the direction of providing for special interests and special needs of recognized groups of students. Something of this reorganization appears at Rollins College in Florida and the Claremore Colleges in California. These movements are still experimental and nothing definite can be said about them, but students will do well to follow the developments taking place.

At the University of Wisconsin, the widely heralded Experimental College has been set up and is now in its experimental years. This movement has attempted to revivify the intellectual interests of a small group of students by giving them the chance to study a whole civilization in its entirety instead of fragments of all civilizations in their isolated parts. Whether the American college teacher can rise to the level of this task, and whether the American student will respond effectively to this particular movement are still questions which only the future can answer.

At Antioch College in Ohio reorganization has gone somewhat further and has provided a program by which students alternate, for five week periods, between the work of the campus and sharing some actual job in the world. In many ways this Antioch plan achieves a personal and intellectual reality for the student not found at any other school. This reality, however, does not commend the plan to all. Some "students" find the process too "real" and too slow. The regular course is six years.

In certain other centers, notably at Brasstown in North

Carolina and at Ashland, Mich., efforts are tentatively being made to develop schools for young adults on the model of the Danish Folk High Schools. This program is likely to be thoroughly tested out in a wide variety of communities in the coming years. Although successful in Denmark, the movement has not been operated long enough in America to offer any basis for estimating its significance with us. The real question at issue in American education is as to whether children and youth are still, in this age of efficiency, to be compelled to spend years of hard work educating themselves, or whether we shall be able to develop a school that will *give* them an education.

A Schoolman's Fallacy.—Welcoming every intelligent effort that is being made to deal constructively with the problems of education and of schools, to-day, it must still be pointed out that practically all these proposed changes, from the elementary school to the university, are tainted with the subtle but very real fallacy that they are changes not in education, but in schools, to be carried out by school men in school houses. Education can never be made over in school houses or by school men, and no change even in the school will long persist. Nothing is more obvious and in a sense more discouraging than the fact that all the movements which have been initiated in school houses in the last twenty years to reform school procedures have almost completely been assimilated to the old school procedures and have lost their significance. They have not reformed the schools or education. The school has swallowed them. Until the fact is clearly grasped that education is a function of the whole life of the child and of the whole community of which the child is a part, and that, therefore, it cannot be changed significantly in school houses by school people, but must be

changed, if it is changed at all, in the whole structure of
the whole community—until this fact is seen and grasped
and acted upon, there will be few real changes either in
schools or in education.

It was pointed out years ago by Compayré, the great
French educator, that "to the changing conceptions in
psychology, changing conceptions in pedagogy constantly
correspond"; and that "every ethical system contains
within itself the germs of an original and appropriate
system of pedagogy." If Compayré were writing to-day
he would have to add that "every economic and political
system contains within itself the controls of its own appropriate system of pedagogy." Educational reformers
may fulminate to the end about the need of educational
reforms. School men are far wiser in their own generation. They know that nothing much can be done about
education, since *that* is determined more by the community than by the school. But something *can be done*
about schools. They can be brought more into line with
current methods and conceptions. They can be made
more *efficient.* They can be better organized. They can
have more adequate systems of finance and of "pupil accounting." They can be made to show the sorts of results
that are admired to-day.

Of course these trends may not please the educational
reformers. But—educational reformers will have to learn
to begin their reforms where they can have some chance
of accomplishing something—not in the schools but in the
folkways of the age.

The schools are helpless. School systems are political
systems resting upon the economic system. Most state
superintendents of schools and county superintendents of
schools and many city superintendents are politicians,
rather than educators. This is inevitable—and it is a

step in the right direction. When they shall have taken the next step—a long step—and become educational *statesmen*, rather than educational politicians, one way to school reform as educational progress will have begun to open.

But we shall see more of this later.

CHAPTER XXVI

WHAT THEN IS EDUCATION?

Great and heroic men have existed who had almost no other information than by the printed page. I only would say that it needs a strong head to bear that diet. One must be an inventor to read well. As the proverb says, "He that would bring home the wealth of the Indies, must carry out the wealth of the Indies." There is creative reading as well as creative writing. When the mind is braced by labor and invention, the page of whatever book we read becomes luminous with manifold allusions. . . . Colleges have their indispensable office, to teach elements. But they can only highly serve us when they aim not to drill, but to create; when they gather from far every ray of various genius to their hospitable halls, and, by the concentrated fires, set the hearts of their youths on flame. Thought and knowledge are natures in which apparatus and pretension avail nothing. Gowns, and pecuniary foundations, though of towns of gold, can never countervail the least sentence or syllable of wit. Forget this, and our American colleges will recede in their public importance, whilst they grow richer every year. . . .

Action is with the scholar subordinate, but it is essential. Without it he is not yet man. Without it thought can never ripen into truth. . . . The preamble of thought, the transition through which it passes from the unconscious to the conscious, is action. Only so much do I know as I have lived. Instantly we know whose words are loaded with life, and whose not.—EMERSON, in *The American Scholar*.

Definitions of education are numberless. Commencement orators usually explain that the word "education" comes from "e" and "duco" meaning to "lead out." This definition finds application at commencement time, at least. But during the school year, schoolmen argue that children have to be *taught* if they are ever to know anything. Parents are both proud and uncertain; the public is frequently weary; and the world seems hopeful and hopeless by turns as to education.

Contradictory Theories.—The situation is quite as difficult as it appears in these contradictory attitudes. If the world were completely finished with all its parts perfect and the social order all "set" for the future; and if every individual were just an "immature adult," education could be completely organized; schools could be entrusted with every phase of it; and the results could be definitely predicted in advance. An occasional child might resist or rebel, but the school and the community would know what to do with him! The present would copy the past; the future would copy the present; and the only possible change would come of defects in these copyings.

But it is doubtful whether such a finished world could even *produce* children. Hence all discussion of such an education is probably fantastic.

At the other extreme of the argument we can see that if the world were utterly free from custom, and all traditional organization and emotion, education could be the free development of the individual; and each generation, even each child, could create its own world and live its own life free from any limiting controls, whether inherited from the past, or imposed by contemporary society.

But it seems likely that in such a world nothing could be organized, even momentarily. Hence, all further discussion of "education" under such conditions seems fantastic.

In the actual world education seems to include both control and freedom. Society has not within historic times ever found itself exclusively preferring either of these for long; its leanings have usually been in the direction of *control*. Freedom is an ideal—but in an insecure world control has a comforting reassurance.

Historic Facts.—Education, as we know it, has always gone on in a community. Every such community has had a long historic past, and it is therefore usually quite completely organized in its own forms of habit, custom, and institution, and with its own patterns of behavior. Into such a community children are born. Occasionally, a child has characteristics strikingly its own and a nature that will resist the impacts of community custom and institution. For the most part, however, children born into such a community offer small resistance to anything the community may see fit to do to them. They are plastic materials and the community is made of hard molds. Each child eventually fits perfectly these social molds. At any rate, each "good" child does. Of course, this should not obscure the fact for us that frequently there is internal resistance to these "perfect fits," and an irritation that may last for years or until death.

Education as Community Process.—Looked at objectively, the process of education is simple. The world as we know it is rather fully organized. A child is born into this organized world. It is born into a family, and a family has organization, with customs and manners and ways of its own. The family is part of a neighborhood or community or city which also has ways of its own even though many of those ways are either fragmentary or negative. The street, the playground, the school, are

areas of activity with ways of their own. Each of these
ways has objective existence, and it becomes a pattern of
behavior to the growing child.

Every child is born into an organized world. It is a
plastic organism. It has some instinctive, unlearned capacities for response to the stimulations of the world, and
it has enormous ranges of uncompleted capacities for response to the farther ranges of the world's stimulations—
and therefore for learning. The human nervous system
includes more than nine thousand million neurones—each
theoretically capable of becoming a "pathway" of some
adaptive response. Children vary in their responses to
the molds and patterns of the organized world into which
they are born; but all make some responses—and are
educated to and by the responses they make. Our education is made of our responses to the world.

The organized world exists for educational purposes as
great congeries of patterns of behavior and stimuli to activity. The child exists as a congeries of potential responses to these stimuli. Learning comes of the responses
which he makes. The patterns that exist about him are
stimulations to activity and in so far as his response fits
the pattern, he becomes adjusted to the world which is
the pattern. The pattern is, therefore, exceedingly compelling; it provides a program of action which satisfies
the need of action in the neuro-muscular system; it provides a social acceptance that satisfies the emotional need
of the child; and it provides social adjustment that promises security to the community. Hence, all parties to the
situation are more or less satisfied.

Standard Patterns for Variant Individuals.—A single
group of children will vary greatly in their ways of responding to the patterns provided them by their world.
The community is not greatly concerned to protect these

variations. It is rather concerned to make sure that they shall all make standard responses to the standard patterns and thereby develop acceptable "social" natures. This was the character of all primitive group education, which was always "social," and ruthless, with respect to the individual.

'The conventional school curriculum is a series of standard patterns purporting to "give" mental and physical habits. It is organized for the purpose of inciting proper responses in the children of the community, and thus assuming proper habits. It is assumed that these proper responses will mold all the children in satisfactory relationships to the community and the world.

As a matter of fact, children vary enormously in the extent to which they accept these academic patterns. A very slight percentage of the children take avidly to them; they like to go to school. These become our typical "scholars"; many of them keep on going to school all their days, as teachers. A considerable percentage accept the patterns as unavoidable and use them as much as they can. They do not achieve standard behaviors, but they are greatly impressed both by the success of others and their own failures—and they learn to live and work with their eyes ever on their "betters." The remainder of the children find the patterns either unendurable or unintelligible. In the former case they rebel; in the latter case they fail. The former group may become geniuses, eccentrics, or criminals; the latter group morons, imbeciles and idiots.

The great defect in the method of the academic school lies in its stating curricular materials almost entirely in terms of responses, i.e., *answers*. These answers are all good enough, but they are answers to questions the child has never asked; and they make unnecessary the child's effort to construct answers of his own. The so-called new school attempts, more or less intelligently, to organize its "curriculum" out of wide and rich ranges of stimulations, i.e., problems, which will be real to the individual child, and to which each child must make his own responses, i.e., define his own answers. In this way it offers the chance for creative expression on the part of the children. But of course any such school can never be sure just what answers the child will make; and society will not, for a long time to come, accept an education that lets children make up their own minds in their own ways. To be sure, many children do just that, but not with the consent of the community or the school! And they mostly turn out to be "bad"!

It is obvious that if educational procedure cannot control the ultimate responses which the children will make, it cannot guarantee social or mental results. The community, therefore, cannot be quite sure that these undetermined responses will make "good citizens"; and the school cannot fully calculate how to give credit for them. Now the world wants its children to "turn out well," and the school wants to be able to certify its graduates to the university. Hence, both community and school tend, bit by bit, to change their emphasis. The community wants an education that molds its young to proper responses and behaviors; the school wants to be able to give grades and credits. A school that works in *problems* cannot be sure of its grades. Only the school that deals with answers can be sure. The result is that even the new school gradually ceases to be "new," and becomes assimilated to the conventional processes of education. It is the fate of any *school* that it must come, soon or late, to a conventional curriculum made up of *dictated answers*.

Education and World Experience.—It is argued by some that an education in terms of his own problems deprives the child of any share in the accumulated experiences of the world. Getting his own answers he misses the answers the world has accumulated. But the fact is that children are enormously imitative. Too quickly they demand patterns for their responses. The problem of defending the child from conventional patterns until he has developed some initiative, some sense of his own right to select and criticize patterns, is very great.

This is the supreme test of the teacher. On the one hand he must defend the individual child, in the search for his own responses, from his own inertias and from the current drifts of the community and the tyranny of conventional patterns of behavior; and on the other, he must make sure that the child shall not be either deprived of the stimulations which the world's experiences should provide him, nor left at last drifting about in a chaos which is the result of a superficial search for his own answers. Bit by bit, out of his own experiences, the normal child will come upon the need of wider experiences than his own unaided powers can provide. When this need becomes clear to him his actual intellectual life may be said to have begun in an objective fashion.

This need of help is met by the conventional teacher by turning the seeker into some museum of old patterns. The intelligent teacher, on the other hand, can turn that need upon wide varieties of possible answers to problems, together with the suggestion that the world always has room for new patterns, new answers. In good time, therefore, the individual may find himself working more or less freely in the world of many answers without becoming subordinate to any one of them. He learns how to use the world's experiences without being destroyed .

What Is Learning?—Learning is, first of all, adjustment to environmental conditions. These conditions are physical and social. To some degree, physical conditions have natural patterns. Hills and valleys, trees and streams, birds and flowers, plants and animals have their own forms and call for their own types of responses. That is, they dictate what learning with respect to them shall be. This is not wholly the case, because the human mind imparts invidious emotional qualifications to many of these natural forms. Even nature, at the hands of man, becomes good and bad, clean and unclean. Certain birds, animals and plants are not proper subjects of knowledge. Certain natural processes and functions are specially vile.

Social conditions are, as has been pointed out, almost universally patterned upon past ways and these ancient patterns are almost universally tainted with emotion. Ways of doing things are always right or wrong, good or bad, proper or improper. Primitively, children absorb these processes and these emotional valuations through the actual experiences of living. They do not learn these patterns in the sense of committing them to *memory;* they commit them to their nervous systems. The pattern is before them, and the nervous system is molded in conformity. They feel the emotion and the emotional *quale* inheres in the habit structure so that when the act is repeated the emotion is experienced anew, in some degree, at least.

Long before there is any formal instruction in modern schools, the normal child has absorbed into his subcortical neural areas many wide ranges of community patterns. He has responded to the ways of the family, the street, the playground, and has made such adjustment to these ways as he must in order to live among them; and his nervous system has been formed by these responses. He has taken on the ways of the family, the street, the playground, and these ways have become part of his nature: his "second nature"—his *habit*.

This is what the behaviorist means when he calls attention to the enormous importance of the first few years in the education of the child. Everything the child experiences in later life will be in some measure compelled to pay toll at these sub-cortical gateways of his experience. Everything his "mind" will ever later confront will have a certain contamination from these earlier habit and emotional achievements. Everything the school attempts to teach him will have to run the gauntlet of these early habits, emotions and interests. This is not the whole story. The emphasis which the behaviorist has placed upon these early years may be overdone, as we shall see, but this is a very large and important part of the story. A school ignores or violates these childish emotions at great risk. The community is careless of the emotional fixations of its children at even greater risk.

The beginnings of learning are, therefore, pre-intellectual. They are habitual and emotional. The child gets his early habits and emotions from his immediate world, of the home, the street, the playground.

Once the child spent his whole life in such an immediate world; but no more. The world of the human being to-day is no longer a local world of habit and emotion. We no longer live in a world that is immediately perceptible. We live in worlds that reach far beyond the range of our perceptions. We live in a world that requires *ideas* for its presentation.

Hence, if the individual is to be able to live in this actual world of the present, he must emerge out of the primitive world of immediate stimulus and response, and from primitive domination by the emotion patterns of childhood. He must still know stimulations and make responses; he must still have patterns of emotion if his life is not to dry up at the roots. But his responses must be able to delay until reflection can take the place of the primitive reflex, and until broadly humane emotions can operate in place of the reflex emotions of the folkway ages. The primitive and childish world must not be scorned, as at present, and buried under an avalanche of academic culture which, it is hoped, will keep it safely still. Nor must it be allowed full play to develop into a luxuriant growth of ruffianism, hooliganism, and the like. The educated individual of the future will live in the world of universal space and historic achievements; but his roots will still be in the primitive energies of the race, though the patterns by which those energies operate will not be primitive, but civilized. What is involved in these all too finely spun arguments?

Our Social Aims as Aims of Education.—In our western world, to-day, there are three great aims which are more or less consciously advocated by more or less self-conscious fractions of the community as objectives of their groups, and, presumably, as objectives of education within their groups. The first and most articulate of these groups, in this mechanical age, is of course the business and industrial fraction of the world. The expressed aim of this group is *efficiency*, although it is not clear just how far this group would carry this aim! The impact of this expressed aim on the school is seen in the gradual transformation of the school room and the school system into an elaborate efficiency instrument for doing something not clearly defined anywhere, but religiously sought for almost everywhere. The school organization has become a great instrument of mass production. The superintendent of schools has become the manager of a factory system and, in most instances, he no longer makes any pretence of being an educational statesman or leader; he is, often, not even interested in education; he is merely the symbol of the smooth functioning of the system. When he goes golfing, the day's work is done adequately; and when he is fired, as he frequently is nowadays, the system runs on just as well without him.[1]

The second of these blocs of society we may call the humanitarians, or theoretical democrats, and their express aim is *social justice*. This is an enlargement upon an earlier aim of this group, which was charity, and is far more inclusive. It is, in fact, so very inclusive, that few, aside from the theoretical democrats, believe that it can ever be achieved in any full sense, and not all of them are sure. The impact of this social aim upon the schools is not very clear. The advocates of theoretical "social justice" are frequently regarded as disturbers of the *status quo*, and are often denied the right to speak in schools.

The third of these fractional parts of society is what we may call the artistic group, and their express aim is *creative freedom*. This aim is held at least verbally by all artists (using the word in the most inclusive sense). But it is obnoxious to most of the upholders of the doctrine of efficiency and it is probably quite generally misunderstood by humanitarians. The impact of this social aim upon education is seen in the "new school" movement, and in all such trends as the "project method" in the academic school.

These three aims, *individual efficiency, social justice, and creative freedom,* are usually presented as mutually

[1] This was the testimony of Chicago teachers during the year 1927-28, when the city system was without a superintendent.

exclusive and therefore permanently antagonistic. We are told that we can have any one of them or even any two of them; but that we cannot have all three. We must take our choice.

How Shall Society Choose?—But the fact that aims are conflicting does not mean that we cannot have all of them. Any human society *must have* all three of these aims if it is to persist. The fact that these aims contradict each other is not conclusive. Life is not a logical syllogism. Efficiency may trample upon social justice and scorn creative freedom although they contradict and deny each other. But the resolution of such contradictions is not to be found in denying facts, or in avoiding the issues, or in escaping from reality. Life itself betrays endless contradictions. That is our hope of freedom. Contradictions do not destroy us. Out of such contradictions intelligence has some chance of emerging. We must neither deny nor ignore contradictions—both because that would be a denial of facts, and because modern psychology recognizes that it is only out of conflict and contradiction that intelligence has a chance to emerge. The fact that the modern world holds a number of antagonistic aims is proof of our latent spiritual wealth. If we accept the implications of these conflicts we shall give proof of our intelligence as well. If we try to solve them, we may find ourselves and our more human world.

Community Awareness of These Contradictions.—Accepting then these three social goals—efficiency, social justice, and the creative freedom of the individual—despite their contradictions, or even because of those contradictions, what are the means at the disposal of the community for developing an education that shall guarantee the achievement and progressive integration of these social aims? The answers to this question will not be found specifically in schools, although it seems likely that schools, or at least educators, must take the responsibility for them. The answers will be developed through the years in the development of a human community, and the adequate re-investment of humanity in the life of such a community. We must get back of institutions to individuals and community realities, if we are ever again to have a real education for at least ninety percent of the human race. What help have we to-day?

For developing *efficiency*, we have all those economic and social organizations which call for continuous individual refinement of technique, which often results in the most exacting skills. Schools may have some share in this, for this aim is not too diverse from the aims of many schools; but the real work will not be done in schools. For the purposes of *social justice*, we have something of a sense of justice in the present natures of men and women, and especially of little children; and intellectual facilities for the study and analysis of situations and for the determination of what seems to be justice and what injustice. Some schools are prepared to have a considerable share in these analyses. For purposes of *creative freedom*, we have ever a rebellious younger generation, and much opportunity for escape from the deadlier controls of the past. These facts lie in three dimensions: they imply a world of length and breadth, and also of depth. The life of the community is real. Men live in real worlds of at least three dimensions—action, reflection, and emotion.

Many will retort that the community does not provide any such opportunities as are here set down, and that if it should try to provide them it would find itself involved in the endless contradictions and conflicts implied in such contradictory efforts. Well, it is true that no contempo-

rary community is wholly committed to any one of these
three goals; few have any large interest in the last two;
and none is now prepared to make itself over so as to
include all three of them. But, on the other hand, in
almost all communities there are groups that do agitate
for all of these aims; and it is also true that, in the long
run, whatever is fought for by an intelligent minority can
be eventually made part of the common life. Tradition
and inertia are not eternal. Both can be overcome. It is
not contended that all these opportunities exist in our
present communities. It is merely contended that they
are sought for by larger or smaller and more or less intelligent groups, and that they are implied in the aspirations of all communities. Since they are here, in part,
men will never be content until they are fully realized.

What Can Education Do?—The content of an education that will accept the validity of all these aims and
that will eventually develop the instruments of its own
creative emergence will remain problematic for a long
time to come. It is a problem. It is *our* problem. The
answer is *not* in existence. We must get the problem before we can get the answer. But we can foresee some of
the factors that will have a bearing upon the answer.

Looking at the matter from the point of view of the
individual, we find certain actual capacities which that
future education will use more effectively. The normal
child lives in a world of experience. He has desire for
greater experiences. He would make the world his own.
He early develops habits and skills in using the world.
In youth, at least, he knows no natural limitations to the
extension of these habits and skills. Given adequate
opportunity, he seeks expansion of his experiences, and
integration of their meanings in and into a world that
satisfies his longings for experience. Those experiences

conflict and contradict one another. That is his fun. He wants a world in which there are problems. The child is even now "material" for the creation of this human world!

Future education will be characterized by *creative imagination*. The education the western world needs—and at times wants—is not *now in existence*. That education must, and will, accept the inescapable social aims set forth in this chapter, as its aims, and it will devote its creative intelligence to the task of *finding out* how those aims can be translated into the *means* of their own realization. Future society will be an efficient society; it will also be a more nearly just society; and it will make more room for the creative freedom of the individual. It will do and be these things—else it will be *nothing*.

These aims are contradictory at present, from the standpoint of social organization, which is but slowly becoming aware of them and in which they must contradict each other in a primitive way. But contradiction does *not* mean the *end* of being. It should be the *beginning* of *intelligence*. An education that has anything of the spirit of science in it will accept all such contradictions as the beginnings of its real work. The *end*—no matter how far off or how long delayed—will be an integrated world in which a good life will include not merely bath-tubs, but neighborliness and poetry as well.

It cannot be done? Science knows no "cannots"!

PART FOUR

A COMMUNITY INTERPRETATION OF
EDUCATION

CHAPTER XXVII

INTEGRATION

It is somewhat perplexing to see students acquiring great blocks of information on certain topics, or developing a special technique of study along certain lines, and equipping themselves for industrial and professional tasks in virtue of those special abilities, while the background of their life on which their economic activity will be displayed is completely neglected. The student may pass through his college courses without its being necessary for him at any stage to review the principles underlying human behavior; without his being required to take stock of the hidden source of his own interests and beliefs and habits and moods; without his becoming aware that those moods and beliefs and interests, which are going to give his individual life its special values, have definite biological determinants which work according to certain definite laws, and some knowledge of the control of which may make all the difference between stability and instability in his life. A college education does little to prepare any one to meet the fundamental issues of life. There is a fundamental discrepancy between the possession of an academic culture and the lack of any grasp of the principles of mental health.—C. MACFIE CAMPBELL, in *Mental Hygiene and Education.*

The academic school has always assumed that an "education" meant taking on something pre-existent to, and larger than, the individual being educated: it includes ready-made knowledges, as found in the school curricula, and "preparation" for accepting the world, with its existent moralities, its existent civic relationships, its current religious attitudes, its forms of marriage, and its offered "jobs" in the business and industrial fields. "Education is preparation for life!"

The new school, in its most consistent expressions, insists on the other hand, that "education" is not anything pre-existent; it is something that emerges newly in the actual experience of each child: "education is not preparation for life: it *is* life!"

Meanwhile, few ever stop to consider that, whatever else it may seem to be, education must always be *seen* to be an *integration* of personal experiences, of the world and the self, into *experience*. Children and youth are going to get something from both these areas of experience; they are going to touch the world of pre-existent things, and they are going to develop something hitherto unknown in the world. But, while the schools quarrel, and teachers do conventional things, in both types of school, the children, for the most part, are still torn in two, in the same old ways. The *learning* they take on becomes what Bergson called "a parasite mentality," rarely entering fruitfully into the processes of their development, but always eating upon that development without giving much in return; and the *development* they achieve without guidance from the past leaves them, most likely, stranded squirmers in the quagmires of their own impulses. But *learning plus development* is not the answer. We must find an educational area so inclusive that both learning and development will be found within, as natural components of those complete processes which make up the fulness of experience. Integration must be real, not merely additive.

Integration in the Older Education.—In all the "taking on" of the *race's experience,* however remote the performance may have seemed, there has always been some integrating of personality; in the case of some few a very real integrating, in the case of the many not much, and when *much* not very relevant or real. In rural and village days, *reading a book* often meant much to a youth— but mostly by accident. The academic school has rarely known what it was doing; it was just carrying on, in the expectation that something would happen. The integrative processes it set going were accidental, selective, narrow, pedantic, exclusive, and frequently perilously near to resulting in dislikes, divisions, dissociations and neuroses. The academic curriculum selected certain types of children for survival in the schools; and it selected certain areas of the child's being for emphasis and development. Such areas were usually small, sometimes bitterly so. Selection was frequently determined, even in non-religious schools, by theological and moralistic conceptions, excluding most or all of what was "natural." This is the old Platonic dichotomy: the individual's personality was severely divided between the "carnal" and the "spiritual," or "mental." The "spiritual" should be selected for survival, the "carnal" for repression, suppression, extermination. As we have already seen, the personal and social results of such schooling are now apparent. It was ever a good education for the production of "leaders" and fanatics, on the one hand, and colorless subordinates on the other. If occasionally a well-rounded *human being* slipped through those processes and escaped alive into the world, small thanks were due the system: this happened in spite of the system. The most that can be said for this older system is that, under prevailing theological and intellectualistic interpretations of life and the world, men's practices were often more humane than their theories, and the race did not entirely perish in the relentless intentions of the system.

Integration in the New Schools.—The newer education stands for "the development of individual personality." Does this mean the actual *integration* of personality? Not always. Integration implies an effort on the part of educators to make sure that all phases of experience shall be taken into account. The new education, in its emphasis upon "individual development," usually sees things in a too narrow perspective. It does not see the part played in individual growth by the whole life of the community. It sees development as too narrowly "subcutaneous"—inside the skin of the individual. The individual so developed will be integrated within himself, and he may be colorful, interesting, and more strictly "himself." But the implications of such development are *individualistic*, atomistic, not social. It may be that future social orders will be made of social atoms, grains of sand. It may be that in the future struggles for survival, the atomistic individual will be the one to survive. That will be something new in the world. The grounds of prophecy are ever precarious. It seems likely, however, that if we are to have a human *society* at all in the future, the "unit" of that society will not be merely a social atom. Time alone can tell.

Integration of Modern Stimuli.—Meanwhile the world at present is much of a chaos, with infinite variations in feelings, emotions, activities, attitudes, and even some bits of "thinking," but with few patterns of richly human organization, even in the family, or the church, or the state. Our institutions seem "washed out." Business affords us some patterns, and industry, too; but those patterns are very narrow, "specialized," thin. They make us efficient, but they do not make us thoughtful, imaginative, humane, sympathetic, broadly interesting. The modern world is rich in stimulations—richer than

any age the world has ever known. But the education
that results from these wide ranges of stimulations is not
always equally rich. The world dissipates us and our
energies, and does not quite know how to conserve the
values suggested in these wide areas of stimulation. We
feel the pulls of the world, and we respond scatteringly,
not knowing what these pulls mean, and therefore not
having adequate responses. We turn hopefully to old
institutions for help, only to find that their advices are
mostly antiquated. We read all the latest books—the
"masterpieces" that have been produced in the last six
months—and are highly exalted and then "let down,"
without recourse. We develop new instruments, religions, schools, parties, societies, arts, and art movements,
only to find in the end that we have further depleted our
emotions. We revel in sensations; we squander emotions
like drunken sailors; we save little but memories from
the débris.

The task of life to-day, from the standpoint of education, is this: to accept all the world offers in the way of
stimulation and release of energies and emotions, but to
see that stimulation and release are but part of the
process of living; to seek also to find means, in renewed
institutions and in community living, by which all these
stimulations and releases may be wrought into integrated
personality through the years of childhood, youth and
maturity.

No one knows, to-day, how this is to be done. Most
of us are afraid of the wide implications of the task. It
seems to implicate us with cosmic forces, with universal
patterns, with pasts and presents and futures, instead of
leaving us happy in the possession of a few well-organized
institutions, like the school, and a past that tells us what
to do. We are both ignorant, and wise in ways that are

wrong. We need imagination that can, provisionally, take the place of knowledge, as hypotheses take the place of knowledge, temporarily, in the scientist's experimentations.

Education is always a *wholeness* of experience, never a part, or a detail. If we are given details and nothing else, we do not wait for the "other details" in order that we may construct a whole. We have no way of knowing that there are "other details"; or if we should find that out, we do not know how many "others" there are. We can do but one thing, namely, make the detail that is offered us take on the semblance of a whole experience. Of course, this gets things all mixed up later, but that is the fault of the teacher, not of the pupil. For all the future, education must take closer account of this fundamental of psychology. Mental development is not made of details. It is made of wholes, and *the whole is never the sum of parts;* it antedates its parts, and is always larger than the sum of its parts.

In this final Part IV of this book, we shall consider the future of education in the light of such imagination as we can summon to our assistance. Here nothing is final, everything is prophetic. The way of the prophet is ever precarious. Discoverers will later show wherein the prophet erred. But still later discoverers will show wherein the earlier discoverers erred, so the score will be even. We shall not here be looking for *answers*. We do not now need *answers*. We need to become aware of the *problem*, or the *problems*. We need provisional trails into the unknown, suggestions for investigations that rise beyond the academic, and something perhaps in the way of a great hypothesis, the framework of the future within which educational progress will likely get ahead. To such provisional statements as seem probable we now turn.

CHAPTER XXVIII

THE NEEDS OF CHILDHOOD AND YOUTH

Greeting his pupils, the master asked:
What would you learn of me?
And the reply came:
How shall we care for our bodies?
How shall we rear our children?
How shall we work together?
How shall we live with our fellow men?
How shall we play?
For what shall we live?
And the teacher pondered these words, and sorrow was in his heart, for his own learning touched not these things.—Foreword to Chapman and Counts' *Principles of Education.*

Whatever the facts may be in other lands, young Danes develop serious interest in questions about life and the world . . . They want to know what meanings life has, if any, and if any one can tell them; they want light as to their own proper vocations in the world, if they are to have vocations; they want to know the meanings of the relentless sex-hungers that gnaw at their bodies and minds; they want to get some sense of their own relationships, or lack of relationships, to the age in which they live and, maybe, to the ages; and for a short while, at least, many of them are curious, and some are afraid, in the presence of the mystery of death. . . . The student feels that he has a right to have his own questions . . . that not to ask them is to suffer partial death, and that not to be permitted to ask them is a sort of spiritual murder; and that all things else are significant in the

331

measure they help us answer the questions of life and work, of love and happiness.—JOSEPH K. HART, in *Light from the North.*

Our first irritable response to questions as to the needs of childhood and youth may be that childhood and youth need what the world has decided they should have, namely, the things which our social institutions offer them. Maybe so; but young people are not, these days, taking these offerings with overwhelming enthusiasm. And when they are asked what they themselves most want, their answers do not always agree with those of the older generation.

Underneath All Institutions.—Hence, in this chapter we shall deal with this question as if there were no institutions; that is to say, we shall try to discover what it is childhood and youth need in their own right. The list will cover a number of specific items. It is by no means complete; it is merely suggestive:

1. HEALTH. Childhood needs vital, natural, abounding, self-forgetful health. Not scared health; not self-conscious health; but health habits that are automatic, and a feel of health that is real. Hence, children need a healthful community, a community that is healthful physically, mentally, morally; a *whole*-some world in which to develop wholeness of living.

2. NATURE. They need nature and the chance to be natural. The implications of this statement are not as narrow as they seem to be. This is not a lesson to be assigned. It is a state of mind to be lived, as will later appear. It may be that art and statistics will some day supersede nature, but that day is not yet.

3. PLAY. They need the chance to play with all the abandon of natural creatures. Intelligent communities provide the means of play and social recreations suited

to the age levels of childhood and youth. *Education* is impossible without play!

4. WORK. They need contact with the work that is going on in the world and in good time the chance to dabble in that work, and then to participate in it while they are exploring the world and getting some feeling for the vocations of life in which they are all to share. The fact that the modern world makes no provision for such a program does not settle the matter. *Education* is impossible without work!

5. PEOPLE. They need people; that is, they need to experience social contacts and feel social relationships with people of their own age and of older ages in natural gives and takes. A modern *school grade* is a barren world.

6. ADVENTURE. They need real adventure and endless planning for vigorous, stimulating adventures that will stir their imaginations and thrill their nervous systems healthfully, and enable them to develop the emotional discipline that can meet life wholesomely. Most city adventurings are unwholesome for children. The essence of *science* is adventure!

7. BEAUTY. They need beauty in their homes, in the neighborhood, in schools and churches, in the whole life of the community; and in their own lives in the forms of wonder and happiness and quiet and expectation. Life without beauty is brutish.

8. PROBLEMS. They need problems suited to their age-levels—problems which must be met and which cannot be dodged; problems for eyes and hands and brains to solve; problems not out of books or set by teachers, but problems out of life and materials and developed within their own years. There can be no *intelligence* without problems!

9. ENTHUSIASMS. They need enthusiasms and the chance to love interests and individuals profoundly; and probably the chance to hate some things as well. But these loves and hates should be real—not something foisted upon them.

10. WONDER. They need a bit of wonder: intimations of unrealized experience to come, and some sense that there are larger things in life than the things they already know. That is, they need to have feeling for an objective world, with reverence in the presence of that world, but not a fatal subordination to the *status quo* in nature or in society.

11. CIVIC EXPERIENCES. They need the chance to have actual civic experiences and in due time to be confronted with civic responsibilities which are not snatched away from them at the very moment when these responsibilities are most real, as is usually the case to-day, especially in the so-called "school civics." They must learn to be civic by being civic. This can't be *taught* out of books. It must be learned in actual experiences.

12. KNOWLEDGE. They need, bit by bit, to develop knowledge. This, of course, is inevitable. But most knowledge should rise out of their own experience with things and conditions, and it should be knowledge that calls for the larger knowledge of the race and that leads to understanding of the world in which they live. Knowledge should *thrill*, not stupefy, children!

13. NATURAL ESCAPES. They need escapes from their own too narrow individualisms and peculiarities into a wholesome social life in the community and world: from institutionalism into the larger world; from the too narrow present into some sense of the past and the future. Most childish escapes to-day tend to be pathological

rather than healthful. In cities children have to live too close to their parents and the adult world.

14. HABITS. They need underlying structures of habit which will gradually organize into useful skills and social assurance, and which will emerge into a real vocation and a share in the economic life of the world that will bring satisfaction to mind and spirit because of its reality.

15. SYMPATHY. They need the gradual development of sympathies and sentiments which enrich into the feeling of a humanity that is big enough to save them from sectarian dogmatisms and partisanships.

16. CRITICAL TECHNIQUES. They need, as they come through adolescence, and into the early years of maturity, to develop technique and skill in the handling of problems, facing their own conflicts, so that with experience they will become masters of themselves and of their part of the human world in which they are to live.

17. IDEALS. They need ideals that shall be compelling and real: ideals of freedom and progress and law; of truth and beauty; of knowledge and moral excellence; of science; of humanity and religion: ideals that will lift them above petty things into the realm of ethical realities.

18. INTELLECTUAL MASTERY. They need to begin to have, say at eighteen or nineteen, some sense of beginning to achieve intellectual power, and the larger freedom that comes of this sense of power; a technique of thinking that can release them from antiquated habit on the one hand, and from mere rebellion against habit on the other; that can give them the courage to be creative of new habits at need, new institutional relationships, new personal worlds, even as the men and women of history whom they are taught to honor have been creative personalities.

19. The Defense of a Community. All children begin with group support, the family group. Until they are organized, i.e., mature, they will continue to need social support. But where shall they find this neighborhood or community support and defense, to-day? They will grow completely *human* only as they have a human world into which to grow. They need communities that can grow with their growing needs from childhood until maturity and well-ordered personal lives are reached. To-day, mostly, they soon lose all touch with anything of the nature of a community, and most of them spend their lives in some fragment of a world. We shall see more of this presently.

These then are some of the needs of childhood and youth. It will be seen that most of these needs cannot be met in schools. They will be supplied to childhood and youth, if at all, in some thoughtful reorganization of the world which will bring back to us something of that former *community life*—which was everywhere the soil of human growth until the development of modern industry brought about the disintegration of all things old and set up the reign of a devastating "individualism" in the world. This cannot be done? Then education will continue to be scholasticism to the end of time.

In order to make this whole subject a bit clearer, specific comment must be offered on a number of these needs here listed. Each of them should be discussed at length, but space will not permit.

Unconscious Education.—The most effective education most of us ever experience happens to us when we do not know we are being educated. Some take their conscious efforts to "get an education" very seriously—from two to four percent of the population. Most of us are shaped, for good or ill, by the things that happen to us. We are the victims of the happenings provided or allowed by our community situations. We are molded by the organized, or now mostly disorganized, life of our communities. A "propagandist" is one who arranges conditions so that the attitudes he wants us to accept will seem to have come to us in the most natural fashion. We are "taught" more or less by schools; but we are *educated* by ten thousand items never found in schools.

The home and the family as a social institution works from earliest infancy to the end of life, one way or another, upon almost all of us. Whatever its practical influences upon its children may turn out to be—and homes destroy as well as conserve childhood—"the home" is a profound influence as an ideal, all through life. In the later years of adolescence and during early maturity it has for most a reality and a stimulus hard to escape, as we stand between the home of childhood and the new home of our later, creative years.

One of the most effective educational forces is sex, with all the experiences that gather around this cosmic impulse. The imaginings both beautiful and sodden; the realizations both poignant and disillusioning; the ultimate habits, constructive and destructive; the institutional forms, or lack of them, that come with our mature years.

Conflict of the Generations.—With the passing years, the establishment of a new home, and the coming of children, a profound question arises and must be settled, namely, which generation is to lead, the adult with his ancient and sacred ignorance and much knowledge that isn't so; or the children with their new and essential impulses, most of which are so superbly arrogant and ignorant? If the parents bring up the children there is usually no progress. There is mere repetition of all the conventionalities and banalities which the past has enforced upon its children. But if the children bring up the parents, the old patterns of life may be made over and the world may move on a bit.

Nature and City Life.—Nature, using the term as a sort of blanket for all the stimulations that come to children in the open world, is the great call to adventure. The modern city largely fails us here. The out of doors was once a normal means of escape for children from the repressions and suppressions of the family and the social world. To be sure, parents and teachers and preachers did what they could to make nature fearsome, filling the woods with bugaboos and the fields with snakes and hornets. But most country and village children escaped those fears and made friends with what they found out doors. Out of just such friendships have come the great naturalists of the ages; men and women who have little by little driven the dragons out of nature and made the world the valid house of mankind. Nature has thus educated the race. Books about nature did not educate Aristotle or Boyle or Faraday or Franklin or Edison, though books may have had some small share in their education. Nature herself did most of the work. Longfellow wrote in his "To Agassiz":

"Then Nature, the old nurse, took the child upon her knee,
   Saying, here is a picture book thy Father hath written for thee."

In the modern city, young people denied access to nature in the old sense, but needing nature none the less, frequently turn in upon themselves, and find thus the shortest cut to nature. Here we find some explanation for much that is, from one point of view, abnormal— even destructive—in the social life of cities. Nature will not be denied. The world of cities may succeed sometime in developing a type of creature who will be purely artificial and fitted to the apartment-house style of living; but the ones who can live such a life will be not natural human beings, but curiously perverted beings, the selected survivors of our current city life, whose characteristics will enable them to endure that restricted kind of living without fatal irritations.

Play as Educator.—Play is an equally effective teacher of childhood and youth, and in some cases, also of age. Play may be, as Spencer thought, merely the using up of excess energy; or it may be as Schiller and Groos thought, the imitation of adult activities in preparation for the actual practise of these activities; or it may be as Stanley Hall says, reverberations of latent activities which have been wrought into the nervous structure of the generations because we are the children of our ancestors, reverberations out of unconscious experiences; or as is most likely, it may be all of these together, or in some varied integration.

Why do delicious tremblings of excitement go up and down our backbones when we watch a football game? Why do we shove down the field with our team and all step down a step in the bleachers, or fall back with taut muscles, resisting with all our might when our team is being pushed back? We, too, are taking part in the simulated conflict; we are taking part by proxy as our ancestors took part in reality in battles that were of life and death. It remains to be seen how long the human race will keep its capacity for these delicious thrills, if most of us never actually share the battle itself.

But playing games has a more specific part in education. Games are patterned plays and the best of them have high disciplinary value. We are developed and organized by the games we play; and naturally the race has developed and selected for survival the kinds of games that would best educate for the life the child and the race must live. Unfortunately, the changes in the bases of our living from the country to the city have in a measure dislocated the values and the meaning of our old games. Few of the old games can be played in the crowded city. As one result we have lost track of the meaning of many important types of play.

Types of Play and Games.—Three stages have been noted in the development of play interests and three types of games correspond to these three stages. Children first play in a segregated way. Under six years of age they tend to play singly, but they like to have company not far away. Little girls, for example, play for hours with dolls. If two or more of them play together, still they play singly, merely within sight of each other. Each is engaged in getting her own behavior disentangled through the weaving in of motherly activities with her own neural patterns. Each talks things over endlessly with herself or with her dolls. She cannot have another person, young or old, interfering. She is engaged in becoming acquainted with herself or with her various selves and any outsider would be a real intruder. Few people know how to identify themselves with one of the selves of the little girl and so carry on with her that "imaginative social process," as Cooley calls it, by which she is slowly getting to know herself, the immediately surrounding world of the home, and the social world in which she lives. Sometimes she visits her neighbor near by, but mostly she must work things out in these early years pretty much alone. She must imitate the world about her in her own way. She becomes a woman by acting the various rôles of women. She learns to cook by cooking; to sew by sewing; to visit by visiting; to carry on conversation by talking; to be a mother by being one.

Like developments may be observed in the career of the small boy.

Group Play and Group Games.—When the child has become a bit sure of himself, he can play more with other children and so he comes to the second stage, that of group play and group games.

In the group game children play together, yet each one still plays his own individual part. The play group is made up of A and B and C. A plays for all he is worth in his own way as do all the others. The strength of the group is the sum of the strengths of the individuals.

Group play usually takes the form of a group game—a contest with a group on each side. One of the famous group games of the past was "Prisoner's Base." This was played by two groups, all the members of each group being equal in rank and being unequal only in their native strength and intelligence. In this game, each individual on each side played with all his might, and the victory tended to go to the side which was able to show the largest sum of individual performances.

The individual child should have this chance to play unrestrainedly in company with his fellows, for all he is worth. He must show himself what he can do and all that he can do; and he must show others what he can do and all that he can. He must not be satisfied until he has shown these things. He should not be deprived of the chance to show the world what he can do in his own individual way.

Team Play and Team Games.—But once he has fully demonstrated these abilities he is ready for the third stage of play—team play and the team game. This readiness comes in general about the age of thirteen or fourteen. Children who attempt to play team games before they are old enough, spend most of their time quarrelling about private prerogatives in the game, as is seen in most baseball games which are played by boys who are too young to be able to learn how to be good members of teams.

Team membership represents a special stage in the development of the individual. It produces a differently organized type of nervous system. The characteristic of the team game is the subordination of the individual to the group. Baseball is an illustration of a team game, and the "sacrifice hit" is an illustration of the way in which the individual player must be willing to submerge himself for the sake of team victory. The team player must not in all ways play his utmost. He must always do the thing that makes for the success of the team, even though it means his own eclipse. The "sacrifice hit" is the symbol of this. The player must be willing to put himself out in order to advance another player or to "bring him home." This is not an easy thing to do. It is not a thing that should be asked of any one who has not had experience with group games, in which he has demonstrated to himself and to others that he could have hit the ball over the bleachers if he had been permitted to do so.

We have very little of real team play to-day, either in schools or in the world (team work is not usually taught in schools), because we have so little understanding of the significance of play in education and growth; or of the way in which team play naturally develops on the basis of normal development of individual and group play.

Summary.—Play then is necessary, educationally, on these three levels of development:

First, in the young child it releases latent powers and

interests and helps him to begin to practice living and to find out what sort of person he is and what he likes to do; by means of play activities that are largely unpatterned but richly stimulated he begins to explore himself and his world.

Second, in the form of group games play enables him to demonstrate to himself and to the world what he individually can do and all that he can do, in increasing measure as his powers unfold. He need not boast or brag: he can demonstrate and be held to realities.

Third, in the adolescent years, in the forms of team games, it helps him to learn how to meet the demands of "team work," and to build up the relationships through which real "team work" becomes possible within himself, and later in his active life in the world. That is, he learns how to *cooperate*. But such subordination as is implied in "team work" is largely impossible, and it is altogether *immoral* save as the individual has learned his own powers and has told the world about them through his earlier group experiences.

The educational meaning of *work* should be developed here next. But something of that has been suggested in Chapter XXIV, and space will permit no further elaboration. The educational meanings of the other items set forth in this chapter must be left to the imagination and research of the student and reader.

CHAPTER XXIX

THE EMERGENCE OF INTELLIGENCE

The type of interest which originated in the hunt remains dominant in the mind down to the present time. Once constructed to take an interest in the hunting problem, it takes an interest in any problem whatsoever. The man of science works at problems and uses his ingenuity in making an engine in the laboratory in the same way that primitive man used his mind in making a trap. So long as the problem is present the interest is sustained; and the interest ceases when the problematical is removed. . . .

The strains thrown on the attention of the primitive man were connected with his struggle for life; and not only in the actual encounter with men and animals did emotion run high, but the memory and anticipation of conflict reinstated emotional conditions in those periods when he was meditating future conflicts and preparing his bows and arrows, traps and poisons. The problem of invention, the reflective and scientific side of his life, was suffused with interest, because the manufacture of the weapon was, psychologically speaking, a part of the fight. . . .

Modern inventions are magnificent and seem quite to overshadow the simpler devices of primitive times; but when we consider the precedents, copies, resources, and accumulated knowledge with which the modern investigator works and, on the other hand, the resourcelessness of primitive man in materials, ideas, and in the inventive habit itself, I confess that the bow and arrow seems to me the most wonderful invention in the world.—WILLIAM I. THOMAS, in *Sex and Society.*

We see long before we *know* that we have eyes. We quench thirst with water long before we know we have thirst—before we have learned the words that mean the need and the act. Use comes before discovery of use. Use is natural and implicit; discovery transforms, and not infrequently malforms the natural conditions of use. But, sometimes, too, discovery improves upon the natural conditions of use, as when we learn to use pure water, and so to avoid typhoid fever.

How Primitive Thinking Inverts Experience.—It was necessary, of course, that the race should eventually become aware of its own existence and attempt to discover the conditions of that existence, if it was ever to become intelligent, "looking before and after." Now human existence is a natural affair like any other natural affair. Fragmentary consciousness of the conditions of existence carries with it real dangers—"a little knowledge is a dangerous thing." And man's first knowledge of himself was fragmentary.

Awareness is rooted in memory of past experiences but it faces future contingencies. Intelligence dealing with future problems faces them in the light of the past. Man has to begin where he is and work forward and backward. Hence, from the standpoint of thinking, the present comes not merely before the future but it also comes before the past. Trying to be intelligent we must begin with that stage of experience which is most intelligent—that is, the present. Thereafter we discover the past; thus history is inverted. The present comes before the past and the present is accordingly read into the past.

Now the past, when discovered, is made of customs and fears. That is not a pleasant picture to the newly intelligent man. The story of the past worked out by the intelligence of later times has always been inverted. It

has always been seen first as intelligence, then emotion—
specifically that of fear—then custom and action based
on custom.   From the writers of Genesis to the historians
of the whole pre-evolutionary period, man first thinks,
then fears, then acts according to his thought because of
his fears.   This is a universal natural interpretation of
history, but it is an inversion of history.   When one has
been thinking, he begins to write where he leaves off
thinking, and he works backward along the course by
which he came to his thought till he comes to where he
was before he began to think—that is, to his emotions
and customs.   His inversions of his own story are perfectly natural.

Our personal experiences are usually similarly inverted.
Casual psychology is upside down.   Our habits appear
reasonable to us—hence, they must be the product of
reason.   We rarely face or argue the reverse of this,
namely, that our habits appear to be reasonable because
our reasoning is the product of our habits.   Our emotions,
too, appear to us to be the emotions of a reasonable
being; we must have selected our own equipment of emotions.   That is to say, according to casual, traditional
psychology, the first man was intelligent; he exhibited the
emotions that such a man should have; and he developed
the habits that would be the instruments of a reasonable
program of living, and that would defend the values of
life which he had chosen.

From this same point of view the world itself is a *plan*
—a rational creation.   Adam was a rational creature.
He knew everything.   He could name all the animals.
He was trapped into a "fall," and the human career has
been badly ordered ever since; but the "right way of
living" is perfectly obvious.

The academic school follows this interpretation of life

and conduct. Whatever may be said of a *"child,"* a *"pupil"* is to be dealt with as a rational person, whose business in life is to build up *large stores of knowledge,* in order that he may know how to *feel* properly about all the issues of life, in order that he may know how to *act* in all the decisive moments of life. First we must *know;* then we must *feel* and *act* on the basis of our knowledge!

Nature may do things in other ways. But nature is something to be denied and escaped. "Rational man" must "move upward, driving out the beast and let the ape and tiger die!"

Intellectualism.—The academic school interprets education as having to do with "mind," that is, intellect, and with inculcating intellectual materials. Schooling begins with "lessons," information, the "ripe wheat" of life's long cultivation. Equipped with facts, the child must find satisfactions, interests, emotions in his facts, and then he must put his facts into practice. "When a boy knows a thing he goes and does it!" Some teachers make some concession to "human weakness" behind the principal's back, but any such concession seems treason to the nobler, that is, the intellectual, nature of man. A real education is made primarily of facts, informations, principles, laws. The test of the moral character of the individual comes when he shows whether he admires or detests these facts, principles, laws. If he admires them, he acts according to them, and thus demonstrates his right to call himself a human being. If he detests them, he fails to act upon them, and thus shows himself unworthy to belong to the real human race. He is a "low" fellow, a criminal, a moron—an enemy of the best: and he is not entitled to share the "benefits and emoluments" that inhere in those who learn, and admire, and obey.

So, scholastic education turns natural experience upside

down. It puts intellect before and above experience, and therefore it puts intellect outside experience—above the world. It denies that intelligence develops through ordinary social experience; and it ignores the initiative of the individual child in creating the world in which he is to live. It is interested not in experience, but in *knowledge*. It provides the ages, and the age, with the spectacle of the pedant—the theorist who can take the universe to pieces before your eyes, and tell you exactly how it is made; but who has never yet been able to put it back together again. As teacher, the intellectualist charms his students; he tears life and the world to pieces for them. But he also lets them down; he is compelled to leave the world in pieces before their eyes.

Since for the pedant, however, life is intellect and fact, not reality and emotional experience, the fact that he cannot put the world together again does not bother him; the world in pieces, with each piece labelled, is *rational*— even though it does not run. What has the little matter of "running" got to do with the far more important matter of understanding? Let practical men attend to the running. Intellectual men have more important functions!

Natural History of Intelligence.—So school inverts most of the natural procedures of experience. But *life* goes at things in a different fashion. The child *does* things first. In the process of doing, he finds out whether he *likes* to do such things, and if he does, he goes on doing them until slowly he may find out what they mean. The child *begins* with activities, and ends with understanding, just as the world seems to have done. Which is the more natural procedure—the child's or the school's? Or are they both natural—each in its way?

If we are to discover the natural qualities of experience,

we must escape from the intellectual inversions of the schools. The child is born into a world that is already organized: the family, the clan, the neighborhood, the state, industry, the church—all these are in existence before the child is born. The child is born with a neural organization adequate to its primary needs; but it does not *know!* It will spend years adjusting this neural organization to the complex conditions of the social world—conditions that are *not* predicated in this native organization of the child—and in becoming aware of its own existence over against these environing conditions. The child does *not inherit* society—he has to *learn* it all.

The child's first adjustment activities are responses; expressions—not impressions. He acts, and learns by his activities; he responds, and learns by his responses; the native responses of his being are released in the stimulations of the world about him, and he learns by such responses both what the world is like and what he himself can and must do about it. He learns by his *expressions,* not by his *impressions.* *Knowledge follows upon experience*—in the development of the child.

Some of the episodes in this natural history of mental growth are found in our common talk. For example, we say, "I didn't know I was that sort of a person; I didn't know I could do that!" Or, "I don't know yet what I think about such and such a matter. I haven't yet made up my mind." Or, "I don't know the meaning of such and such a word; I have only the vaguest feeling about it." That is to say, we discover ourselves and make up ourselves as truly as we discover the world; mind actually comes into existence in experience; it is truly made up; and words begin with us as feelings, not as definite meanings.

When we say, quite naïvely, that we "make up our

minds," we state a fundamental fact of psychology, and about the nature of individual and social mind. When we ask what sorts of persons we are, we are searching for equally fundamental facts. What deeps, what uncertainties, what chasms, what possibilities are implied in these questions! As human organisms, we first act, or respond —thus beginning the development of habits; we pass primitive judgments—of liking or disliking—upon those acts because we *feel* them and their results; we may stop there and never go further; but if we are properly stimulated to do so, we may eventually become sensitive and discriminative about our acts and their condition, and aware of conflicts of acts, habits, and situations, and so we may begin to analyze—and *think!* We may develop analytic, presentative, critical intelligence!

But such intelligence is the product of experiences and experience, not the precondition of it!

Some Pertinent Historical Considerations.—The human race inherited most of its physical organization, including its nervous system, though it seems likely that the human brain is a *mutant* from antecedent anthropoidal brains. In matters of habits, human beings have much in common with the animal world in general. Many of our human emotions are functionally identical with animal emotions—so that even anti-evolutionists sometimes call persons they do not like "brutish."

But the development of human society is a new and changed chapter in the history of life. It is its own history, not merely an enlargement upon animal history. Human civilization was not inherited from man's animal ancestors. It is the creation of man himself in his own history. And man's mind is a product of man's own social history, not of his animal ancestry.

The first stage in human history was spent in building

up great structures of custom and habit—"folkways"—in enormous variety, each group taking its own more or less accidental way along the years; and the selection of these for survival; those groups that survived kept their folkways from destruction, but they quite properly believed that the reverse was true—that their folkways kept them from perishing. Thus their folkways came to have a sacred quality; in time they became sacrosanct—to be violated at the peril of the individual and the group.

These structures of custom and habit carry with them their own appropriate emotions of fear, anger, hope, hate, love and the like. In any conflict of habits or customs, these emotions are variously released. They are so intimate, so personal, so real that they give the clue, and the cue, to Reality itself. The gods often speak in them.

Beyond emotion lies the realm of "thinking." But by comparison, thinking is cold, impersonal, calculating, inhibiting, and devastating. Hence, emotions are to be conserved at all costs (in the primitive mind) and thinking is to be avoided, escaped. Methods of avoiding going from emotion to thinking have been many: we can weep; we can pray; we can ask advice of others; we can read a book, especially the Bible; we can become sick; we can feign insanity, or actually achieve it; we can get religion; we can undertake programs of furious activity; we can retreat into old habits and customs; these and other methods have been tried and found not unsuccessful in avoiding the toil and the nuisance of "thinking things out."

The Place of Intelligence in Experience.—But in some instances men have been brave enough to "face the issues," at least in a measure. Out of the conflicts of primitive group customs and emotions, human intelligence has slowly emerged—through the ages—with many setbacks and many false turnings in some few instances, in some few groups; to become the promise of critical and scientific understanding in recent centuries. Out of human experiences and the conditions of experience slowly emerges understanding of experience and its controls, and the analytic development of the conditions of new and more desirable experiences!

Intelligence, then, in this sense, is the product of experience. Experience is wider, deeper, more extensive than intelligence, or critical understanding. Experience, itself, is mostly irrational, pre-rational, non-rational. It is natural: it is of nature. The habits of human beings are quite as much parcel of nature as are the habits of animals. The impulses of human beings are quite as much of nature as are the winds that blow. The emotions of human beings are quite as much rooted in nature as are the emotions of animals. Intelligence is also natural, but it is the expression of a level of nature not present in the animal world; not generally present in the primitive human group, and not always welcome in the modern polite world.

"Intelligence" does not create experience, although, given its chance, "creative intelligence" begins to emerge very slowly in childhood. But, in general, children spend years as victims of patterned activities, which are imposed upon them, eventually to become habits, by home and street and neighborhood and school. The world does what it can to make them routine creatures, determined by old patterns. It is mostly a fortunate accident when personal initiative escapes from the control of custom and goes adventuring widely in the world of experiences.

The race itself was probably hundreds of thousands of years old before such a phenomenon as Greek intelligence emerged out of the primitive shadows. The little child is two, three, five years old before he begins to exhibit qualities that are properly to be called critical, although he has been discriminative from birth. We dimly envisage an age when the race will seek release of individual and social initiative as the most precious thing in the world.

Childhood and youth, especially the latter, might be periods of opportunity within which, along with an ever-widening experience, should develop understanding, judgment, creative imagination, poise. Out of such widening and integrating movements and counter-movements, the young adult might find how to live adventurously, naturally and wisely—in a world that was in existence before he was born; a world that is refractory and jealous of its own ancient ways; yet, a world that should, somehow, make room within the old for this new individual, with his own creative imagination, his own judgments and his own critical understanding.

It is just here that we come to the point developed in Chapter XXII on education through group memberships. There we found that membership in groups does now raise issues that might lead to a critical intelligence if we knew how to lead on from conflicting emotion to understanding of emotions and their organization into tools of analysis, comparison and creative reconstruction. Knowledge of this sort is in existence, though strangely it is not much in the schools. We shall deal with it in the next chapter. Here we must make an additional comment upon the failure of the school to grow a social crop of real intelligence.

The Academic School and Intelligence.—The academic school does not, in general, understand, or care for, this sort of intelligence; it ignores the possibility of such intelligence, even when it does not actively obstruct the emergence of it. The academic school is usually scared at the signs of innovating intelligence, not having the slightest idea what to do with the child that manifests it. But in after years, the same school is fairly good at claiming credit for the development of such intelligence, when it once has appeared. A university may not be able to deal intelligently with a Lindbergh when he is one of its "students"; but it can give him an honorary degree after he has demonstrated his quality unaided.

The New School and Intelligence.—The New School does not greatly understand this sort of intelligence either, at least not in its social rootages and significances; but the New School does what it can to make the release of such intelligence possible; it is happy when it finds signs of such intelligence; it helps to provide the best conditions (at least within its purview) for the further development of such intelligence; and it is willing to send such intelligence out into the world without making foolish claims as to its own share in the result.

But it must be fairly obvious, by this time, that intelligence is a social product, not the product of any school. The intelligence developed in former generations, when all schooling was of the old-time academic sort, was not the product of that old-time school, however much it may claim credit for it. That former intelligence was the product of community life, its work and play and general interests—and the school's part in it was small and often of no consequence; and even when of consequence, the result of accidental conjunction of circumstances.

The intelligence developed to-day in New Schools is very real in all the earlier years—the years within which it is possible to give the child real conditions of development inside the walls of a school. But the problems of the later years, youth and early maturity, when the conclusive patterns of mind are being formed—either toward old customs and traditional folkways, or toward the open world and the liberal mind—with these problems the New School has not yet learned to deal convincingly.   It has no true community of its own—which will help it stand for its earlier ideals in its later years.   Hence, battered by parents who want their children to go to college, and by colleges that will not accept anything but conventional "minds," it is compelled to "do the best it can do" in a hostile world.   Few really progressive schools have been able to live more than ten years.

So, while the world needs released intelligence more than anything else that can be imagined, it probably gets less of it from all the agencies of education than any other product.   Habits it gets in plenty, such as they are; and knowledge, more than it can use; but how much of critical understanding?   It is the only kind of education that is worth working for.   It is the one kind of which we may say that we have less than we need.

The very conditions that make its development imperative, namely, the chaos of group conflict in the modern world, are the very conditions that would make its emergence possible, if we could learn how to "grow" it.

CHAPTER XXX

THE MEANING OF COMMUNITY

Education is not apart from life; it is just the adult generation giving its own world to the new generation. And be sure the adult generation will not give a very different world from that in which itself lives. The adult generation cannot keep its own private evils, traditions, greeds, autocracies, shams, follies and insincerities, and ask the school, working in the midst of these effective influences, to produce a new generation committed to good, to science, to altruism, to democracy, to honesty, to wisdom and to sincerity. The democratic problem in education is not primarily a problem of training children; it is the problem of *making a community* within which children cannot help growing up to be democratic, intelligent, disciplined to freedom, reverent of the goods of life, and eager to share in the tasks of the age. A school cannot produce this result: nothing but a community can do so.—Joseph K. Hart, in *The Discovery of Intelligence*.

Thinking which was a rage is become an art. The thinker gives me results, and never invites me to be present with him at his invocation of truth, and to enjoy with him its proceeding into his mind. . . . The revolutions that impend over society are not now from ambition and rapacity, from impatience of one or another form of government, but from new modes of thinking, which shall recompose society after a new order, which shall animate labor by love and science, which shall destroy the value of many kinds of property, and re-

place all property within the dominion of reason and
equity.—EMERSON, in *Lecture on the Times*.

Membership in a group roots the individual deep in experiences of social reality.   Trees have more than one
root.   Living things have many roots and they draw their
substance from many depths and diversities of soil.   A
human being similarly needs rootages in many kinds and
types of groups, if he is to escape arrested development.
As we have seen (cf. Chapter XXII), the world provides
the soils for just such rootages.

Becoming Civilized.—It is not true that the new-born
child is by biological inheritance assured of a civilized
human nature.   Human nature must be achieved by him
in the processes of his growth and education.   If he draws
his substance from any single group or any narrow range
of groups, his human nature will likely be lopsided, particular, narrow.   If he grows up in a provincial group,
his human nature will probably turn out to be provincial.
If he draws experiences from many superficial groups,
his human nature will turn out to be superficial.   If he is
to become a real human being, he must get his roots down
deep beyond the academic, into the world that is human;
he must feel the impact of racial types, of social groups,
of many ranges of institutional organization; and he must
have the sense of having shared and been shaped by the
interminable interweavings of groupings that make up
the human world.   He must do more than hear of these
things: he must share them.

It takes all kinds of groups and groupings to make a
world.   These groups and groupings will often seem to
bring the individual nothing but chaos.   But we must
remember that the world was made out of chaos.   Education need not fear chaos; educators may well be fear-

ful when there is no chaos. An over-organized world is probably a dead world.

But membership in many groups brings complications of habits, loyalties and interests, as we have seen. These complications and conflicts are real. They are also necessary—if the member is to become social, intelligent, and individualized. The ancient doctrine of well-meaning moralists that there could be no conflicts of "duties" in this world is disproved by the facts of every individual's experiences. Membership in unlike groups inevitably means conflicts in personal growth. The only chance of escaping from conflict is by remaining free from group memberships, or finding some other way of ignoring the facts of experience. These conflicts disturb the group member with respect to uses of his time and the importance of his interests. He is drawn in many directions; he would use his time for many purposes; he would do many things—each as some specific group loyalty holds him. He would work and he would play; he would study and he would worship; he would gamble and he would save; his group memberships nourish his life; make the world varied and interesting; tear him to pieces.

The Uses of Groups.—In reality, this multiplicity of groups answers to the growing individual's undeveloped needs and latent interests in ways but little recognized by educators. The fact that a group interests an individual means that he probably has some need of the things the group stands for: the group's interests feed his own uncertainly developed interests in some way, and he would experience more of the matter. *Interest* is a sense of unsatisfied need. He will be drawn to every group he touches that offers him any satisfaction for these unsatisfied needs. His real education depends upon the discovery and the release of his own native interests and the satisfaction of his needs. If the community provides group memberships of sufficient diversity, number, and range to stimulate every latent interest of his nature, there is a chance that he will achieve an education rich in emotional satisfactions and in diversity of directions. If the community does not provide him with such wide ranges of group membership, he will, at some point, fail to achieve this discovery, release and nurture of his emotional needs, and he will always be the poorer for this lack; but he may never know that fact!

One great defect in modern living appears in the fact that our disorganized communities fail to provide many individuals with a sufficient range of group memberships to assure this all-round development of their emotional and volitional natures. Under such circumstances they become lopsided, poverty-stricken in some aspect of their beings. Another defect appears when a community provides too many group stimulations; when the individual becomes over-stimulated in certain directions or, as one might say, "over-grouped." Here, in the efforts of the individual to make the most of everything he comes upon, he is likely to become superficial and merely frivolous. A bit of frivolity is good, but too much is—more than enough!

Group Conflicts in Individual Lives.—It was pointed out above that group memberships in many directions inevitably lead to conflicts within the individual: he is pulled in many directions by his own group attachments. These conflicts may prove destructive if they work themselves out undirected. If membership in many groups is not to prove in the long run destructive of personality, conflict must be balanced by processes of integration that are equally real. Every conflict in the individual must, in general, lead to a larger integration, if it is not to do the person more harm than good. Ignoring or repressing conflicts in experience is about the most disintegrative of all educational procedures. Over-emphasis upon conflicts may be almost equally destructive. The former process destroys by developing areas of repression that may become pathological; the latter, by dissipation of energies that may leave the individual nothing to live upon.

Education, that is, development of experience, involves two movements, two processes: first, a continuous differentiation of experiences, so that day by day, two experiences grow where only one grew before; second, continuous processes of integration, whereby over and above all differentiations, something of unity and wholeness in experience is maintained, or secured. "Ideas" have long been the stock in trade of the school man. "Sensations" are much in vogue with youth, and the world of publicity. Few will argue that "education" can be made entirely of differentiations. Most will admit the need of some integration "from time to time." Schoolmen recommend their "ideas" for purposes of integration. But, for the most part, the only integrative processes that will have the feel of reality to the individual involved will be those that operate from within, that organize the conflicting factors in his experience by developing their own intrinsic meanings.

Unfortunately, this method of dealing with the personal conflicts of individuals has never been much prized by the race, either by the commonalty, by educators, or by philosophers. Nor have the implicit processes here suggested ever been explicitly presented as educational technics. Instead, under the dominance of group dogmas, the very existence of such conflicts in individuals has been regarded as proof of moral delinquency, that is, as evidence of trafficking with other groups. For the cure of such delinquency they have usually had to submit themselves to the external shaping of some accepted institution.

For example, the church stands ready to advise the individual to give up all his conflicts as being essentially evil, to accept its doctrines as finalities, and to "trust and obey." The academic school will, with great good will, advise him that his personal conflicts are of minor importance or of no importance in the light of eternity, and that he should learn his lessons and accept the findings of "truth" or of "science" and make them sufficient to his needs. If his conflicts should lead him into outbreaks against conventions, the policeman or the judge may send him to jail to cool off! And if his conflicts should produce actual breakdown of a pathological character, he may be sent to an asylum for mental hygiene where for the first time his case may be dealt with with some intelligence.

That is to say, most of our institutions have been utterly ignorant, even contemptuous of the emotional and intellectual difficulties of the individual who, being rooted in many group relationships, is trying to find moral integrity for his being. This, we now know, means "thinking things through," personally, courageously, to a positive end. The last thing in the world the traditional church or the traditional school, or the traditional political party, or the traditional business man, or the traditional home would advise a youth would be to "take time off and think these things out." Socrates was sent to death for advising Athenian youth to do just that— and for aiding and abetting them in doing it—for teaching them *how* to do it!

Education and Group Conflict.— Education in the modern world certainly cannot much longer fail to recognize the reality of the individual's intellectual difficulties as the outgrowth of these inescapable personal conflicts. The modern educator, like the old Greek pedagogue, must accept the problem of helping the individual achieve personal and social integration. The individual grows up in a wilderness of groups. The modern community is not real enough, not sufficiently organized, to provide the old-time social integrations as a matter of course. There can be no real education without integration. The school cannot provide the integration the individual needs. But *education* should be able to do so!

This integrative task has two phases which answer to each other. In the first place, this struggling maze of conflicts, which the modern individual is, must move toward actual personal integration. That is an internal, personal problem, and a long problem, extending over the plastic years, at least; and it can be worked out effectively by no one but the person concerned. No institution, no other individual—teacher, preacher—can perform within him the processes of integration that are essential to his intellectual and moral maturing. The one who is doing the growing must do the growing. No magic can do it; there is no royal road to integration. It is an internal process, not an imposed one. This integrative process—which is never finished—involves conflict, analysis, contrast, comparison; evaluation, experiment, testing, judgment, reasoning, synthesis, and action that tests results on new levels of understanding and behavior. In short, this is the growing aspect of experience. These intellectual factors emerge in the midst of the process. Real integration is the intellectual aspect of experience, as we have previously seen. Intelligence if it ever appears at all, emerges in the midst of conflicts.

But on the other hand this process of personal integration, extending naturally over many years, must have natural or social supports that give it the *feel* of reality and at least occasional completeness. This social support of integration must be more than institutional—it must be *human*. The only organization that has ever held all human qualities in trust as aids to personal integration has been some sort of *community*.

A community is a congeries of groups, more or less integrated. Each such group provides rootage for some social factor that is fragmentarily human. A *community* not only includes many groups, but it also provides room for group conflict and group criticism; and if it is stable enough it will compel the member of these various groups to rise above the level of mere group existence and assimilate, make use of, integrate all the various values of all the various groups within his own experience as he comes to maturity within this complex situation. That is, a real community compels members to "think things through"! Nothing but a community can bring this result to pass.

Now groups are very real, and they lay their impress within the neural structures of the individual, turning him in many directions, giving his being many and varied facets. But *community* is not so very real, to-day. Hence, most people are torn much, but integrated very little: they have more sensations than they know what to do with. They have many experiences, but not much experience. They have many sensations, but not much thinking. They have seen many trees, but rarely the woods; many houses, but rarely the city; many lands, but not often the world.

That is to say, integration is not a process, or series of processes that can go on *ad hoc*, of themselves, in a vacuum. Men, women and children are real: they are differentiated, varied, many-sided phases of the world in which they live. If, to complete their educations, they are to be organized, integrated, made whole—that, too, must be provided for by the existence of some sort of world that is organized, integrated, whole. The failure of individuals to achieve this wholeness to-day is not primarily to be charged to their own private accounts, but to the fact that contemporary life affords few, if any, organized, integrated areas of social experience—few, if any, old-time communities that have sufficient reality to assure complete integrations in their members.

Can the Individual Save Himself?—There are some few people, perhaps, in any sort of world who are capable, because of some very fortunate combination of circumstances, of developing a sort of personal integrity, or even a real moral individuality, without much help from an equally well-organized community. But such persons are very few. The great deficiency in education, to-day, for millions of young people is not the fact that they are easily torn to pieces by the stimulating groups that compete for them in the chaos of the modern world—for such differentiations are necessary to a real development—but the fact that the adult world provides them with nothing equally compelling in the way of integration. They lose themselves in the interesting chaos of the world, the city, and that is well. But they do not—many of them—ever "find themselves" again! And that is their destruction.

There are institutions that call to them—churches, schools, parties, jobs, classes! But each of these usually has some ax of its own to grind. Where is "humanity" in this crisis? Where is wholeness, where is integration, where is the world—the community? Old fragments of it querulously complain that "youth is going to destruction." But nothing inclusive enough, disinterested enough,

to win the will of youth appears.   Some young people fall
back upon the old fragments of the world—and try to
make the best of their defeats.   Some set up little "solutions" of their own—"communities" or "groups" that
offer answers to their need.   But the failure of all such in
very short time is proof of their inadequacy.

The Submerged Community.—Two aspects of the situation at least remain to be discussed.   The first of these
is the fact that every center of "community chaos" to-day
holds within itself enormous areas of interest and value,
of which the very existence is unsuspected.   The old community has broken to pieces under explosive forces too
great to be contained within it.   The growth of the city,
the spread of races, the development of transportation
and communication: no old-time community can withstand the pressure of such forces.

But the break-up of that old community did not totally
destroy its human qualities; they were merely submerged
in the welter of other interests and in the new activities.
The most broken neighborhood is still the home of innumerable bits of a true humanity.   Every such disorganized "community" needs exploration, investigation, discovery, the bringing to light of whatever human values
may be hidden there.   Under the feet of the teeming
modern crowds are the streets of ancient cities.   Unsuspected in the byways of the world are fragments of ancient cultures.   We are finding this out, here and there.
Incapable, because of our disorganization, of producing
any sustained great works of art, we find bits of old arts
here and there and exhibit them to ourselves as proof
that we have "taste," even though we have little creative
power.

Those former cultures may not be sufficient for these
new times; no age can live entirely as parasite upon the

past, even its own past. But they do prove that "humanity" is not entirely gone from us. Also, they suggest one of the great sources of the new culture, the new civilization, the new community of the new day. That new community will not materialize out of "thin air"; it will not come down from heaven, ready to be occupied by men. It will come, if it comes at all, out of the materials of all old communities and cultures, as these are subjected to the creative needs of the new day, organized by the creative imagination of the freed mind, and fulfilled in the spirit of a free science. The future must have its own forms and spirit; but always that future, if it is to be alive and not merely academic, must find its roots in the past. The submerged communities that are all about us will furnish much of the material out of which any future community is to be developed.

The New Pedagogy and the Modern Pedagogue.— This brings us to the second phase of the situation noted above. Chaos is with us in much of our social living and in our education. The cure for chaos is not to be found in ignoring it, or in denying it, or in denouncing it, or in running away from it to some delectable island of peace that lifts its fronded palms in the air in the midst of some distant stream. The cure for chaos is still what it was "in the beginning." For the world was, at least once before, "without form and void," with waters covering the solid land. But "a spirit brooded upon the face of the void," and presently "cosmos" began to emerge out of chaos. Our modern world-chaos probably needs just such a "spirit" moving over the surface of the waters.

In lieu of such a "spirit," we might do with a few real Greek "pedagogues" who could still find the fragments of a human world amidst the seeming void, and who could bring those precious fragments to childhood and youth, not as materials to be learned, but as experiences to be lived, and as the hope of a city, a community, a world that should be worth living in, and so bring healing and light to them in their need. School teachers, in our times, are not pedagogues in the old Greek sense. The very word pedagogue has lost its original meaning, and is now almost a term of opprobrium; while "pedagogy" is a subject for satire.

But the task of making the community that we need, and of developing pedagogues who can bring healing and wholeness to the experiences of childhood and youth is too big a task for the modern teacher, caught in the "system." It is a task for real *pedagogues*—citizens of the whole city, whose heads lift above the clouds; statesmen whose imaginations are able to envisage integrity of environment, even when all about them is nothing but primitive chaos.

We shall return to this need of the pedagogue and the educational statesman again, before we conclude.

CHAPTER XXXI

THE DRAMATIC MOMENT IN EDUCATION

The hunting life is of necessity one of great emotional interest. . . . Game and sport are still words which mean the most intense immediate play of the emotions, running their entire gamut. These terms are still applied most liberally and most appropriately to hunting. The transfer of this hunting language to pursuit of truth, plot interest, business adventure and speculation, to all intense and active forms of amusement, to gambling and the "sporting life," evidences how deeply embedded in later consciousness is the hunting pattern. . . . Men reserve the hunting occupations to themselves and give the women everything that has to do with the vegetable side of existence, and all activity that involves drudgery. . . . With change to the agricultural life all other than hunting types of activity are (if women do not suffice) handed over to slaves, and the energy and skill acquired go into the game of war. . . . The adjustment of habits to ends, through the medium of a problematic, doubtful, precarious situation, is the structural form upon which present intelligence and emotion are built. . . .—DEWEY, in "Interpretation of Savage Mind," *Psychological Review* (Vol. 9).

Jesus answered and said unto him, Verily, verily I say unto you, except a man be born anew he cannot see the kingdom of God. Nicodemus saith to him, How can a man be born when he is old? . . . Jesus answered and said to him, Art thou a teacher of Israel, and understandest not these things?—*John's Gospel.*

The academic school, confronted with the great masses of "knowledge" we now possess, has been able by many things to rationalize its historical and hence, accidental, position, and to act as if *education* were an intellectual process, and as if "getting an education" were identical with taking on facts.   Hence, in most academic schools the typical procedure has been some variation upon the old assignment: "Take the next ten pages."   In a school year of two hundred days, the prospect of listening to one hundred and ninety-nine repetitions of that remark will release emotions of pleasure in very few pupils.

Normal Human Experience Emotional, not Intellectual.—The fact is that normal human experience, in childhood and youth, when it is not too closely circumscribed by adults or institutions, is enormously varied.   It is full of dramatic moments; it is always about to make some wonderful new discovery; it rises and falls with excitement, pressing climaxes, anticipated realizations, the joy of great victory or the almost equally pleasant sense of temporary defeat.   Childhood and youth gets its most stimulating effects, not primarily by adding line to line, precept to precept, but quite casually, accidentally, unexpectedly.   Education is largely the by-product of dramatic exploits, of moments when something vital is happening, or about to happen.   Later when *real* things occur, even facts and precepts cease to be dead echoes out of a meaningless past; they become living meanings in a vivid present, and they open the way into a future rich with promise.

The greatest single crime in our scholastic education is the school's denial of these dramatic moments in the experiences of childhood and youth, and its reliance upon the line upon line, precept by precept type of instruction. It is true that teachers often attempt to "develop the emotions" of their pupils: they "pump up" the feelings of the children by calling attention to words, phrases, sentiments which they think "beautiful," and which they want the children to "enjoy." "Is it not beautiful?" they ask. Most such questions are sheer impudence!

Natural Basis of Education.—The human race, in the course of its evolutionary history, has developed a number of characteristic mental textures. Each great age of evolutionary history has probably left some trace of its own type of neural organization within the structures of the nervous system. Everywhere the race passed through ages of more or less precarious existence when its continuance depended upon its skill in the hunt. Weapons were primitive and not very effective. The hunter was compelled to come close upon his quarry if he were to capture or kill it. He had to stalk his game cautiously: life and death were in the issue of success or failure. If he succeeded he lived; if he failed, he died. Life depended upon his skill. Survival meant the selection of a type of neural organization that was sensitive to these dramatic situations: the descendant of a winner was likely to be a winner, too. Those who failed, failed by and large, because they were not sensitive to the factors in the dramatic situation. When they died they probably left no descendants and thus their duller neural organizations were eliminated from the world.

That does not mean that all who now live are sensitive to the dramatic aspects of experience. Group life has always protected some incompetents—and education can dull the native hunger of the nerves for excitement. But it does mean, probably, that most children and young people do have hunger for dramatic experiences—experiences that involve plots, climaxes, rising tides of emotion, and the heightening of life, generally. Educators must become more clearly aware of these natural hungers, "interests," anticipations, and give them larger share in the processes of education.

Emotions in Childhood.—Children of the hunting generations have inherited much of this sensitive neural organization. Their nervous systems are responsive to the moving things in their environment. They can stalk the wild things of the woods, and the little less wild things of the streets and the back alleys. The tragedy of city life to them is that there are so few opportunities to stalk real game in the woods, and the substitutes the city offers are usually fraught with perils. Their nervous systems are hungry for the sorts of dramatic-suspense situations that selected their type of nervous system for survival, and the world offers few such experiences to them in these days. The hunting life put its premium upon the neural organization that could wait in the midst of dramatic stress, fully under control, and that could strike at just the right moment, and strike with fatal accuracy. The hunter who could play the game of waiting in that way won and lived. His descendants, to-day, feel the need of similar experience; but the world is wary of giving them. Delinquency and criminality may be, for many, but perversities of this hunger for the dramatic.

Children once re-lived that dramatic past in their games. Country children used to play games based on hunting patterns: Hide and Seek, Grey Wolf, and various other "wild Indian" games. Games of this type seem largely to have disappeared; or to have been so modified as to have lost their dramatic qualities.

Children of small communities, to-day, seem to have few games. They wander about, after school, in search of something to do. They invent games of the dramatic sort, sometimes. But their inventiveness is limited by unfamiliarity with the old materials and situations, on the one hand; and, on the other, baseball and various "athletic" programs have invaded the areas once reserved to these more primitive types of games. Baseball provides emotional release, of course, as we have seen; but its emotions are native to a much later and more mature level of experience than are those of the hunter meeting his quarry face to face.

The city has, as yet, made no adequate provision for the dramatic and emotional needs of childhood. The city is an adult world, and the drama and emotion of the city are those of the adult. The child must take the "leavings." Face to face adventures with automobiles and other forms of rapid transit there are in plenty, but the odds against the child are too great, too unfair. Even a lion might give a hunter a moment's chance for life; an automobile is a machine, and knows no mercy. He who gets in its way is destroyed. This is not *dramatic adventure;* this is certain death!

Emotion in the Academic School.—At school children find slight provision for the release and satisfaction of their dramatic needs. Day after day they live through some arid variation upon the undramatic "take the next ten pages." This is nothing like stalking a deer in the wilderness; it is altogether like hiking, dead tired, across a barren desert that stretches on monotonously before to the vanishing horizon.

By contrast, practically all the materials of our school curricula have come out of the dramatic past of the race. All our geography is the result of explorations filled with the most thrilling adventures. All our history is wrought of materials woven out of heroic careers. Even our mathematics has come of such dramas as the annual overflow of the Nile and the re-ordering of line fences which would make it unnecessary for the Egyptian farmers to murder one another. All our sciences have developed by investigators who have stalked their facts and laws in quite the same way the primitive hunter stalked his quarry. Nothing is more characteristic of the dull régime of our scholastic "education" than the extent to which practically all the primitive emotional deeps of human experience are either denied or ignored, leaving for purposes of education only the gross heaps of "established fact": "Take the next ten facts!"

Stories of scientists like Galileo, Newton, Darwin, Pasteur, illustrate the argument. Each of these men lived and worked in situations that were profoundly dramatic in the most primitive sense of the word. Pupils mostly miss this fact. They learn the *results* of investigations, without ever suspecting the drama of those investigations. They have heard that Newton saw an apple fall; but they have not heard that he saw, in the falling of the apple, the like falling of all the stars of the heavens. They do not know that Darwin stalked facts of evolution for five years all about the coasts of South America, and that he then worked fifteen years to get those facts marshalled into orderly array. They have never heard of the life and death conflict that raged in the soul of Pasteur when he debated whether he should use his new rabies serum on the boy bitten by a mad dog. They learn the facts, *post hoc;* they rarely share the dramatic moods through which those facts were laid bare; and almost never do they realize, in their laboratory work in science, any of the dramatic joy of the real investigator. So even science, the drama of the last four hundred years, fails to dramatize experience for them; it also becomes dull, factual, dogmatic. And even the graduate of scientific courses finds no difficulty, and no incongruity, in joining the range of the dogmatic and the unimaginative.

Escaping from the Esthetic.—Attention has previously been called (Chapter XXIX) to the way in which education inverts experience, turning the world of history and psychology upside down, and inside out. We must now consider a further illustration of the same principle. If nature were ruled by *logic*, learning intellectual lessons would result in intelligent living; a rational principle taken into the mind would show itself in rational conduct. But the world is not governed by logic, at least, not by the logic of the books. Hence, in actual experience, the more the majority of individuals are schooled in factual learning, the more they incline to *passivity*, rather than to *activity;* until eventually, those who take this sort of education most seriously arrive at the inverted conclusion that "to think is better than to do." But this "thinking" probably means reading books, rather than real thinking. Too often, the "thinking" developed in schools ends in a "cultured passivity." As Hamlet said: "The native hue of resolution becomes sicklied o'er with the pale cast of thought!" The outcome of "thought" is not healthy action, but a sickly estheticism! This is too frequently the result of scholastic education. Running away from school may be the only means by which an active child can save his "soul."

There is danger that this word "estheticism" may be misunderstood. Life needs esthetic experiences, but "estheticism" is the doom of healthy living. It is produced by institutions, in so far as they substitute ready-made experiences for real experiences, and thus permit passivity to take the place of normal activity. It is not here argued that men, women and children must be forever active; it is expressly agreed that every one needs moments and hours of deep, quiet meditation, even vegetation; but those moments must be the product, and the need, of that individual's own experience, not something foisted upon him as a substitute for his own experience. The great immorality of our age is not doing "evil" things, but in doing nothing, or in being a parasite upon the past. Esthetic experiences are necessary to a normal and sound experience; estheticism consumes what it feeds upon and turns normal experience into a pallid imitation of itself. If we are to have a sound esthetic and ethical experience, we must learn how to emerge from the estheticism of our present schoolishness. In order to present this emergence in the most dramatic fashion, some specific contrasts will be set forth.

Two Attitudes.—Grammar has long recognized a category of classification which is called "voice." Under this category, as any grammarian knows, there are two classes, the "active" voice, and the "passive" voice. These two "voices" represent two distinct ways of accepting the world. Normally, each of us is both active toward the world and passive to it, in turn. We *strike* the world, and we *are struck by* the world. As long as both these types of experience are judiciously mingled in our living, we can maintain a fairly healthy equipment of attitudes; we can be molded by the world, and we can impress ourselves upon the world.

But *education* almost always tends to over-develop one or the other of these types of attitude. We become over-arrogant toward the world, especially toward our social world, and try to rule it; or we become over-humble in the presence of it, and accept whatever it offers us. Either development is pathological, and victims of the process are all about us. In general, schooling, for a variety of reasons, has always tended to over-emphasize the passivity of children: the "good pupil" is almost always a passive, obedient, receptive child, whose whole "will" it is to do what he is told. As a "subject" of an autocratic or feudal society, such an outcome would be admirable; it is the "subject's" duty to do what he is told to do. But for the child who is to be a "free member of a self-governing society," such an education is, it goes without saying, utterly wrong. The academic school tends to turn out passive types; the world needs active types, creative types. The New School promises these creative types. It does not fully realize upon its promises, partly because it has never fully envisaged just what is implied in the promise. It will be valuable to set down in parallel columns the diverse characteristics of these two contrasted types, in order that both the academic school and the new school may see more clearly what it is they are both producing or promising. They will be presented under not entirely unequivocal class-names.

Esthetic and Ethical Types.—Warning the student not to take these two type names too literally, we may proceed to differentiate them:

The Esthetic Type	*The Ethical Type*
1. The child is passive	1. The child is active
2. He receives impressions	2. He expresses himself
3. Learns to enjoy things	3. Learns to create things
4. Assumes conventional tastes	4. Develops personal discrimination
5. Education deals primarily with use of leisure	5. Education looks forward to a social vocation
6. Individual loses interest; becomes more blasé	6. Individual becomes more active, interested, effective

7. Finds satisfaction in being "appreciated" by others

7. Finds satisfaction in work and in doing social and creative things

8. Education emphasizes the consumption of goods

8. Education emphasizes the production of goods

9. Eventually, the individual may have to live by his "wits"

9. Always prepared to live by the exercise of socially desirable skills

10. Education ends probably with a store of *knowledge* dealing with the past

10. Education ends with *intelligence that* can negotiate the unexplored future

11. All the under-structure of the individual's life is of wishes, appetites, desires unrelated to the "knowledge" that has been imposed from above; hence, he is never free.

11. The understructure of native impulse has been integrated with experience and wrought into patterns of behavior adjusted to the world; hence he is free.

It must be said, again, that these classifications are not to be taken in too literal fashion. They do indicate directions which education, or experience, tends to take. The esthetic attitude, fostered not altogether intentionally by our academic schools, produces the passive type, the timid member of society, the follower of fashions and trends, who easily accepts the domination of strong characters. The ethical attitude, fostered not altogether intentionally by some of our progressive schools, tends to produce the non-conforming barbarian, effective but not very charming to live with. Custom clings to the esthetic type, as being more in line with the trend of institutionalisms. Progress looks to the ethical type, as more likely to do the reconstructive thing necessary to redeem both the individual and the institution. Probably intelligence will eventually help us to develop a program of experience and education which will save enough of the ethical type to assure some cultural survivals. But the details of such a program are not now in existence: they await critical experimentation, through the long future.

Defeat of the Dramatic.—Now, it is just the present over-emphasis upon the esthetic aspect of experience, in all our institutions, but especially in our schools, that is responsible for the elimination of the dramatic factor in education, and, probably also for the practical non-existence of any true esthetic values in our American life. The esthetic, properly considered, is a function of normal experience: experience must have its esthetic moments. But when all experience is made passive and becomes "esthetic," then no part of it is ever truly esthetic. Passive experience is not necessarily esthetic; usually it is characterized by an *estheticism* that is futile and degrading. The essence of the esthetic is not passivity or the feelings that dominate a mood of leisure; the essence of the esthetic is that rise and fall of emotion which is characteristic of experience in its creative moments, and especially in those moments of recovery when, as the creative mood is passing, all forces conjoin to gather up all vivid meanings and bring them into a new unity—a unity which is complete in itself, satisfactory in all its presentations, and of universal significance.

But such experiences will rarely, if ever, come to the individual whose whole life is spent in passivity. Academic education just to the extent that it develops a passive estheticism is the consistent foe of any true esthetic.

The dramatic is a function of natural living in a world

that presents problems, or precarious moments of any sort; and the esthetic is a function of the precarious situation and its solution, whether to defeat and death, or to a more inclusive living. The school child gets a bit of questionable joy out of playing the teacher for a fall. But, on the whole, school has been, and still is, about the most monotonous area of the child's experience. By comparison, the street is a wilderness of primitive adventures. Teachers make efforts to inject drama into lessons by means of fortuitous questionings or conditionings; but though a child may be able to fool himself by means of a jack-o'-lantern, he is not long fooled by the artifices of teachers. Experiences are real to children, and they easily puncture the bubbles that are held out to them as real worlds.

It is not as if, in a world like this, we were put to it to invent dramatic situations. Life is still filled with conditions that imply dramatic stresses and profoundly esthetic revealings. We have sterilized living. "Safety first," is our motto: "Take no chances" is our slogan. To be sure, we have made a world in which conditions are "stacked" against the child. Bishop Potter said, many years ago, that the automobile had divided the city population into two groups, "the quick" and "the dead." And we want to live. So we take no chances and we teach children to take none. But the race was not developed in any such program; and the nervous system of the average individual is beaten down to this monotony of living by nothing less than the most severe disciplines. Even then, most of us carry about with us all our lives a latent, wistful hunger for excitement, for escape from the commonplace. Youth refuses to-day to accept the maxims of safety and the "prudent counsels of commerce." Youth will have drama—even at the cost of life. Life without drama is not life, but a slow waiting for death. No schooling that ignores all the dramatic moments in living will ever for long have the right to call itself *education*.

The Lying Eminence of Drudgery.—We try to compensate for the tedium of dull hours by arguing that "all great men have worked hard at detailed tasks which must often have been distasteful to them." Such a statement is just near enough to the truth to pass for it with many. It implies that men have grown great by being drudges. There is no basis for this anywhere in the world. Great men have done dreary tasks, of course; but they knew something about why they were submitting to the drudgery: they could see some sort of end from the beginning. No man ever became great by drudgery. On the other hand many who might have been greater than they ever became were defeated by meaningless drudgeries imposed upon them. It is one thing to do hard, drastic work because one sees its place in a program of understanding; it is an entirely other thing to do hard, drastic work at the command of some taskmaster, without seeing any of the reasons or purposes in it. The deadly puritanism that esteemed work the more worth while the more distasteful it was had no worthy basis in psychology. It was a hang-over from an earlier theological psychology. It has been responsible for enough frustrations in the past; the present and the future do not need it any longer.

What we do need is some sense of joy in life and work; some feel of the dramatic; the plot of circumstance; the gathering of the crisis, the problematical; the climax; the clash of interests and the play of elemental forces; and the dénouement, out of which we may emerge into wider understanding and a more complete community of living. "The play's the thing!"

CHAPTER XXXII

THE EDUCATIONAL CURRICULUM

A system of education is part and parcel of the living tissue of society. What affects the one cannot leave the other unchanged. The daily search for bread and security, for love and adventure and companions, that perpetually absorbs the energies of men and women; the selfish struggle for power and privilege that constantly engrosses the attention of individuals and groups; the violent storms of passion that occasionally sweep through the social order; the wild irrational moods that sometimes seize on the minds of the masses; the enlightened movements for civic reform that now and then catch the popular imagination; the bitter clashes of sect and class, of race and occupation, that inevitably attend the evolution of institutions—in a word, every vibration that agitates the social structure must sooner or later reach the public school.—George S. Counts, in *School and Society in Chicago*.

No agency in American life has been sufficiently concerned with the whole situation. Although the task is difficult, there is great need for a new synthesis, a comprehensive orientation of the relation between the school curriculum and the content of life on the American continent to-day.—Harold Rugg, in Foreword to *Twenty-sixth Yearbook of the N.S.S.E.*

Three factors enter into each educational event, namely: the experiencing individual, the experiences themselves, and the leadership (or lack of it) by which those experiences are selected, determined, organized and interpreted. All else, though important, is subordinate. The child, the situation and the teacher—these are necessary. "Situations" may be of two sorts: academic and real.

The Educational Curriculum.—We must emphasize a distinction between the *school curriculum* and the *educational curriculum*. The school curriculum is that body of selected and organized knowledge and activities with which teachers and pupils are concerned in school houses; the educational curriculum is that wider range of activities, attitudes and knowledges with which men and women (including teachers) and children (including pupils) are concerned in every nook and corner of the community, and through all the ranges of life and experience. The school curriculum is a more or less important selection from the educational curriculum, which sometimes supplements, sometimes denies the latter.

Once there was no such thing as a school curriculum. The education of the younger generation was left to the care of the community at large. Life itself was the curriculum. That is to say, *education* is older than *schooling*, in the experience of the race. Even to-day children are two, three, four, five or six years old before they start to school or kindergarten. That is to say, education begins before schooling in the life of the modern individual. The school curriculum quite evidently was organized long after education began, and inside the processes of education. This is history. It is also psychology. It is not, but it should be, *pedagogy*.

Education as a Social Process.—If, therefore, we are to find a clue to the organization of a satisfactory school curriculum we must first find the organic function of schooling in the whole process of education. Hence, we must continue to employ the word *education,* not as if it were synonymous with *schooling,* since that would beg the question at the start, but in its real meanings in the experience of the child. Neither tradition nor our current institutionalism can be of much help here. We must get our help from history and psychology.

We cannot stop short of the facts. Education must be identified with the totality of the individual's experiences, of whatever sort, volitional, emotional, intellectual, and wherever gained: his skill or no skill, his mind or no mind, his taste or lack of taste; whatever he is, or possesses, or exhibits of personal capacity or incapacity. Somewhere within or about these experience premises of the individual an explorer might discover some remnants of his schooling. But we shall never understand, or be able to direct, or achieve any intelligent control over the processes of schooling until we escape from the schoolroom conception of education and learn to think of schooling as a chapter within the whole growing experience—in so far as it is anything at all.

At present the school assumes a practical monopoly of the word education. It makes its own curriculum, or attempts to do so; sets up its own tests of its own effectiveness, or tries to do so; and selects its own teachers on the basis of its own understanding of its job, or claims the right to do so. Because of these facts, there are almost no schools that will give any kind of credit for experience gained outside the school, no matter how valuable that experience may be; and almost all schools will accept the credits of other schools, without going back of the record, and hence without knowing whether those credits stand for any real increment of experience or not. That is to say, in the development of the tradition, schooling has become a matter of *credits,* having in large measure parted company with education, which is always a matter of *experience*.

Some Schoolish Abstractions.—This schoolish attitude has produced two extraordinary abstractions in our modern world: first it has abstracted from the whole experience of the race certain intellectualisms which are held to be superlatively valuable, and these it has cumulatively organized into the school curriculum; and second, it abstracts from the whole experience of the child certain intellectualistic effects, for which the school can accept casual responsibility, and which it attempts to identify with *education*. In its most extreme form (and institutions always tend to extremes) the school identifies capacity to achieve these intellectualistic effects with educability; and large numbers of so-called "educational psychologists" are now engaged in working out the refined mechanics of this alleged educational process. From these two schoolish abstractions, educational leadership and common sense must consistently and continually appeal—to the whole life of the race, to the community, and to the whole experience of the child. *A whole child in a human community*—nothing less than this can be the ultimate ideal of education; and no short-cut results, achieved by intellectual and ethical violence, can be acceptable as substitutes.

We accept this schoolishness partly at least because of our mental and moral laziness. We know, when we face realities, that our children are always educated by the life they live, by the experiences they enjoy and suffer, by the expressive activities they undertake and carry through, by the problems they solve. We know that the neighborhood, the community, the back alley feed our children quite as much as does the school. We know, when we are courageous enough to be honest, that beyond reading, writing, and a little "figuring," the final impress of the school upon anywhere from 75 percent to 90 percent of the children is essentially nil—save for that social life which children find at school but outside the school room. We know that children *must live* in the community, *some* community, after school days are over; and therefore, that the school must not make them very different from the community, even if it can. We know that education is what the whole community does to children and youth, not merely what the school does.

Community Realities.—We know that in the course of eighteen or twenty years, the average child takes on the ways of the community: its goods and its evils; its passions and its prejudices; its friendships and its enmities; its loyalties and its stupidities; its wisdom and its follies. We know that the community, or the conglomerate of stimulus and experience in the midst of which and by means of which the child grows up, will be the real educator of the child, shaping his mind, nourishing his emotions, forming his habits and his will, or no-will; and we know, that in the main, the academic school teacher will be a more or less anxious but helpless spectator of the whole process.

None the less educators center most of their constructive energies on the school, in the belief that the school, or the teacher in the school, with a little or even a great deal of talk, in a few months or years, can cure whatever the community is producing that is undesirable, through all the months of the years. Knowing that abstract intellectualisms have little if any relevance in a concrete moral situation, we, none the less, expect the school by means of abstract lessons in "civics" to make good citizens out of the children of the community, and that, too, without in any way disturbing the right of the community to retain its own bad citizens. The folly of this method is obvious in its results.

How Shall a Curriculum Be Made?—Certain modes of procedure seem obvious. Must we not begin by ignoring the school as a factor in education, and first examine our community life, local, national and even international, in order to find out just what is happening to children at the present time? If we assume, as most schoolmen do, verbally at least, that children should have the chance to grow up to be intelligent, open-minded, unprejudiced, sharers in the common tasks of civilization, what real chance have they in the average community to-day? To be sure, they are advised by their parents, teachers, ministers and politicians to follow noble ideals and they are given memory gems to *learn*. Meanwhile they are given community processes to *imitate*.

But assuming that children are as real as stalks of corn, and assuming that the community is the soil in which they are growing up, and, giving to the preaching of parents, teachers, preachers and politicians the persuasive value that it really has, what chance has the average child in the average community to grow up to become an intelligent, open-minded, unprejudiced sharer in the great tasks of civilization? *Until the school knows something about the answer to this question,* it has no basis upon which to get ahead with its own curriculum-making; it must continue to deal in the intellectualistic materials of the traditional curriculum, hoping that, somehow, the lessons learned in school will have some influence in behavior. The first task then of the educator must be that of finding out what education children get outside the schools. No school program can be intelligent that avoids or ignores this aspect of the problem. This experience outside the schools is the basic stuff of education for all but a very small number of children.

The next task of the schoolman, if he is to cease to be a mere institutionalist and become an intelligent worker in education to-day, will be to determine, by and large, how much of this non-schoolish education that the child gets is necessary if our civilization is to be democratic and intelligent. There is no reason under the sun why valuable experience achieved outside the schools should be denied or ignored inside the schools, and there repeated in a dull and discouraging fashion.

The school—let the matter be here definitely stated— has no fixed, or final, or absolute function. The school that is needed in a democratic social order cannot claim immunity from the constantly changing conditions of the democratic community; it cannot hide within a tradition, and claim certain ranges of action or certain areas of experience as its own by immemorial right. The school in a democracy cannot be stated in terms of the known values of arithmetic, but only in terms of the uncertain and shifting values of an algebra. Schooling cannot be stated in a definition, but only in a formula, whose terms are unknown quantities and which has to be solved anew in each new stage of social organization if we are even to preserve the ancient values of living—to say nothing of achieving new ones.

Limitations Upon the Casual Education of the Child.—Before stating that formula, we must call attention to the fact that there are two aspects of the community experience of the child that must be critically considered. These are, first, that some of the experiences which children accumulate in the current community life are decidedly undesirable and demoralizing. Community tradition is a dank pool in which filth, hate, prejudice, war, superstition, fear, morbidity, repression, inhibition all have large place along with whatever sweetness and light humanity has discovered and conserved. The casual experience of the average child, therefore, needs some correction, and some protection against the morbidities of the past. This protective function can easily be over-done, of course, so that "good children" are frequently not allowed to play with "bad children"; but also it can be underdone.

In the second place, the child's experience needs posi-tive development, expansion, stimulation and organiza-tion. There are ranges of possible human experiences not to be found in the current living of any one commu-nity; and there are intimations of wider ranges of expe-rience not yet achieved in any human community, but promised in the anticipations of our creative humanity, just as, say, the flying machine was promised in the hopes of men in the year 1900, although no flying machine was then in existence. This expanding of experience beyond the bounds set by our casual community living must be the function of some agency that is wiser than is the com-munity as a whole. Most communities can be persuaded to provide for the realization of their own hopes, even though the community as a whole may be unable to un-dertake that task itself. But such undertaking must be seen as a legitimate part of the life of the community, not as a private matter, or as a way of escape.

Here, then, are two phases of the general task of edu-cation which the community by itself is not quite able to perform: first, the defense of the child against the ex-treme morbidities of the community's own traditions and fears; second, leading out the child's experience, posi-tively, beyond the limitations of common knowledge and understanding. Humanity must find ways of escaping from its own morbidities and fears inherited from its accidental past; and of achieving that larger, more commanding future promised in its hopes and in its tools of intelligence. These tasks the community will do well to turn over to specialized agencies of education. These tasks are the function—and the justification—of the community's social instrument of education. Can a school do these things?

A Formula.—If we are to state this function in an algebraic formula, we shall have something like the following: the real task of the community's educational instrument is to provide those factors of experience which are not already provided by the community itself. The school must complete and integrate individual experience.

In other words, the school must escape from its traditions, which hamper it and keep it from doing its work, and it must become a real educational instrument, understanding its work in a scientific way. Historically, the school is the youngest of our institutions, and its work must be supplementary to the services of all the other institutions; psychologically, it claims to stand as the instrument of intelligence in experience, and, as such, it can scarcely demur if one points out that hiding within an ancient tradition is not so much an intelligent performance as it is the denial of intelligence. Little by little, the school is being forced to accept the logic of its own professions, and state its own function according to some such formula as the one given.

Some Corollaries.—Two corollaries emerge now from which, it seems, there can be no appeal. First, the making of a school curriculum is not wholly the schoolman's job. If the school is ever to escape being schoolish and become truly educational, the school curriculum must be conceived as of a piece with the whole educational curriculum; that is, it is part of that total of valuable experience which is the heritage of the children of the community and which will be the education of those children.

Second, the community as a whole makes the real curriculum—with what results we know. If education is ever to be more satisfactory than it is to-day, the whole community must recognize its share in making this real curriculum. The school must give over trying to set itself off from the community; its work must become integrated to the casual educational processes of the community, both by acceptance and by criticism. It is easy for the schoolman to withdraw into the school room and make his own curriculum, and then to blame the community for the failure of his academic enterprise, as many school men now do. When the school man learns to think of his task as integral with the whole process of education in the community, he will try to find out what that real task is: how to work out its various implications, and how to enlist the whole intelligence of the community in helping to provide a really intelligent program of education for the children. The community will have to become conscious of its devastating share in education before we can get on to a greatly constructive program.

This enlisting of the whole community to a share in the task of making an intelligent education is all the more necessary because just as soon as schooling escapes from the school and becomes education, learning will escape from an irrelevant scholasticism and become relevant social intelligence; that is to say, it will begin to *make a difference* not alone in the life and experience of the individual child, but in the life of the community. In the long run, in a democracy, unless schooling is to be a futile repetition of a meaningless past (and that would be the death of intelligence and, hence, of democracy), curriculum-making must be seen to be something more than the mere making of a school program: it must be seen to be—what it is—*community making* as well. It will become one phase of the great task of *adult education.*

The school, as we have seen, cannot do much alone toward making a different community. But, if a community can be enlisted, intelligently, in the making of a more intelligent school, it will be definitely engaged, at the same time, and in the same degree, in making itself a more intelligent community! The great scholastic error has always been and still is, that the school is the schoolman's domain, and that changes or modifications in the school or the curriculum are to be determined wholly by the convenience or interest of the school officials. Schoolmen must run the schools!

But, surely, we must now admit that a new fact brought into a school must, in the long run, produce a change in the community. A change in the curriculum of the school that has no effect upon the life of the community is not a change at all: it is an illusion. It is a mere shuffling of the cards—that leaves the deck the same as before. On the other hand, a change in the life of the community that has no reflection in the work of the school shows that the school has become or is becoming isolated from the realities of the community and is finding its tests and its support in some academic tradition; and that has always been the end of *education.*

The Failure of Educational Psychology.—Educational psychologists, of the psycho-physical tradition, have hoped to solve this problem of the rift between the school and life by developing a technique by means of which the intellectualistic materials of the curriculum may be made to produce corresponding intellectualistic effects in the minds of the children which will be worthy of school credits. They hope for a day when all children will be graded early in life in respect to their so-called "educability," so that they can be sent to schools specially prepared to deal with their particular levels of ability. This plan ignores and denies education, and places all its faith in *schooling*. If and when that result shall have been achieved, the academic drift will have become universal, and the irrelevant school will have been accepted and officially warranted by "science." Science will have put its seal upon its own negation—drift!

From such things, not in toto, but as finalities, educational intelligence must make its firm dissent. The community as a whole is the ultimate educator of human beings, whether children or adults; and a whole, or growing human being, not an intellectualistic acrobat, must be the aim of education.

In the accomplishment of this aim, some educational instrument must be devised by the community to do certain things the community itself cannot do. Something like a school we must always have.

But from the intellectualisms and remoteness from life which make up the curriculum of the present school and from those intellectualistic effects which now emerge as school credits, educational leaders must continuously and consistently appeal—to the whole life of the community, of which the school will be only a part—and to the whole experience of the child, of which his "intellect" should be only a part.

Accepting all the work of all the educational experimenters as valuable in its proper place and proportion, educational philosophy must continue to assert that the ultimate tests of both life and education are to be found not in school rooms nor in laboratories but in the expanding life and culture, beauty and joy, of our human communities, and in the growing control of the individual over his own life and destiny as an expressive, cooperative and yet critical member of that human community.

Education as a whole must find out how to achieve such broadly human results. The *school*—or whatever will eventually take the place of the school as the community's specific agency for doing what common experience cannot do—will have its share in this process, or these processes. But that share will be only a supplement. It will never be the whole of education!

The reason why it must never be more than a share will be set forth more fully in the next chapter.

CHAPTER XXXIII

EDUCATION AS INTEGRATION OF PERSONALITY

The most important aspect of a mode of organic behavior at any time or place is its unified totality. The whole man is the primary agent of response, all partial responses which analysis may reveal being subsidiary to and dependent upon the fully rounded dynamic character of the total response. Instead of saying that instinctive and other forms of behavior are a sum of reflexes chained together by a process of accretion which works either in the process of evolution or through the formation of specific habits, we should say just the reverse; namely, that vague, total, and undifferentiated response becomes, through a creative effort, differentiated and discrete. Out of the whole generate the parts; out of a primitive diffuse total-response come both instincts and reflexes through racial development, and likewise all habits and voluntary responses through individual development. . . . In order to find the right rhythm for any specific adjustment a procedure of trial and error is at first indicated: not however in the sense of a perfectly aimless and chaotic response, but only in the sense of discovering within the matrix of behavior, at first crudely and incompletely defined, a pattern that can be felt as adequate. When the right response is hit upon, the entire act is transformed. The internal structure of the behavior, until that moment vague and uncertain, now fits itself together as a complete and economical pattern—in a word the movement achieves a *melody* which it had previously lacked.— R. M. Ogden, in *Psychology and Education.*

The heredity of the modern American is increasingly diverse. His ancestry is of the whole human past. He often combines within himself enormously varied strains from scores of races. In some instances the integration of these diverse strains is not complete and he grows into a more or less divided personality. Education has but recently learned the meaning of integration.

Diversity in the Modern World.—The modern social world is exceedingly diversified. Its distractions are innumerable. The old small community integrations have largely disappeared. Racial types by the score rub shoulders on the streets of our cities, the adults getting no closer together. Distinctive fragments of the old folkways come into conflict in every neighborhood in the city. The city is a wilderness—of non-communicating groups.

These social distractions of the modern world, stimulating the diverse heredities of the modern individual, are producing the most disorganized personalities the world has known, at least since the brilliant days of Athens. When we add to all these things the effects of travel to all parts of the world, we get a rather significant picture of the modern person—varied, distracted, "wise," superficial!

We must admit that differentiation of native possibilities is necessary for the enrichment of personality. This is the basic process in education. For this purpose a world rich in all kinds of physical and social stimulations is necessary to the education of the individual. Some such world of nature and action was the background of that widely praised education which characterized America in the eighteenth and nineteenth centuries. The nineteenth-century American was not educated by schools but by his community.

The Need of Integration.—But integration of personality must always follow upon differentiation, or the result will be disintegration. For every enrichment of personality by decentralization of interest, skill or taste, there must be a compensating integration which binds up into a new forceful whole all the factors of this enriching being. This new unity must be an integration, not merely tying up a bundle.

In primitive times almost the whole impact of the community was integrative, or repressive, perhaps. Education was then too narrow. The primitive group was a closely knit community and it threw its repressive functions round about its members until they became as completely organized as was the community itself. This, without compensating differentiation, ends in stagnation.

That is, much of this primitive education was not integrative in the proper sense of the word. It molded the individual. It selected certain factors of experience as proper for him and compelled the repression of all the rest. It failed to be integrative in the sense used here. It selected, eliminated and molded. It did not integrate. It produced *good group members,* not integrated individuals.

The educational significance of the community is found in these integrative processes. The diverse materials, activities and interests of the world call out distinctive responses in the individual—in so far as he is able to respond. But it is the world as a whole—or some community as an integrated world—that rounds out personality and compels upon the individual an integration that corresponds to its own integration; an integrated community will, by and large, turn out integrated individuals—*whole* personalities. A distracted community will turn out distracted persons.   An over-organized community will turn out persons "sot in their ways."

Disintegrative Impacts of Institutions.—The impact of modern institutions upon children is frequently disintegrative.   Each institution appeals to some specific facet of personality and elaborates, even exaggerates, that phase unduly.   The modern world is characterized by people who are over-developed and under-developed in various ways.   They have too much religion and too little business; or too much politics and too little morality.   They advertise their memberships in institutions by their every move.   "The tired business man" is one of these exaggerations.   The religious fanatic in an age of science is another.

The whole history of the race has been a series of exaggerated alternations between over-integration and disintegration: over-integration of nations, communities and individuals.   Nature reveals two intimate processes—differentiation and integration.   There can be no expansion and enrichment of life without the former; there can be no permanence to life without the latter.   But neither statesmen nor educators seem ever to have understood these facts.   Both have overdone the integrative movement at times until social order has become institutional tyranny; then it has swung in the other direction until it has achieved wide disintegration.   Education is now but dimly perceiving the necessity of both differentiation and integration as continuing movements in human experience, not mechanically imposed but naturally grown.

At present individuals are rebelling in great numbers against the iron-clad tyrannies of our old group moralities as expressed in institutions and group opinion.   In this rebellion they have been aided by many things, for example, the distractions of wartime; the cynicisms that followed the war; and the rapid development of mechanisms such as the Ford which have aided the escape from institutional control. The "older generation," educated in the older community moralities and forms, has been scandalized by these rebellions; but it has scarcely understood their meaning and has scolded youth a good deal for its disintegrative tendencies.

Scolding is, of course, no solution for these problems. The post-war world is not contained and cannot be contained within the bounds of pre-war institutions and concepts, and we have no post-war community wise enough to give us new institutions and concepts. There must be definite disintegration of many old invidious institutions; there must be rich differentiation of emotion, intelligence, and will in the midst of these disintegrations; and there must come out of both the disintegration and the differentiation a new and rich integration of emotions, intelligence, and will to live. But these things can come not of themselves, but only as factors in *a new community life* and a new type of individual. Intellect can never save the race *ad hoc*. But intelligent development of conditions that will compel new and desirable integrations will provide "salvation."

What Is Integration?—We must recognize definitely with respect to all our institutions, but especially with respect to schools and education, that there is an infinite difference between molding a person and integrating a personality. Our historic and current institutions have assumed a molding authority over their own members, and have asserted a similar right over all individuals. They have even pronounced curses upon individuals who have refused to be molded by their express patterns. Once institutions, claiming divine sanction, could make good on their right to control and mold individuals. But likely that day is past. Even compulsory "education" may have had its day!

The process of molding persons is external and invidious. It selects certain aspects of personality for survival and it suppresses or represses or destroys as far as may be all other aspects of personality. The pathological results of such selecting and molding processes are, of course, all about us. They fill our institutions for the mentally unstable. They are the specific objects of study of Freudian analytic psychologists: they are the pathological specimens we all know—the neurotics, the dissociated personalities, the hysterics, the abnormal of nearly all sorts.

These types are to be found everywhere. Since our institutions are absolute and belated, they are adjusted to almost no one. Hence, almost every one who has been subjected to the molding influences of institutions, whether in the home, the school, the state, the church or the industrial world, is more or less abnormal, disintegrated. This is the meaning of the statement sometimes made that "the abnormal is the normal." The concept of integration is still alien to most of our thinking. The state insists upon loyalty and conformity; the church upon conversion or confirmation; the home upon obedience; the school upon learning; and industry upon efficiency. All these concepts imply molding and mechanization—not integration.

An integrative process would take account of all elements in personal development and undertake to cultivate all these elements in such ways that a living, growing, self-directive individual may emerge. It is certain that the various factors that inhere in any specific personality will show contradictions. A molding process would solve

these contradictions by forcefully suppressing all but one
factor in them and then developing the selected factor.
The integrative process would solve such a contradiction
by analytic understanding of the factors that enter into
it, and by helping all such factors come to terms with one
another so they can all be incorporated in an organic way
in the solution, which will be something new in the world.
This is the real problem of the teacher to-day. But it is
a problem not yet glimpsed by many teachers, and only
partially glimpsed by the psychiatrist. It is the problem
of developing an "intelligent life."

Thus we see that the older molding processes are invidious, selective, repressive, and under the control of
institutional or folkway attitudes representing the survival of some ancient fragmentary concept of life, usually
of a theological cast. Integrative processes, on the other
hand, are inclusive, analytic, intelligent, natural, and they
look ahead to an ever-widening enrichment of experience
and to an ever more inclusive world. Molding processes
seek to keep the world as it is. Integrative processes
would let the world become whatever it must become in
order to release all the values latent in our conflicts. Integration is always bringing something new to birth!

Integration in Schools.—The academic school has
never in its long history known this concept of integration. It has never consciously practised integration as a
present and future technique. "Good teachers" have
often done so—without quite knowing what they were
doing. The school has taught *old integrations*, wrought
out by great teachers and artists in ages of other disintegrations, as patterns for the present and the future.
This is why the so-called "humanities" have been so
highly esteemed in education. The "humanities" have
achieved their great reputation because they are old pro-

grams of integration worked out by great spirits in the presence of social disintegrations not unlike our own. But an old integration taken literally can merely defeat the mind of the new age in its inescapable task of doing in our time what that older mind did in its time. There is a beauty about classical interpretations of life that we eagerly long for. The significance of such interpretations is not, however, to be found in making them molds of our present life. That significance is to be found in discovering how men in other days worked out such beautiful integrations—until we too learn how to develop the "humanities" we need for our own day and its problems. We need to use the social and intellectual methods of the classical scholars and artists, but not their results: we must achieve our own results.

So the academic school has tended, not to integrate its pupils, but to mold them. It is not to be wholly blamed for this, at least, to-day. The school is not a social situation inclusive enough to provide integrative possibilities. The school provides only certain intellectual factors: it is not a human community; it is an intellectual instrument developed in the days when men lived in communities. The fact that we no longer live in communities is not to be charged against the school. The only thing that can be rightly charged against the school is the fact that it has not realized that we no longer live in the old community ways and that therefore its own method must be reconstructed to meet the new conditions of life and learning. The school did not make the modern world; but it might, at least, undertake to understand the world.

Anything less than a community which includes very wide ranges of physical and social activities, very rich opportunities for the expression and differentiation of feelings and emotions and, therefore, endless opportuni-

ties for intelligent analysis of the conditions of action and
values of action as expressed in emotion—anything less
than such a community cannot provide the setting, the
factors, and the stimulations for these continuous processes of differentiation and integration which should make
up the total of a real education to-day. Repression and
instruction can never be *education!*

The School's Part in Education.—The school might
have a vital place in these processes of differentiation and
integration; but schools do not at the present time envisage themselves in such rôles. If we may recall the
story of an earlier chapter (III), the disintegration of
group personality when the old group life broke down and
gave way to a larger but fragmented community, we shall
better understand the meaning of both differentiation and
integration. If we recall the story of the Greek pedagogue who helped young people understand the changing
world, find themselves in this new world, and organize
themselves in the midst of those disintegrations, we shall
have a graphic picture of the process of integration. Integration is a social-intellectual process that must develop
in the very midst of the conditions that call for it. It
cannot be imposed upon dead moments later! The pedagogue must live in the midst of the conditions that make
him necessary. The academic school made its great,
though quite natural, mistake when it assumed that the
processes carried on by the pedagogue were processes of
learning; that, therefore, they could be distilled into the
forms of knowledge; and that they could be carried outside the situation calling for them—to a school beyond
the areas of confusion, where they could be taught in
quiet—as lessons—in a timeless institution. The academic school assumes that the experiences developed in a
number of specific conflicts and integrations can be

brought together, generalized into a universal integration
and taught as an "education."

One result of this retreat of the academic school from
the situation that called the pedagogue into being is to
be found in the modern college student, who has taken
on immense areas of knowledge, every item of which once
had relevance to some specific social situation, but very
little of which will ever have such relevance for him—and
this for two reasons: first, because he will not be able to
recall the exact knowledge needed to meet any specific
situation at the moment when he needs it; and second,
because he will not come upon a social situation needing
knowledge at the exact moment when he is in command
of that bit of knowledge. Hence, he will have many bits
of useful knowledge which he can never use because he
will never be at the place of use at just the right time;
and he will meet many perplexing social situations which
he will not be able to deal with in terms of knowledge
that he possesses theoretically, because he will not be able
to dig up just the right knowledge at the right time.

The best he can hope for in general is that he will have,
now and then, the right bit of knowledge to meet a con-
fronting situation. Most frequently he will be in the position of "Skippy," in the comic strip who ended his evening prayer by saying, "And make Duluth the capital of
Vermont." When his surprised mother asked him why
he made such a curious prayer he replied, "Because I put
it that way in my examination and I want it to be right."
In other words, the typical student in the academic school
has great numbers of perfectly good answers to perfectly
relevant questions, but it is only by accident or by luck
or in response to prayer that he gets his particular answer
attached to the right particular question.

Habit-building is integrative—but old habits may war

against necessary new habits. Information may be integrative, but usually schoolish information gets no further than into the memory. "Discipline" is integrative; but if it wars against "new experiences" it becomes obstructive of differentiation and, hence, defeats that larger integration which should be the continuous increment of the years. Knowledge would be integrative if it were taught, or acquired for integrative purposes. Usually, to-day, its function is disintegrative: it destroys old assumptions, frequently without offering anything to take their place, as has been shown so fully in China, in recent decades.

The living processes of integration can use habit-building, information, discipline, knowledge, habit-reconstruction—everything in its business. It is not con-struction, but natural growth. True growth differentiates old structures and enlarges old functions, but keeps the integrity of the organism at all hazards. This is what education should do: the *end* of education is not intellect, but an integrating personality, in whom emotions grow ever freer, experience of the world grows ever wider and yet more organized, analytic intelligence becomes ever more inclusive and capable, and the will-to-act becomes ever more sure in any situation in which action is indicated.

No school can ever assure such an education. Nothing less than an integrating community, of which something of the nature of a school is a part, can surely bring it to pass.

CHAPTER XXXIV

EDUCATIONAL STATESMANSHIP

A false humility, a complaisance to reigning schools, or to the wisdom of antiquity, must not defraud me of supreme possession of this hour. If any person have less love of liberty, and less jealousy to guard his integrity, shall he therefore dictate to you and me? Say to such doctors, We are thankful to you as we are to history, to the pyramids and the authors; but now our day is come; we have been born out of the eternal silence; and now will we live, live for ourselves, and not as pall-bearers of a funeral, but as the upholders and creators of our age . . . Now that we are here, we will put our own interpretation on things, and our own things for interpretation . . . there is a better way than this indolent learning of another. Leave me alone; do not teach me out of Leibnitz or Schelling, and I shall find it all out for myself.—EMERSON, in *Literary Ethics*.

The belief that thought and its communication are now free simply because legal restrictions which once obtained have been done away with is absurd. Its currency perpetuates the infantile state of social knowledge. It blurs recognition of our central need to possess conceptions which are used as tools of directed inquiry, and which are tested, rectified and caused to grow in actual use. —DEWEY, in *Experience and Nature*.

The development of the academic school in America has been accompanied, inevitably perhaps, by the growth of the office of superintendent of schools. For a little while in the passing of the century of school development

405

the superintendent of schools promised to be the educational leader of his community—an educational statesman. That promise has faded of late. He is now, and is likely to remain for a long time to come, simply the executive of the school system, holding a position analogous to that of the superintendent of a factory. He keeps accounts—he hires and fires. He carries out the policies of the school board.

The Superintendent of Schools.—His work is almost completely concerned with the organization and operation of the school as a going concern. He must keep the school machine humming away peacefully; he must defend the school against local prejudices and traditions; and he must do what can be done to keep the school going in the face of those changes in the contemporary world that are difficult to avoid or ignore and that seem to threaten the work, even the existence, of the school. Whatever happens, the school must go on!

That is to say, all about us are changing knowledges, changing psychologies, changing social aims, and changing social organizations that should normally influence the activity of a social institution and perhaps throw it into confusion. The superintendent must keep all such influences out of the school as far as possible. There are problems of many kinds that impinge upon the free operation of the school! The schools must be kept going in spite of all such problems. The school's the thing: the children and teachers must be tallied, accounted for and paid off in grades or checks; the community must be kept happily unaware; the school-board must be constantly mollified; and all the records must be in perfect up-to-the-minute order.

From the standpoint of modern factory efficiency methods it is an inspiring spectacle. The school becomes increasingly a human factory from which pours an endless stream of young people *finished*, but without interest of any sort such as the school professes to stand for; with just such interests as the products of other factories have, namely, to find their places in the big machine and do their part in the world. They are schooled as other materials have been tooled. They are ready for their places in the world.

The Failure of Leadership.—This development of the school machine—unforeseen and probably undesired—is resulting in something near to tragedy, even for the superintendent. The machine is becoming so effective that it can run on without the superintendent, as has been abundantly shown in American cities in recent years. Minor defects can be turned over to trained mechanics for repair. It would be a bit of sardonic destiny if the efficient machine should finally reject the chief machinist.

But this position of the superintendent of schools as chief machinist has become an anachronism—from the standpoint of education. The local community, the nation at large, needs educational leadership to-day, and it finds little such leadership. The schooling of children is now the least important of educational responsibilities. The schools will go on undisturbed without a superintendent. They will turn out *schooling* without the constant watchfulness of a head foreman. They have become automatic.

But the community lacks educational leadership. The nation lacks *educational leadership*. Two educational tasks await the appearance of such leadership. These two tasks are quite inescapable if we are to have any real education at all in the future. And these tasks probably await the emergence of men who can escape from their absorption in the deadly routines of school administration and undertake to become educational leaders of their communities, even educational statesmen at large.

The Educational Administrator.—The first of these two tasks is the education of the teachers of the nation and of the local community to a liberal understanding of the *social nature* of education and integration in terms of their own work and to an intelligent defense of that interpretation in their own personalities and before the public. The teacher represents "the future of civilization," getting in its work upon the future generation. At present that future, so represented, is often not very inspiring and it is far from providing the ideals of a free society. This is not always the fault of the teacher. But sometimes it is.

The second of those tasks is bi-polar: on the one hand the community must be helped to accept wider intellectual and social outlooks—the humanities and the sciences, long praised in schools, must become the actual moods of the community, if the school is long to be permitted to do more than praise them; and on the other hand, the school group must learn from actual contacts with all the varied interests and concerns of the community what are the vital realities of life, and, therefore of education, and what education must do to make itself significant in its own local world. The child is of the local community. Education must, of course, be more than a local community interest; it must bring all times and all lands to the nurture of the common life. But the normal child is rooted in some sort of real social world, and an education that ignores or destroys the roots of the child's experience is no more intelligent than would be an agriculture that cuts off the roots of the stalks of corn for "ideal" reasons.

In other words, community realities and values in education cannot be left to the mercy or the interests or the initiative of the superintendent of schools, who is, to-day, usually neither an educational leader nor a community personality. Education is a problem of social and community statesmanship. The educational statesman must know schools and school practices, of course, but he must not be submerged in them; he must know more than them. He must know the world in which he lives and works, in its wider personal and institutional organization and impacts. He must know the education going on in the community outside the schools. How otherwise can he be a real educator? In the homes and neighborhoods of the city, in the playgrounds, back alleys and streets, in factories and machine shops and business houses, in the industrial world generally, education is continuously going on, and he must know these things.[1] The educational statesman must know politics and the political world, churches and the religious drift, social life and recreation, both legitimate and illicit; he must know the moralities of the world and of his communities, both the petty and the real; and he must have his roots deep in everything that affects the intelligence of the community. He must have a share in all these things, because in spite of all our idealizations of the school, the realistic education of from 90 to 98 percent of our children and young people is the product of non-academic influences. An educational statesman must know where the education of the community is coming from. He will not attempt to deny most of that education with an institutional gesture!

Ahead, for our whole social order, lies the long, slow, even heart-breaking task of escaping from mere custom, tradition and the mechanics of old institutionalisms into

[1] The most far-reaching education in the world to-day, perhaps, is found in what machines are doing to men, both in the way of disintegrating them and in the way of more or less satisfactory organization of their personal and social lives!

new customs, traditions and institutional relationships that will exhibit more understanding, sympathy and social intelligence. The factory superintendent often declares that he has no interest in any such reconstructive results or aims: his interest is in products and profits. The superintendent of education *must have* such interest; but his interest must be more than emotional, more than official; it must be human, intelligent and real. The superintendent of schools can play the game of the factory superintendent. But a superintendent of education must have imagination enough to see what is happening in his world.

Educational Progress.—Schools will continue to have some share in education of children; but it must be obvious by this time that the education of children for the new age of humanity will never get ahead faster than the mental arrest of the adult community will permit it to go on. The progress of any school is conditioned by the intelligence of its community. The superintendent of schools usually accepts that fact and lets it go at that; and gives his attention to perfecting details of the machine. But the superintendent of education will understand that he may not let things go. He must meet the educational task of his time. He must make education a matter of adjustment to the moving, changing world. He will know that the best way to bring about educational progress is by developing a broader community intelligence. Hence, he will spend his energies, not on the petty details of school mechanics—if for no other reason than that a school machine runs itself very well—but in helping his community understand what education is, what education the coming years demand, what education the children and youth of the community must have in view of the coming years. He will be an educational statesman, not merely a section hand, or even a foreman in an educational factory. He will not tamely submit to the dictations of a belated community. He will make that community his problem, until he learns how to bring it up to the level of intelligence upon which it will permit a real education to take the place of dead scholasticism and the rattling of school machinery. And as a free man he will occasionally pay his mind out on the "dead wood" that clutters colleges and universities.

At present, every progressive movement in America, including whatever is really progressive in our academic schools themselves, is more or less completely submerged in the chaos of our war-time disintegrations and our primitive fears. We scared ourselves near to death in wartime, and have not recovered. We are still frightened by all sorts of shadows. Our pre-war institutions just run on, more or less sadly. There is little statesmanship of any sort in the world, and almost no educational statesmanship. Our school superintendents are mostly institutionalized administrators, recommended not by their understanding of the world, but by their graduation from some big university; and they work away at their own narrowly conceived technical tasks of making the school run. Teachers are dominated by them—so that intelligent criticism of a superintendent by an intelligent teacher is regarded as of the nature of treason. The public is impressed by them—even when it knows that school results are not satisfactory.

In place of this type of institutional leadership, we shall some day have educators who are outstanding personalities in their communities; whose very presence will be instinct with the spirit of both science and good will; who will represent the eager, sincere efforts of their communities to find more intelligent living; and whose life-long task it will be to help bewildered civic and educational instruments find themselves and learn how to cooperate to a single great end—the intelligent great community.

That end is not to be achieved primarily by the education of children, as now, to present-day forms of living. That end will be approached just in so far as we further the intelligence of the whole community. If any should fear that such a statement implies the neglect of children, the answer may be made at once that any furthering of the intelligence of the community will be a program from which the children cannot be excluded. The hope of children is in advancing community intelligence, not in school systems.

In every neighborhood, even in the fragments of the world that pass to-day for communities, there are vast riches of materials and processes that might enter into the expanding experience of the children, if there were any one about with imagination enough to see those things and make them available. The Greek "pedagogue" did just this in an age similar to ours, and we must rediscover something of that same old method. A statesman of education would be intelligent enough to do such a thing—and many another equally desirable.

The Freedom of the Schools.—There are those, of course, who argue that if the politicians would "let the schools alone," they could get ahead with their real job of educating the children and thus they could "save civilization." But the schools are *not going to be let alone.* All such pleas are a waste of time and breath. The doctrine that schools should be free from all interference on the part of the community and that an expert staff should be allowed to operate the schools unhampered by any community criticism, always breaks down in the presence of changing social conditions. The task of education has never, in spite of school legends, been turned over to the school; and it never will be turned over to any school, for the simple reason that it cannot be. School people, including the superintendent, cannot withdraw into their private areas of professional prestige and ask the public to send on their children and "then let us alone." Education is a social process and the community will always be concerned in what the school is doing. Soon or late, the community will check up on the whole program of its schools; whether intelligently or unintelligently will depend in part at least on what educational leadership has done to develop intelligence in the whole community.

It seems, from current situations, pretty clear that unless the superintendent of schools becomes big enough to be an effectual factor in the education of the whole community, he will not long have the chance to work even at the schooling of the children of the community. That is to say, unless he learns how to become something of an educational statesman and undertakes to develop all the educational resources of the whole community—not merely the schooling of the schools—he will not long be accepted even as a foreman of the school plant. He must develop in the direction of the Greek "pedagogue of the community," or else find himself isolated in a subordinate position, the prey of every passing political vulture.

CHAPTER XXXV

THE SCHOOL OF THE FUTURE

The family and neighborhood, with all their deficiencies, have always been the chief agencies of nurture, the means by which the dispositions are stably formed and ideas acquired that laid hold of the roots of character. The Great Community, in the sense of free and full intercommunication, is conceivable. But it can never possess all the qualities that mark the local community. It will do its final work in ordering the relations and enriching the experience of local associations. The invasion and partial destruction of the life of the latter by outside uncontrolled agencies is the immediate source of the instability, disintegration and restlessness which characterize the present epoch. . . . There is no limit to the liberal expansion of personal intellectual endowment which may proceed from the flow of social intelligence when that circulates by word of mouth from one to another in the communications of the local community. That and that only gives reality to public opinion. We lie, as Emerson said, in the lap of an immense intelligence. But that intelligence is dormant and its communications are broken, inarticulate and faint, until it possesses the local community as its medium.—DEWEY, in *The Public and Its Problems.*

Prophecy is a precarious trade. Conditions change rapidly these days and every change in conditions makes less likely the fulfillment of any prophecy based on present situations. But the meaning of intelligence is found in the adjustment of individuals, groups, and institutions to changing conditions. Intelligent adjustment involves

414

forecast of the future. The conditions of adjustment must be presented in advance of working out the mechanisms of adjustment. Hence, intelligent adjustment implies not merely adaptation of the adjusting organism to an environment but also the reconstruction of the environment to meet the real needs of the adjusting organism. That is to say, intelligent adaptation lies always in the future and must, therefore, always have in it an element of prophecy. So to our prophecy!

The Mind of the Inventor.—Not realizing the social implications of what they were doing, inventors have for a hundred and fifty years been making machines that have not only turned old mechanical methods out of use in favor of new mechanical and industrial orders, but in the very same breath they have turned old economic, political, social, moral, religious and intellectual orders out of house and home, without thought and without care. The chief of these inventions, the steam engine, has completely unmade the old rural and village community, and has made the modern industrial city with its millions of people, milling in congested area.

If by some chance of scientific fortune, the electric age had preceded the steam age, the effect upon civilization might have been very different. Electric power can be utilized at any point within 500 or 1,000 miles of the place where it is generated and in any quantity, from $\frac{1}{16}$th of a horse power to 10,000 horse power or more. Steam power, on the other hand, must be utilized within two or three hundred feet of the place where it is generated. If electric power had preceded steam power, the industrial revolution might have taken place without any corresponding social revolution—the older community life might have escaped disintegration and the building up of great cities might have been long delayed and much more gradual.

But the fact that steam power preceded electric power meant inevitably the drawing away of tens of thousands, even millions, of people from their earlier habitats and piling them up in great industrial centers, with all the social chaos that that has involved. And now since the steam engine has piled up the cities, electric power is made subordinate to the present social and economic situation and is used, largely, as transportation power as means of delivering the workers to their posts near the steam engine.

Of course, James Watt and George Stephenson foresaw none of these things. No one could have dreamed of the social results of these physical inventions. Even to-day, with the facts plainly before us, it is almost incredible. We do not think of them as real; we have achieved only the dream stage ourselves one hundred and fifty years after James Watt. So much has physical invention upset the orderly working of our minds.

The Problem of Mind.—For three hundred years, then, and specifically for one hundred and fifty years, inventive mind has been engaged in reconstructing the physical bases of existence and making tools which should bring larger areas of natural resources and power under control. With these facts there can be no quarrel, though the results of these facts are not altogether to our liking. We shall not do well to blame James Watt for the evils of to-day.

But on the other, this is the fact: the present economic and social order, or disorder, is, in large measure, a by-product of the inventions of the last three hundred years. It is not the *product* but a by-product of mind. Mind is not in it: mind passed by, busy with more direct things! What then?

able to feel that he is of its wholeness a part, and not merely a part of some fragment of it. It must provide for all that is human. It must have within its bounds and available to its membership young and old, actual processes of work: work that has both economic value and educational significance. It will have civic order of such sort that children can have the sense of growing up into this order, participating in it and understanding it. It will have the equivalent of the finest religious life of our times, which will provide childhood and youth opportunity to develop feelings for something larger and finer than themselves. It will have cultural interests, artistic, recreational and social, that will give the child and the youth room for the release of all their creative powers. And it will provide all the factors of education that are needed by children and young people. This community will have its own self-respect and integrity; but it will not be provincial in the sense of being cut off from or antagonistic to other communities. It will feel its relationships to other communities and to the world. Its members will have self-respecting capacity to achieve understanding in dealing with other communities, and with the world, because they will be rooted in the reality of their own community. Such communities are now developing in specific areas along the Atlantic seaboard and elsewhere, too, perhaps.

The Nature of the School in Such a Community.—In the community of the future there will not be one school; there will be any number of schools devoted to any number of diverse activities and aims. Democracy is realized not in sameness but in diversity. The texture of individual variation must be adequately woven into the whole fabric of community life so that each individual will be developed vigorously in his own right and so that each community will have an indigenous culture, the product of its own culture-past and its present individual variations. Whatever will relate the individual intelligently, sympathetically, creatively to his community and the world must be provided as far as possible in the common life. The economic, political, religious, social, recreational interests of the community must again become educational. Beyond these helps, it will be the business of the community, working through some intelligent educational instrumentality to make wider provision for the complete education of childhood and youth and the adult as well.

Individuals must be helped to achieve such efficiencies as they desire or as will make them effective participants in the industrial and social life of their community. They must achieve such personal freedoms as will enable them to be creative in whatever direction their interests may lead. The realms of mind and science must be ever the concern of the intelligence of the community. The problems of discovering the effect upon the moral and spiritual life of the community of any readjustment in the physical or industrial environment must be endless matters of concern. And for all these reasons opportunity for freedom of thought, freedom of research, freedom of teaching must be ever kept open. If we are to have a human community we must have *mind*.

The interrelations of intellectual development, with all other aspects of development—physical, economic, social, biological, moral—must more clearly be foreseen by the educational forces of the community of the future. The part-time school will play a much larger rôle in such a community; we shall not have so much need for abstract mind developed in academic isolation. We shall need concrete minds developed in the give and take of adventurous living.

How Shall Such a Program Be Accomplished?—The task of community building in this educational sense, by which education itself is to be redeemed from its own academic fate and in some measure, at least, the "great dichotomy" is to be healed, implies attention to the education of adults rather than to the education of children. The education of children has got about as far as it can get until the adult world yields a bit. For the sake of progress in the education of children, it may be necessary to pay less attention to elementary education for a time and to deal with the far more pressing problem of the education of adults. Men and women must be educated for real participation in a world friendly to science and intelligence. An illustration of this task comes from post-war Germany. The adult German mind was not sympathetic after the war to the change from monarchical institutions to republican institutions. The very fate of the revolution has depended upon the capacity and the will of the adult generation in Germany to re-educate itself to the acceptance of the republic.

The American mind faced the same problem on a smaller scale, at the close of our own American Revolution. But the American mind never accepted the problem and never solved it. It remains unsolved in large measure to this day. The American mind is even now morally and intellectually scarcely more ready for the real implications of democracy and science than is the German mind to-day for the reality of the republic. We need adult education for our future quite as much as Germany does. This fact ought to be recognized, especially by all those educational institutions in America that are dealing with

young people between the ages of seventeen and twenty-
five. Here is the great crisis in the education of the individual, and this is where a genuinely democratic and scientific education on a national scale will be won or lost.

Adult Ignorance of the Meaning of Education.—
A chief obstacle to the development of a real education
is found in the stagnation of adult understanding. The
school has always been an intellectual, bookish institution. As we have seen, it began that way as the result
of an historical accident; and it was proper under the
conditions that produced the school. But the adult mind
of all successive generations has never been able to escape
the form of that accident. Schoolmen and laymen alike
hold that the school's business is "the cultivation of the
intellectual life" of the pupils. It stands to reason, does
it not, that the intellectual life can best be cultivated by
the use of intellectual materials? Not one-half of one
percent of the adult public holds any other point of view.

Yet, children are not intellectual creatures. They may
become intellectual some day, if permitted to do so. But
nearly everything the adult world permits to them tends
to operate to keep them from becoming intellectual, primarily by forcing the intellectual upon them ahead of
time. Children are biological organisms. What we call
childhood is not properly human childhood at all, but biological childhood, which achieves maturity at nine or ten,
and old age at eleven or twelve. Human childhood begins, properly speaking, with puberty and adolescence, or
at eleven or twelve, perhaps. Hence, at eighteen, boys
and girls are just the right human age, namely, six years
old, to start to school. The most intelligent of modern
nations, Denmark, has grown intelligent through the development of a great school system that takes children at
eighteen, without other prerequisite than age, and helps

them to find out how to face the world intelligently—in their own intelligence.

But it is likely that this paragraph will seem to practically all adult readers the quintessence of nonsense. It is the unabashed ignorance of adults that stands in the way of genuine education, whether for children or for themselves.

A National Program in Education.—We have much talk to-day about the need of a national department which shall put education on the same dignified basis with agriculture and which will make our nation seem to be as much interested in children as in pigs. There is much to be said for such a national department but most of what has been said is argument against the proposal rather than for it. It were far better that we should have no national program in education than that we should have one in which the analogy of the department of agriculture's care for pigs was transferred to a department of education's care for children. The education of children requires a different kind of program from that adequate to the successful raising of pigs. Complete centralization of the care of pigs might result in a more desirable standard pig. But only the machinists in education want to turn out a standard child.

We do need a national program in education, but it should not be under the direction of the academic schoolman of to-day. For such direction would mean the apotheosis of the academic school. A national program in education should be directed by educational statesmen who can see that the real problem of education to-day is not better schools but better communities; and who would, therefore, be interested not primarily in the centralization of a great national school system but in the decentralization of educational interest and in the development, in a broadly social sense, of every local community in America, and of schools as agencies of intelligence in all local communities. We are too much concerned with the schooling of children, and not enough concerned with the education of the whole people. A national department of education presided over by a Socratic "pedagogue," whose prime interest would be the "bringing to birth" of every community in the nation, would be supportable. A national department of education that would help to decentralize educational interest and attention, and that would intelligently undertake to develop the latent resources of all our local communities would be desirable. But who ever heard of a centralized department supporting a program of decentralization?

The trend of government in the immediate future will be more and more toward the center. The only chance America has of escaping the demoralizing effects of this trend lies in the possibility that we shall have a few educational statesmen who will rise above their petty and pretty institutionalisms and stand, even with their backs to the wall, for the educational freedom of local communities, for the free play of all educational influences through all our living, for something of genuine individuality.

CHAPTER XXXVI

THE PROBLEM VS. THE PROBLEMS OF EDUCATION

We talk glibly about laws of learning and psychological principles which are rarely laws or principles in the true sense of the terms.—V. A. C. HENMON, in *Journal of Educational Research*, May, 1925.

There are many problems of education, as the preceding chapters have endeavored to set forth and to dramatize. Many of those problems, as aspects of school and educational effort, are to be found listed in the appendix. This is a book of problems. "Getting an education" consists not of getting *answers,* as most teachers imagine, but of getting *problems,* as all practical men know so well. Hence, no excuse is offered for attempting to increase the number of problems in the awareness of the readers of this book, save the old statement that he is a benefactor of the race who makes two—of anything—grow where only one grew before. Of course, increasing the number of problems must be done fairly and decently. The original baffling problem must be split up into two or more less baffling smaller problems; but these less baffling ones must always be envisaged as factors in the solution of the original problem. In "getting problems" we share the future tasks of the race and the larger intelligence that comes of problems met and solved. In "getting answers" we merely share the past achievements of the race, the old technics, the old ways, the old habits, and the accepted and often sterile knowledge of that by-

gone past. The real student, the active and vital partici-
pant in the tasks of to-day, must be reconciled to the con-
frontation of problems, his own problems and the problems of the modern world. Teachers—of old materials—
may claim exemption from the problems of to-day; but
surely no *educator* can do so!

The Problem of Education.—But a positive education
ends not in the mood of differentiation, but in that of
integration. Hence, a positive program for educational
reconstruction must end on the note of integration. Over
and above all the *problems of education* rises *the problem*
of education. To that we turn, briefly, in this last chapter.

That problem is the thread that binds all these chapters together into a single whole, the question that runs
all through these pages, namely, to-wit: How can youth
avoid the dead hand of the past, and still secure for its
own uses the living tissues of the past? Or, how can the
new generation escape the domination of the passing generation, and yet come into the possession of the wisdom
that the world has found, to date? The problem is old,
of course—as old as the days of the Athenian Sophists,
at least. The answers proposed through the ages have
been many, some of them of very great promise. In the
long run, however, practically all of them have resolved
themselves into one or the other of the solutions offered
at present, namely the academic solution, as set forth in
Part One of this book, or the individual solution, as set
forth in Part Two. In the first solution, the individual is
absorbed into the group, the community, the past, the
traditions, the folkways, and becomes a fragment of the
larger whole. In the second solution, the individual becomes absolute, and the group dissolves into the atoms.
Neither of these solutions is convincing or final; but as
long as we shall have the former setting itself up as final

and complete, we shall need whatever corrective and hope the latter may be able to conjure up. We shall be able to emerge from these fragmentary solutions into something more convincing only as we see these solutions as fragmentary, and are willing to face the problem, as a whole. "When the half-gods go, the gods may come!"

Statement of the Problem.—*The true educational agency is the community within which and by means of which* the individual comes to whatever maturity he reaches. By and large, the qualities of that community will be reflected in its members, variously, of course, as they have various capacities for responding to its impacts, and as they touch various facets of its existence. The real problem of education, then, becomes that of *making a community* that shall be expressive of humanity, present and to come. "There can be no substitute for the vitality and depth of close and direct intercourse and attachment." The disorganization of our older communities was inevitable, desirable; but disintegration, as an accepted state, is not inevitable, desirable. Its continuance is merely proof of our immaturity, or our inertia.

Nor can we ask some fragment of the disorganized community, for example, the school, to take over the whole problem of integration and handle it, *ab extra*, arrogantly, intellectualistically. We have complimented human nature by this proposal long enough. Human life is real. It is as real as corn and cattle, or any other living thing; and it must achieve its ends, however desirable, by processes that do not violate its own reality. *The problem of education* is the problem of community-making, in the most fundamental sense of the term. The problem of the school is merely a chapter in that more inclusive problem. School is important. But an *unrelated school*—a school that is unacquainted with, or indifferent to, the world within which it is attempting to operate, the world from which its "pupils" come each morning and to which they must go back evenings—is an impertinence. A school that compels children to become "pupils" for some hours each day is in the long run an immoral institution. The vitalities of life are in *communities*, not in *institutions!* "Humanity" is a healing wholeness, not an institutional fragmentariness.

How, then, shall that whole and healing community life be rediscovered and reestablished on the earth? What are the present facts about such community, either *in esse,* or *in posse?* What fragments of such community now hold us, mold us, manhandle us, break us to pieces, turn us lop-sided, bring us to a distorted or real completion and integration?

All the lesser, detailed problems set forth in these pages find their proper meanings within the configuration of this problem. Primitive educations that persist beyond their time; disorganizations that break up old integrations; new organizations that merely drift together like fragments of a shipwreck in an ocean whirlpool; new hypotheses forecasting a more intelligent future; new materials; new methods; new institutional alignments; new philosophies; new psychologies; new logics—whatever the past or the present has uncovered finds its real significance within the configuration of this problem. All these factors give content to the problem. But the problem is more than the sum of these factors; the whole is always more than the sum of its parts. The problem of education is before us, and until men find complete release and complete integration in community life that is fully released and fully integrated that problem will be there.

The Answer.—For the answer to the problem is not in existence anywhere. It is not of the past. It is not of the present. It is of the future, and like any real future it must be *created*. The problem cannot be "measured," for its outlines project beyond the existent present into the non-existent future. The answer to the problem cannot be "measured" or "tested," because that answer is not in existence. As Professor Dewey has said: "Even if it be true that everything which exists could be measured if we only knew how, that which does *not* exist cannot be measured. And it is no paradox to say that the teacher is deeply concerned with what does not exist."

The "answer" to the argument of this book, the answer to the problem of education, is of the future. It is not, therefore, something to be learned. It is something to be invented, discovered, thought about, imagined, wrought out of the materials and the hopes of the world. This gives place for *mind* in education, imagination, scientific method as the modern exemplification of the hunt, dramatic suspense and expectation, accidents and happy guesses, tests and experiments, hypotheses and verifications—in the actualities of living. The answer is not in existence. Hence it is not in books. Hence it cannot be set as a lesson to be learned by students. It is not a "blue print" of a construction to be everywhere set up by "experts" and imposed on local communities. It must emerge, or be made to emerge, by creative insistence, out of, from within the processes of, community living. Nothing but its pale shadow will ever be written down in books, even as the materials of this book are but faint echoes of the actualities with which it is concerned.

This specific book will have missed its whole reason for existence if, at the end of the reading, or the study, the reader or student shall be able to say: "Well, that ends that!" Books settle nothing. At least this book settles nothing. The intent of this book is to unsettle our educational complacencies, and to compel passive minds to realize something of the same *chaos* that now really obtains in the social, economic and educational realities of the world. The word *chaos* just used was deliberately chosen, for it was out of *chaos* that the world was made. "And the world was without form and void; and darkness covered the face of the deep; and the creative spirit moved over the face of the waters."

"And the creative spirit said, Let there be light! And there was light!"

The creative educational spirit of our times must, it seems, likewise emerge from its comfortable, platonic aloofness in its academic groves, and move out into the social chaos of the age, to brood over the surface of the troubled waters, seeking for a new "firmament," and a new light. Our school and campus "platonists," handing down supernal Ideas from their serene heights, have failed to solve the educational problems of the age; have failed to solve even their own problems.[1] The problem of education is submerged in the problem of civilization in general; and *civilization* is being defined and determined, these days, more by what goes on in the chaos of the market-place than by the meditations of the campus or the school. On the very day upon which these words are being written, a local newspaper gives editorial statement to this undeniable fact. The editor says: "Whenever we find teachers in the university attempting to teach, from mere conviction, what no man may know about life and its eventualities, we shall strike vigorously at the practice. . . . The statement attributed to Mr. ——, if meant literally, would have been destructive to that hopefulness without which life cannot be sincere

---

[1] This latter failure was inevitable, since "their own problems" are not their own, but all the world's.

and optimistic. . . . We contemplated a moral point to be driven home."

Some will retort: "The very world of industry that you hold in such reverence and to which you seem to want to surrender the control of education, is the product of discoveries and inventions made in university laboratories. If you want to get to the center of *power*, go where the inventors and discoverers are at work—to the campus and the school!"

But there is here no question of "surrendering." There is here only the question of fact: where is the educational control of the age, as shown by the actual centers of power?

Moreover, Edison, Steinmetz and Ford are not of the campus, and they never were. Even those investigators who work on the campus are mostly but nominally there. Their real affiliations and interests are more and more with business and industry; their interests in "culture" and "learning for its own sake" grow more attenuated year by year.

The ultimate *aims* of education are found in the world of social, professional and industrial affairs; the materials of education come, in the last analysis, from the same source; the methods of education must be adjusted to the processes there used; and any criticisms of methods, materials, or aims, must take its rise out of the real world. If there is to be any real culture in future America, it must, like the culture of Athens, be wrought of the stuff of the life and work of the people; it cannot be made merely of old cultures handed down in bits from academic heights. Platonism is, indeed, a noble ideal: too noble and too ideal for the human race in the America of our times! It is not a question of surrendering: it is a question of beginning where the community really is, and building on the solid foundations of reality—from the ground upward, not from the clouds downward.

Must not educational statesmanship, accordingly, turn again with Socrates to the market-place, and try to discover the real bases of real education in the actualities of the world? Do we not need, to-day as never before since his own time, the inspiring example of this most modern of men, the ancient "pedagogue of community," for leadership in the understanding, first of civilization, and then of education as the technic of progressive perpetuation of civilization? Not his words, but his spirit!

APPENDIX

for the study of

ASPECTS OF CONFLICT IN EDUCATION

With bibliographical materials

INTRODUCTORY CHAPTER

What two specific conceptions of education are now widely held both in the school and in the community, and what is the standing of each? Are these conceptions mutually exclusive, or may they be "harmonized"?

Cobb: *The New Leaven.*
Dewey: *New Schools for Old.*
Hart: *Light from the North*, Ch. 1.
Judd: *Psychology of Social Institutions*, Chs. 14-18.

PART ONE

THE INSTITUTIONAL INTERPRETATION OF EDUCATION

CHAPTER I: SCHOOL

What was the program of a country school in the first half of the nineteenth century? Why was that school so highly esteemed? Was its work satisfactory at the time? Has the country school changed much to date? Is its work as satisfactory now as it was a century ago? What explanation for these facts? How does the city school of to-day differ from the country school of a century ago? Why is the city school so much criticised to-day? Have these current criticisms any valid basis?

Hart: *Educational Resources of Village and Rural Communities.*
Sullivan: *Our Times*, Vol. 2.

Chapter II: The Primitive Group as Educator

Distinguish between *schooling* and *education*. Which is the more inclusive? Which seems the more important?

What are "folkways"? How did they come to be? What was—and is—their significance? Their value? Has the human race ever escaped from them? Are modern communities, or individuals, subject, in any way, to folkways? How do they educate?

How do folkways differ from institutions? What is an institution?

What was *education* in the primitive group? Can such *education* be justified to-day? Does any of it exist to-day? Where? Why?

Briffault: *The Mothers*, Vol. 1, pp. 1-100.
Spencer: *Education of the Pueblo Child*.
Sumner: *Folkways*.
Thomas: *Source Book for Social Origins*, Part 2.

Chapter III: Disorganization of the Primitive Community

What was the size of the "primitive group"? What causes populations to increase? What happens to a village when it grows beyond village dimensions? What is meant by *organization* of a community? By *disorganization?*

What happens to an individual when he goes from a village to the city? When the village in which he grew up grows into a city? What changes in his modes of living is he compelled to make, if any? Can the resident of a city *know* his city?

Can he know an *institution?* Are institutions "good" for a city, or "bad" for it? Why? Which should dominate: the city, or institutions?

Hart: *Community Organization*.
Lindeman: *The Community*.
McIver: *Community*.
Steiner: *The American Community in Action*.

CHAPTER IV: THE FUNCTIONS OF THE PEDAGOGUE

How did boys choose their occupations a century ago? How do they choose them to-day? How did Ben Franklin come to be a printer? How many occupations could have been found in the Boston of Franklin's time? How many are listed in the U. S. census to-day?

Does *education* mean anything in the modern city that it did not mean in the old rural community? Does it call for any new *powers* in the individual? Does it call for any different type of teacher, or teaching? If so, in what respects? Would an old-time country school be adequate in the modern city? Are present city schools able to do what is expected of them? If not, why not? Is their problem one of lack of funds, or does it go deeper than that?

Does the modern community provide any one who performs the functions here said to have been performed by the Greek "pedagogue"?

> Franklin: *Autobiography.*
> Hart: *Discovery of Intelligence*, Chs. 4-7.

CHAPTER V: THE PEDAGOGUE OF THE COMMUNITY

Socrates has a great reputation in history—what is the real basis of that reputation? What were his real services to humanity? What were the real charges upon which he was tried and condemned to death? Was his condemnation in any sense justified? Has any one else ever been punished for like causes?

Did Athens, the city, need the work of Socrates? Does any modern city need similar work? What would a "modern Socrates" try to do? What would be the character of a "modern Socrates"?

Does the modern city resemble Athens in any particular? Have we any "sophists" to-day? Who are they, and what are they trying to do?

> Aristophanes: *The Clouds.*
> Hart: *Discovery of Intelligence.*
> Plato: *The Apology.*

Chapter VI: The Escape into the Academic

What is meant by "learning by experience"? How does this differ from "learning out of books"? Where do books come from? Where have the *ideas* found in books come from? Where did Socrates get his *ideas?* Where did Plato claim he got *his* ideas? What was the real source of Plato's ideas? Does it make any difference whether a teacher teaches in the center of the city or out in the edge of the city? How did Plato's teaching differ from that of Socrates? Why is Plato called "academic"? What does the term mean? Was Socrates "academic"? Why not? Can education be non-academic to-day? Why is so much of modern education "academic"? Does that characteristic improve education, or does it make it less desirable? How would a non-academic teacher differ from an academic one to-day?

Hart: *Discovery of Intelligence,* Chs. 6-10.
Judd: *Psychology of Social Institutions,* Chs. 14-18.
Plato: *The Republic,* Bks. 3-5.
Sullivan: *Our Times,* Vol. 2.

Chapter VII: Plato's Royal Lie

Psychology, these days, is much concerned with *repressions, suppressions, complexes,* etc. What do these terms mean, and what is the basis of the facts they connote? What part has "lying" had in the development of government? Education? Religion? Morality? Business? What is "diplomacy"? Trace the element of lying through Plato's *Republic* and *Laws* by means of the indexes.

Why was Plato so concerned to "put over" a certain type of educational and social organization? Do teachers still hold those same views, anywhere? What "royal lies" are told to-day?

Adler, Alfred: *The Neurotic Constitution.*
Hart, Bernard: *Psychology of Insanity.*
White: *Outline of Psychiatry.*

CHAPTER VIII: THE TRIUMPH OF THE ACADEMIC AND THE GREAT DICHOTOMY

What is the origin of the folk-belief that certain parts of human nature are "high" and other parts are "low"? Where does this belief usually "crop out"? What part does it play in modern religion? In government? In business? In family life? In social life? In education? What foundation has it in actual experience?

What methods has religion developed for dealing with this "dichotomy"? What does government do about it? Are there any laws with respect to it? What does the school do about it?

Accepting the division of human nature into "high" and "low" aspects (for purposes of the argument), consider the various phases of the school in their relation to this division: With which part of the individual is the teacher concerned— with the "high" or the "low"? To which part is the curriculum directed? School discipline? Which part learns lessons? What does *educational psychology* have to say about these two parts? Where is the I.Q located, in the "higher" or "lower" part? Is "intelligence" concerned with emphasizing this division, with ignoring it, or with healing it? What is "morality" in the light of this Platonic psychology? What is "culture"? What is "education" for? In the light of this Platonic point of view, what should one do about work? About leisure? About marriage?

> Dewey: *Human Nature and Conduct.*
> "   *The Public and Its Problems.*
> "   *Reconstruction in Philosophy.*
> Hart: *Inside Experience.*
> New Testament: *Book of Romans.*
> Plato: *Republic,* and *The Laws.*

CHAPTER IX: INTERLOCKING INSTITUTIONS IN THE MODERN WORLD

What are the major institutional organizations of the modern world? For the sake of experiment, how should these be arranged in order to show their relative importance as servants of the "common weal"? As matter of practical fact, which of them is most powerful in controlling public and private action? What is meant by the "economic determination of history"? Does this appear anywhere in the modern world?

Americans talk a great deal of their "free schools." What does "free" mean in this phrase? Does any other institution, or social organization, attempt to control the schools? What place has politics in the control of the schools—in actual fact? What place has religion? What place has business? Does either of these interests care what is taught in the schools? What can they do about it? What do they try to do about it? Is there any cure for this "meddling" with the schools?

Résumé: What is the specific conception of education stated in Part One, and what are the bases of criticism herein set forth? Do those bases seem substantial, and are the criticisms valid?

> Aristotle: *Politics.*
> Beard: *Whither Mankind.*
> Counts: *School and Society in Chicago.*
> Dewey: *The Public and Its Problems.*
> Hart: *Discovery of Intelligence,* Chs. 34-37.
> Plato: *The Republic.*
> Sumner: *Folkways.*

PART TWO

THE PSYCHOLOGICAL INTERPRETATION OF EDUCATION

CHAPTER X: THE INDIVIDUAL

How does the story of the origins of the human race as given in Genesis differ from that given in the school histories—as to the historic facts? As to the psychological implications? Can these two accounts be harmonized? (Better not be too sure!)

In the "natural history of man" which comes first: the community, the group, or the individual? What does the school work for: better individuals, better communities, or better groups? Or none of these? What is "education" trying to do with the individual: make him a better member of society, or a better individual? Or both? Or neither?

Dewey: *School and Society.*
Hart: *Social Life and Institutions.*
Smith: *Education Moves Ahead.*

CHAPTER XI: THE SOCIAL WASTES OF INSTITUTIONALISM

Are institutions natural, or artificial? Have they always existed, or have they come into existence at some time? Are they changeless, or may they be changed? Have they ever been changed? Have American institutions ever changed? Give examples.

Do institutions ever "lose step" with the times? What happens to their "members" under such circumstances? What happens to their "officials" at such times? Whose business is it to defend institutions against change? Why do some individuals, groups and institutions defend abuses, injustices, corruptions, wastes?

Hart: *Social Life and Institutions.*
Lawes: *Life and Death in Sing Sing.*
Merz: *The Great American Bandwagon.*
Sullivan: *Our Times,* Vols. 1, 2.

CHAPTER XII: THE NEW SCHOOL IN ACTION

How has industrial civilization affected education? Why should the coming of big cities, or large-scale industry, make a different kind of education necessary? How does the big school fail to meet the needs of big industry? Why should we talk about "going back to Indian teaching," for our methods?

Just what is the "new school" trying to do? How does its "action" differ from the action of the academic schools? What does the new school mean by "creative learning"? What does it mean by freedom? Can children be kept from feeling anything of the past experience of the race? Should they be so kept? What is freedom?

How do the principles of progressive education differ from the ordinary practices of school? Can a school be completely isolated from the community? Should it be?

> Cobb: *The New Leaven.*
> de Lima: *Our Enemy the Child.*
> Rugg: *The Child-centered School.*
> Sisson: *Education for Freedom.*
> Smith: *Education Moves Ahead.*

CHAPTER XIII: CAN CHILDREN MAKE THE WORLD OVER?

What has been the traditional fate of rebellious children? How have innovators, inventors and leaders of new movements been educated in the past? Has the world had an adequate supply of such leaderships? Can that supply be increased by taking thought? Should children be educated to conform to current practices, or to make them over? Can children at fourteen make their own way in the world? Can they if they are rebellious against the world? Can children of eighteen? At what age, if any, does an individual become self-sufficient? How is the world to be made over if children do not do it?

> Dewey: *The Public and Its Problems.*
> Hart: *Adult Education.*
> " *Light from the North.*

CHAPTER XIV: ACADEMIC BACKFIRES ON THE NEW PSYCHOLOGY

What is psychology? Is it study of individuals, or of groups? Is it study of individuals in action, or in repose? Is it introspective study, or objective observation? Is it a "scheme" of some kind, or is it valid description? Is it a branch of science, or is it some sort of theology?

What sort of psychological program is to be found in the

regular academic schools, the public elementary and high schools? What sort in the "new schools"? Is there any real difference between them? What is that difference? Is it important? Is the psychology of the academic schools behavioristic, intellectualistic, or social? Of the "new schools"?

Are there *many kinds* of psychology in the world, or but one kind? If the former, how can such things be? Are psychologists engaged in deciphering human nature, or in promoting their own creeds?

Coleman and Commins: *Psychology, A Simplification,*
  Chapter 12.
Dewey: *Human Nature and Conduct.*
Hart: *Adult Education,* Chs. 4, 5, 10, 13.

Consult, also, the enormous literature of "tests" and "measurements," etc.

CHAPTER XV: THE DILEMMA OF THE NEW SCHOOL

What is the business of a school—in the opinion of the general public? In the attitudes of the pupils? In current educational theory? In the doctrines of the New Schools? In what sense is a school a tool? Is the school nothing but a tool? Whose tool? Is there any question, to-day, as to who owns the tool?

Is it true that a "school needs a community"? What does the statement mean? What is the community of the "academic" schools? Has the New School any such community at present?

Are there any differences worth emphasizing between the New Schools, and the academic schools? Should those differences be enlarged or diminished? If the latter, how can it be done? Do those differences find any echoes in the community? Can the New School survive without a community to support it? What "creative elements" are to be found in the modern world? Do those elements have any educational program? Can they survive without such a program?

How is it that the New Schools can be fairly successful with children under twelve and less successful with children after that age? Is the fault in the children, in the community, or in the organization of the school? Is the difficulty inevitable? Is it inescapable? What are the New Schools doing about it?

> Cobb: *The New Leaven.*
> de Lima: *Our Enemy the Child.*
> Dewey: *The Public and Its Problems,* Chs. 5, 6.
> Hart: *Adult Education,* Ch. 3.

CHAPTER XVI: THE REAL TASK OF PSYCHOLOGY IN EDUCATION

What percentage of pupils in the academic school really *master* the lessons set for them? Is there a valid distinction between schooling and education? Between learning and education? What elements and factors are involved in education? Are all these to be found in the school? In the New School? Does educational psychology display the factors that make up education?

What does Professor Mead mean by "the self," in the quotation at the head of this chapter? Has this "self" any place in the plan of the school? In education? What does the school program offer this "self"? The New School program? Is the fate of this "self" important to the community? To the individual? Does "education" take much account of it? Do the books on educational psychology pay much attention to it? What is the *aim* of education, according to the educational psychologies?

How does education actually begin in individual experience? At what point in that experience does the school begin to take hold? Is the work of the school organized with respect to its actual place in the life of the community, and of the individual?

> Hart: *Discovery of Intelligence,* Chs. 28-31.
> " *Inside Experience,* Chapter on Education.
> James: *Talks to Teachers.*
> Sumner: *Folkways,* Chapter on Education.

Consult also the large list of Educational Psychologies, etc., to be found in every pedagogical library.

PART THREE

HOW WE ARE EDUCATED

CHAPTER XVII: EXPERIENCE

What are some of the ways in which the word "experience" is used? Would it be fair to say that all education is *experience?* That all experience is education? That every experience educates, in one way or another? What is the "world of experience"? What part has old custom in experience? How distinguish between casual experience and reflective experience?

Hart: *Inside Experience.*
Judd: *The Psychology of Social Institutions.*

CHAPTER XVIII: THE SCHOOL IN A CENTURY OF DRIFT

Consider and criticise the statement by President Pritchett, at the beginning of this chapter. Is President Butler's suggestion that formal education and life work should somehow "get together" practicable? Is it sound psychology, or pedagogy? How were young people actually educated a hundred years ago? How was John Marshall educated? George Washington? Ben Franklin? Is there any "education out of school" to-day? Of what sort? How is it related, if at all, to the education in school? What does "pedagogy" know of this education out of school?

What are the reasons for holding that a "graded school" is better than one that has not been graded? Is there any connection between the facts in this case and the nature of the out-of-school life of the children? What change is indicated for the country school that has moved to the city? Why will not a country school do in the city?

Counts: *School and Society in Chicago.*
Dewey: *School and Society.*
Hart: *Educational Resources of Village and Rural Communities.*

Chapter XIX: Our Educational Achievements

What were the arguments for popular education at public expense developed during the nineteenth century? (See Chapter I.) To what extent have those arguments been justified in our later and present history? If the school is a conservative institution how has it helped social progress? What are the basic types of criticism of the public schools, at present? What validity is there in the criticism quoted from Shaw in this chapter? How has the public rationalized the large percentage of failures in the public schools? Why was the old-time rural school more successful than the present city school? What are the actual characteristics of a college graduate to-day?

> Beard: *Whither Mankind?*
> Butler: *Annual Report for 1925.*
> Fisher: *Why Stop Learning?*
> Hart: *Adult Education.*
> Pritchett: *19th Annual Report of the Carnegie Foundation.*

Chapter XX: How We Are Educated

What actual educational factors exist inside the school? What factors exist outside the school? What does a child experience before he ever starts to school? What happens to him out of school during the school years? What becomes of his "mind" after the school years are over? Why? Is there such a thing as "mind"? If not, why is there so much talk about it? If so, what is it for? Does it often fulfill its functions? Make specific application of the sixteen educative factors set forth in this chapter. Add others.

> Addams: *Spirit of Youth and the City Street.*
> Dewey: *School and Society.*
> Hammond: *The Rise of Modern Industry.*
> Hart: *Educational Resources of Village and Rural Communities.*

Chapter XXI: Extra-Curricular

Why is so much emphasis placed on the *school's* part in education? What is the basis for the belief that uninteresting *school* pursuits are more important than interesting *outside* activities? Why have the extra-curricular activities so enormously increased in recent years? What is meant by "an education"? Do college students get "an education"? How, and where? Relate instances of "education by accident." Should we seek to increase or to decrease the possibilities of such "education"?

> Cooley: *The Campus.*
> Cox: *Extra-Curricular Activities.*
> Curtis: *Education Through Play.*
> Lynd: *Middletown.*

Consult also books and magazine articles by Joseph Lee.

Chapter XXII: Education Through Group Memberships

What "primary" groups are to be found in the modern community? What "secondary" groups? What makes a *group?* What constitutes membership in a group? What "under-grouped" persons are to be found in the modern world? What "over-grouped" persons? Make a "chart" of a normal person, showing his memberships in groups. How does the group "educate"? Is such education "intellectual"? Do schools give "credit" for it? Why? Trace the "group history" of some person, from infancy to maturity?

How do groups usually settle their conflicts within themselves? With other groups? What is the significance of the psychological doctrine that "intelligence emerges out of conflict"?

What is the origin of the materials of our school curricula? How are those materials related to present conflicts in students' lives?

> Briffault: *The Mothers,* Vol. 2, pp. 489-500.
> Cooley: *Social Organization.*

Dewey: *Human Nature and Conduct.*
Sumner: *Folkways.*
Thomas: *Source Book for Social Origins*, Part 2.

CHAPTER XXIII: ARRESTED DEVELOPMENT

What is meant by "adaptation"? By "adjustment"? By
"development"? What is an "arrested community"? Where
may such a community be found? What sort of education
goes on in such a community? What produces "arrest" in a
community? In an individual? What can overcome this "arrest" in the community? In the individual? Is there any "arrest" in the modern academic school? Is there any validity to
the argument that "morons" can be produced in schools?

Briffault: *The Mothers*, Vol. 2, Ch. 18.
Holmes: *What Is and What Might Be.*
Spencer: *Education of the Pueblo Child.*
Steiner: *The American Community in Action.*

CHAPTER XXIV: EDUCATION ON THE JOB

How were children educated before there were schools?
Was such education of any value? What were the educational
values of farm life and work? What help did the country
school offer in the education of the country child a century
ago? What has become of work to-day? What part can a
city child have in any *real*, that is, socially important, work
to-day? What does this mean in his education? To what extent can talk about work, or looking on at work, take the place
of participation in work? Why are child-labor laws necessary?
If children are to be legislated out of industry, how shall they
get the education formerly acquired through sharing in *work?*
What is the modern world doing about this problem, if anything?

Hammond: *The Rise of Modern Industry.*
Hart: *Adult Education*, Ch. 1.
Kallen: *Education, The Machine, and The Worker.*

Veblen: *The Instinct of Workmanship.*
   "   *The Theory of the Leisure Class.*

CHAPTER XXV: RECONSTRUCTIVE MOVEMENTS

What are the real facts about the argument as between "individual attention" and "mass education" in the public schools to-day? Can both contentions be true? What was the justification for the passing of "compulsory attendance" laws? What effects have those laws produced? Can those laws be justified at present? Are there any arguments against them? If the public schools are doing the full job of educating America, why do we have so many reconstructive movements?

What is the reason that no new method, e.g., "projects," lasts very long in the schools? What has become of the "Gary System"? The "Dalton Plan"?

Bourne: *Education and Living.*
de Lima: *Our Enemy the Child.*
Pritchett: *19th Annual Report of the Carnegie Foundation.*
Rugg: *The Child-centered School.*
Washburne: *New Schools in the Old World.*

CHAPTER XXVI: WHAT THEN IS EDUCATION?

What fundamental contradictions in educational theory are existent to-day? Where did education begin? Who were the first teachers? Why did schools develop? What was the original purpose of the school? What has become of that purpose? Where does the child's education begin to-day? What is the most intimate process in education?

What becomes of the variant individual to-day? What is the criticism against education as made of *answers?* How shall a child become aware of *problems?* Or, should he be saved from problems? What are the *aims* of education to-day? What are the aims of the school? Are these two sets of aims harmonious? Should they be? Should the school have aims of its own? Where shall those aims be found?

Counts: *School and Society in Chicago.*
Dewey: *The Public and Its Problems.*

PART FOUR

A COMMUNITY INTERPRETATION OF EDUCATION

CHAPTER XXVII: INTEGRATION

What meaning, if any, has the phrase "integration of personality"? What is the difference between an "integrated" and a "disintegrated" personality? What effect has school on personality of the pupil? Does the school curriculum act as an integrative, or as a disintegrative, influence upon the pupils? What effect has the modern "community" upon its members? Are there any distinctive *integrative* factors in the modern world? Where and what are they? Does business integrate its participants? Does religion? Does education? Does recreation?

Hart: *Inside Experience.*
Odum: *Man's Quest for Social Guidance.*
Steiner: *The American Community in Action.*

CHAPTER XXVIII: THE NEEDS OF CHILDHOOD AND YOUTH

Can the community depend upon the schools to look out for the social welfare? Are the schools interested in the *interests* and *needs* of childhood and youth? What are the schools actually interested in? Criticise the list of "needs" of childhood and youth given in this chapter: take from it; expand it; relate it to community life. To what extent do children actually find these "needs" in the modern community and school? What is the real question at issue between the older and younger generations? How can children get "nature" in the city? What are the recreational activities of children in the modern city? What group games, if any, do they play? What team games? What is the validity of the argument herein made for group games and team games?

de Lima: *Our Enemy the Child.*
Van Waters: *Youth in Conflict.*
"   "   *Parents on Probation.*

Chapter XXIX: The Emergence of Intelligence

In what sense, if any, may it be said that "our reasoning is the product of our habits"? Is it fair to assume that "pupils" are rational creatures, and that they prefer school to all other pursuits? What is "intellectualism"? How is "intelligence" a product of experience? Can the "intelligence" discussed in this chapter be "tested," or "measured"? How may membership in several groups minister to the "intelligence" of the individual? Does it usually do so? Why?

What does the academic school mean by "intelligence"? How does that "intelligence" differ, if at all, from the "intelligence" discussed in this chapter? What does the New School mean by "intelligence"? Is this "intelligence" identical with that of the academic school? What is the function of intelligence in experience, and in life?

Dewey, and others: *Creative Intelligence,* Chs. by
    Bode and Mead.
Follett: *Creative Experience.*
Hart: *Inside Experience,* Chapter on Intelligence.

Chapter XXX: The Meaning of Community

If the new-born child is not assured by his heredity of becoming a civilized human being, what are his chances of achieving that estate? Is membership in many groups desirable for the individual? Under all circumstances? What is a community? What is the educational significance of a community to an individual? What two continuous processes are necessary to the education of the individual? How is each normally provided? What share may a school properly have in these processes? Why is *integration* less common to-day than *disintegration?* What part does "former culture" play in education to-day? Is it integrative or disintegrative? What **real** help does the individual get to-day in his struggles toward personal integration? What hindrances?

Dewey: *Human Nature and Conduct.*
Hart: *Light from the North.*
Van Waters: *Youth in Conflict.*

CHAPTER XXXI: THE DRAMATIC MOMENT IN EDUCATION

If "education" is not "facts" or "information" what is it? What room is found in the school for the natural emotional life of children and young people? What is a "dramatic moment"? Give several illustrations of such moments from actual experience? Are such moments ever found in school? Under what circumstances? Is it healthful for children to have "excitement"? Are the old games of the hunt healthful? In what sense is *science* dramatic? Give examples of dramatic experience on the part of scientists? Does the academic laboratory provide much such excitement? Does modern life provide for more, or for less, of the dramatic in the lives of children? Can the school do anything about this dramatic interest? Is it true that "no man ever became great by drudgery"?

Hart: *Inside Experience,* Chapter on What is Art?
Rugg: *The Child-centered School.*
Stott: *Adventuring with Twelve Year Olds.*

CHAPTER XXXII: THE EDUCATIONAL CURRICULUM

How do children get their educations? Where do they get their facts? Their attitudes? Their emotions? Their habits? Their lies? Their grime and filth? Which is the more dominating, the life of the street or the lessons of the schoolroom? Of what elements is the *educational curriculum* made up? Who makes it up and who is responsible for it? Of what ele-

ments is the *school curriculum* made up, and who is responsible for it?

> Addams: *The Spirit of Youth and the City Street.*
> Lynd: *Middletown.*
> Thrasher: *The Gang.*
> Van Waters: *Youth in Conflict.*

CHAPTER XXXIII: EDUCATION AS INTEGRATION OF PERSONALITY

If the world is increasingly diverse to-day, what is to be
the fate of the individual? Can he escape this diversity? Can
he ignore it? or must he meet it and assimilate it?

Do our institutional memberships help us integrate ourselves,
or do they tend to our disintegration? What is happening to
the "younger generation"? To the older generation? To the
younger children?

What happens in the integrative function? Can *teaching*
help this process? Can the school? What are "old integrations"? What value has the past for the problems of to-day?
Will old answers satisfy our new problems? Why not? What
are the differences between *integrating* and *molding?* In what
sense is the school not a "human community"? Why is a "human community" needed for purposes of integration? What is
the real end or aim of education in this age?

> Dewey: *Democracy and Education.*
> Hart: *Light from the North.*
> Lindeman: *The Meaning of Adult Education.*
> Martin: *The Meaning of a Liberal Education.*
> Russell: *Education and The Good Life.*

CHAPTER XXXIV: EDUCATIONAL STATESMANSHIP

Can the statesman be distinguished from the politician?
Has America had any real statesmen in education? Name several of them and determine what they did. Was the city superintendent of schools, in America, ever an educational states-

man? Name one such. What has become of the superintendent of schools? What are the educational tasks that confront educational leaderships to-day? Who are the educational leaders of America to-day? Where are they leading us?

Counts: *School and Society in Chicago.*
Sumner: *Folkways*, Chapter on Education.

CHAPTER XXXV: THE SCHOOL OF THE FUTURE

Are inventors of new machines good citizens? Are changes in social order brought about by new inventions legitimate? Are inventors of new social enterprises good citizens? Is blind change permissible? Is *proposed* change permissible? Is a New Arithmetic allowable? Is a New School in which to teach that arithmetic allowable?

How may it be said that "our present social order" is a "by-product of mind"? Should we get *mind* into our social interests, as much as it is already in our industrial enterprises?

What prospects have we for the development of new human communities in the future? Or, must education become more and more factual, intellectualistic? What is the likelihood of Shaw's child, born at 18, fully educated, becoming the fashion?

What factors must be kept in mind in forecasting the future educational instrumentalities? What should be the characteristics of a future "human community"? Will such a community need schools? How many kinds? Why must education, for some time to come, concern itself with adults rather than with children? What sort of "national program" in education do we need to-day?

Hammond: *The Rise of Modern Industry.*
Hart: *Adult Education.*
" *Light from the North.*
Steiner: *The American Community in Action.*

GENERAL BIBLIOGRAPHY

For the fuller investigation of the problems here outlined there is much available literature, but some of it is not universally available. The more important authors and books are as follows:

Addams: *The Spirit of Youth and the City Street.*
Briffault: *The Making of Humanity.*
    "   *The Mothers.*
        This is a monumental work in three volumes. It deals in the most comprehensive fashion with the anthropological and psychological factors in social organization and culture, and it is fundamental to any interpretation of education to-day. The first hundred pages of Vol. I, and chapter 18, in Vol. II, are specially significant.
Counts: *School and Society in Chicago.*
        An important discussion of the whole relationship of the school to the community and to education in a big city.
Dewey: *Democracy and Education.*
    "   *Human Nature and Conduct.*
    "   *The Public and Its Problems.*
    "   *Impressions of Soviet Russia.*
        These are a few of Dewey's books that are quite indispensable to the student of modern education. The last one corroborates many of the positions taken in this book.
James: *Talks to Teachers.*
        This is still a book of signal importance to students of educational processes who are not lost in *technics.*
Judd: *The Psychology of Social Institutions.*
        This book is one of the very best arguments for the academic type of schooling. The last half of the book presents in brief compass the point of view from which this Social Interpretation takes its most decisive departure.

Martin: *The Meaning of a Liberal Education.*

A generalized presentation of a real humanism in education.

Steiner: *The American Community in Action.*

The best treatment known to the author of current community disorganization. A necessary book to one who is to understand contemporary education.

Van Waters: *Youth in Conflict.*

The vivid picture of Youth caught in the wreckage of our contemporary disorganization.

Students and teachers are urged to make large use of the Reader's Guide to periodical literature. Every topic treated in this book is illustrated at length by articles in current magazines.

The author's own books may all be regarded as prefatory monographs upon the theme of this book. The list follows:

Adult Education (1927).
Community Organization (1920).
Democracy in Education (1918).
Discovery of Intelligence (1924).
Educational Resources (1913).
Inside Experience (1927).
Light from the North (1927).
Social Life and Institutions (1924).

INDEX